WE ALL CAN READ:
THE READING WORKBOOK

A STEP-BY-STEP INTENSIVE PHONICS PROGRAM
FOR TEACHING ANYONE TO READ AND SPELL.

BY JAMES E. WILLIAMS

©Copyright 1990
by James E. Williams
ISBN 0-9614010-4-4
Second Printing: September 1996

≈

P. O. BOX 8839/ATLANTA, GEORGIA 30306-0839

James E. Williams is a writer, educator, and consultant. He lives with his wife in Atlanta,
Georgia, and conducts reading seminars for schools, community organizations, and companies
throughout the country. For further information contact him at the following address:
P. O. Box 8839/Atlanta, GA 30306-0839/404-874-3993.

For my wife Ellen, whose name means light.

Acknowledgments

I would like to thank my wife, Ellen, for her inestimable assistance and support while writing this book and for the countless hours she subsequently spent editing it.

I would like to thank my parents Bernardine and Gordon Williams for their lifelong love and support.

And I would like to thank Joy Franklin for helping to make this book possible.

Preface

The process of learning to read is a long and profound journey. It is no small matter to grapple with and confront a basic human activity that for whatever reason one has failed to master after the early elementary grades have been left behind.

The method of teaching reading presented in the ensuing pages is founded upon the bedrock conviction that almost anyone can learn to read if that person has access to proper instruction and is sufficiently motivated and disciplined. A further corollary to this fact is that not only can almost anyone learn to read but also that almost anyone with the prerequisite reading skills, regardless of his formal educational background, can successfully teach reading to another.

The human activity of reading is a fundamental expression of man's ability to learn, to shape and mold his individual destiny, to adapt both to his environment and to change, to survive and to flourish. The inability to read in our society is every bit as disastrous and crippling as physical injury must have been in earlier times when survival was intrinsically related to man's ability to follow the seasonal migrations of the herds and the fluctuating rhythms of the cyclical harvests.

The reading program presented in this book is written for those who are learning to read and for those who in some truly meaningful way would like to make a difference in the lives of others. The need is as vast and as close to us as our own city or town or rural hamlet. This book is a potential tool for changing lives, not only the lives of those who receive instruction in reading but those who offer their assistance as well. In the end it is our own self we reach towards in reaching out to another. "

WE ALL CAN READ
Table of Contents

An Overview of
We All Can Read

In this book a step-by-step program is presented for teaching anyone to read and spell. This book is also a tool for teachers as well as people who are interested in teaching someone to read but who have no background in teaching reading. One does not have to have formal training as a reading teacher to be able to offer to another the gift of literacy. Using this book, one need learn only one lesson at a time; it is not necessary to learn the entire program before beginning instruction.

Follow each exercise in order. Volunteer tutors should meet with their students at a very minimum of one hour per week. Two to three hours per week would of course be better, and from an instructional perspective one to two hours each day would be ideal. Obviously the amount of time one has to offer will vary widely from one person to another. Ultimately the most important consideration to make when deciding how frequently to schedule instructional sessions is to determine what amount of time you, the tutor, are able to give without overextending yourself. One hour freely given each week is in the end far better than two hours a week where after a while the time commitment becomes too much, and resentment begins to creep into the process. Schedule only the amount of time per week that is appropriate for you, and continue these exercises through to their completion. If you follow these guidelines, results are assured, and you will accomplish the life-changing and miraculous act of teaching someone to read.

This program will work equally well with young children; however, in reference to scheduling instructional time for children between the ages of four and seven, several factors must be considered. The first is that young children learn best within the context of daily reinforcement. The younger the child, the more true is this fact. Second young children have a shorter attention span, and therefore the amount of time per instructional period must be adjusted for their developmental stage. Finally the ideal time to begin reading instruction is when the child's innate curiosity about reading begins to become evident. Most children by the age of four are ready to begin to learn to recognize and write the letters in the alphabet and to make the sounds that those letters represent.

The pace at which a person will proceed through these exercises will vary according to many factors such as the person's age, reading background, and learning ability. These exercises are designed to accommodate both the beginning reader and readers of a more intermediate skill level. In addition these exercises are designed to help individuals who can read but who were never exposed to instruction in phonics when learning basic reading. These exercises teach the phonetic basis of the language in a succinct and systematic way.

Begin by teaching the sounds of the consonant letters. Point to those letters found on page four, and have the student give the sound that each letter represents. Alternate this technique with making the sound and having your student write the letter which represents that sound. Name for your student the five main vowels. Tell him that all other letters are consonants. Mention also at this point that letters can be written as both capital and lower-case letters.

Clear and legible handwriting on the student's part is a critical element to emphasize while teaching phonics. Handwriting provides a strong kinesthetic component to the instructional process. Always insist that your student write legibly. If your student does not know how to write his letters properly, your first job as an instructor is to help him learn how to perform that task. Don't allow your students to switch arbitrarily back and forth between lower case and capital letters. Insist that they use lower case letters only unless the capital letter is called for grammatically.

Begin each instructional session reviewing all elements covered thus far in the program. A flash card set containing three separate skill levels correlated to the book is available from the publisher. These cards provide a succinct course review as one proceeds through the program. The entire reading manual with all exercises and instructions is available in an audio tape program. These audio tapes have been developed to be used by individuals working without benefit of an instructor or as review material for students with instructors to use between instructional sessions. The audio tapes are also helpful for teachers who want to familiarize themselves with the lessons they will be teaching.

Until page seventy-six both nonsense words and real words are found in almost every exercise. If your student already knows most of the real words on the page, have him read instead from the nonsense words. In this manner you will insure that your student is isolating and blending the sounds together properly. If you are working with a student who is a nonreader or one who reads at a level where he does not recognize most real words, then work exclusively from the real words only. With all other students work with both the real words and the nonsense words.

On each page incorporate a dictation exercise using the letter combinations and words directly from that page. In dictating words, follow the principle that if your student already knows the spelling of the real words, use the nonsense words. In Section One spend approximately half of every instructional hour on dictation. The remaining time is spent in having your student sound out letters and words.

All words are to be sounded out. Do not allow your student to guess. It is not necessary for the student to learn an exercise to perfection before moving to the next lesson. Constant review is built into these exercises. Every principle introduced is repeatedly reviewed from the point it is first introduced through to the last exercise. Use your own judgment as to when your student has sufficiently learned one exercise and is ready to continue on to the next lesson. Keep things moving so that there is a sense of progress on your student's part. Remember to vary the pace. If a student is encountering too much difficulty while reading and thus becoming tense or frustrated, switch to spelling activities for awhile.

Always give encouragement to your student; he might need it far more than you would ever suspect. When progress is made, be sure and make recognition of that fact to him; however, be aware also that there often exists the most subtle of lines between praise and condescension. Never patronize the person with whom you are working. Give honest feedback and constant enthusiasm.

Section One
Teaching Instructions

The letters of the English alphabet are divided into two groups: vowels and consonants. The five major vowel letters are *a, e, i, o,* and *u*. All the remaining twenty-one letters of the English alphabet are consonants. Vowel sounds are made with an unrestricted flow of air out of the mouth while consonant sounds are made by partially or completely interrupting the flow of air out of the mouth. The letter *y* can function as either a vowel or consonant, depending upon its position in a word. In Section One *y* will be used only as a consonant. (Later in the program we will discover in what situations *y* will function as a vowel and also in what situations the letters *w* and *r* will also sometimes serve as vowels.)

The goal for your student in this first section of the book is for him to learn the sounds of all of the single consonants and the short sounds for the five major vowels and to discover how all these sounds may be blended smoothly together to form words. In addition consonant blends and consonant teams or digraphs are taught. A consonant blend occurs when two or three consonant letters join together to create a blended sound which contains the individual sound of each letter. A consonant team occurs when two or three consonant letters combine to represent an entirely different sound from the sounds represented by the individual consonant letters which compose the team.

Begin by teaching your student the sound of the consonant letters. Have your student refer to page four. On this page is found each consonant letter with a picture above it. For instance the letter *b* is located directly under the picture of a bus. The first sound heard in the word *bus* is b. This b sound is the sound which the letter *b* represents. Carefully go through each letter and determine how well the student you are working with knows the consonant sounds. Explain to your student that if he has difficulty remembering any of the consonants' sounds, he should remember the key word pictured above each letter. For *b* the key word is bus; for *c* the key word is cat, etc. After remembering the key word, the student must then learn to isolate the first sound heard in the key word in order to determine the sound represented by the given letter. **When teaching the consonant sounds, avoid as much as possible adding the *uh* sound after the consonant sounds. As an example the sound for *b* is not *buh*; instead the sound for *b* is b. The sound for *c* is not *cuh*; instead the sound for *c* is c.**

Be sure to insist from the beginning that your student properly form his letters. When you dictate words for spelling, insist that your student use only lower-case letters unless there is a specific reason for him to use an upper-case letter. Many students will arbitrarily use upper and lower-case letters in the same word. This behavior indicates a lack of understanding of the difference between upper and

1

lower-case letters. Most individuals who have experienced a lifetime of difficulty in learning to read and write believe the language is unlearnable because it is arbitrary. And the corollary to the belief that something is arbitrary is that it is also, therefore, unfair. Stress from the very beginning that the English language is predictable, that there exists an underlying set of rules, and that by systematically learning those rules one step at a time, almost everyone can learn to read and spell well.

On page five have your student read the page in its entirety beginning from row one through row eleven. He should be able to make the sound represented by each letter on each row. After your student has gone through all eleven rows, reverse the process. The teacher makes the consonant sounds found in the eleven rows, and the student writes the letters which represent those sounds. Repeat this procedure as many times as is necessary until it is obvious your student has mastered the relationship of consonant letters and their corresponding sounds.

On every page in Section One the instructional procedure is identical. First the student will read every word or letter combination on the page. Next the teacher will dictate every word or letter combination found on the page. Students should never memorize words but rely solely upon the sounds heard in dictation in order to spell the word correctly. When doing dictation, do not be afraid to exaggerate the sounds of each letter in the word when it seems helpful to the student. Also each student should be able to see clearly the teacher's lip movement as each word is pronounced. All of the lessons in this book are linked in a sequential and hierarchical order. A student should demonstrate a reasonable degree of mastery of each lesson before being permitted to proceed to the next lesson.

Most pages of Section One are divided into two parts: real words and nonsense words. Nonsense words are essential to use in teaching phonics to older students or adults. Many students have memorized hundreds or even thousands of words and yet have little or no knowledge of phonics. No purpose is served by having them call out words they have long ago memorized. Teaching with nonsense words forces a student to look at the individual letters within words and to associate sounds with those letters. Since many older students and adults have already developed a sight vocabulary, the best way, and in many instances the only way to teach them phonics is by presenting them with words they have never seen before. This rationale for using nonsense words to teach decoding for older students is equally true for teaching spelling. A student will oftentimes know how to spell a word without any knowledge of the phonetic relationship of the sounds and letters in a given word. When a student is asked to spell a nonsense word, he must rely upon the sounds he hears being pronounced. Spend approximately half of each instructional period in Section One on spelling practice.

It is vital to be precise when teaching the sounds of all letters but of particular importance when teaching the short sounds for each of the five vowels. Take as long as is necessary in these initial exercises. These basic sounds are the building blocks for the pronunciation of the entire English language, and thus these pages constitute the heart of the phonics program for teaching reading. Distinguishing between the short sounds of *e* and *i* can be particularly difficult. For this reason you will notice that the sequence involved in introducing the vowels is *a, e, o, u*, and only then *i*. The reason for introducing the *i* sound last is to enable the student to have as much time as is possible to learn thoroughly the *e* sound first before being asked to articulate the closely related *i* sound.

In many instances the person with whom you will be working with will have a negligible background in phonics. It might take such a person a significant period of time to understand the implication of the fact that letters represent sounds and that all of our words can be reduced to distinct sounds which can then be represented by letters. If the person you are working with does not seem to make much initial headway, do not assume the process is not working. Virtually anyone can learn the skills being taught in Section One; however, some people will require much more time than do others. The great mistake often made by teachers or tutors is to conclude prematurely that the person they are working with is not capable of hearing the sounds. A vast body of research has indisputably shown that almost anyone can be taught to discriminate accurately between sounds. You must keep in mind that you might be asking a person to do something he has never been asked to do before in his life and that quite likely at first he might not even understand the principle that letters are symbols for sounds. By introducing the principle that letters represent sounds in English, you are asking the person to view the English language in an entirely new way. If your student is not learning at the rate at which you think is appropriate, do not assume the method is at fault, and do not blame yourself; simply understand some people require a great deal more practice than do others!

However long it takes for the person you are teaching to master the basic sounds of English contained in Section One, take the time necessary for him to learn. If someone you are teaching has difficulty, be gentle and relaxed. **The most challenging part of the whole program is encountered at the very beginning. Once these initial sounds are thoroughly learned, your student is already over the hardest part of the entire program. Encourage your student by reminding him of that fact often. Do not allow discouragement to take hold.**

The Consonant Sounds

Bb   Cc   Dd   Ff

Gg   Hh   Jj   Kk

Ll   Mm   Nn   Pp

QUqu   Rr   Ss   Tt   Vv

Ww   Xx   Yy   Zz

Unit One
The Consonant Sounds

Note for dictation: When dictating the letters' sounds on this page or when dictating words from the following pages, have the students repeat back to you the sound or the word which you have pronounced before they attempt to spell it. Oftentimes students will not clearly hear the sounds because they have never been trained to listen for sounds. One cannot spell accurately what one has not heard clearly. A major purpose in dictation is to establish for the student the direct and consistent relationship in English between letters and their sounds.

The letter *q* is always followed by the letter *u*. The letter team *qu* is classified as a consonant letter team. Underline all letter teams.
qu = the sound *kw*

The letter *s* makes two sounds: Double underline the letter *s* when it makes its second sound. **s̲ = *z* as in no̲se**

The letter team *ck* is a consonant letter team which is used for the *k* sound following the short sound of a vowel. The letter team *ck* is never used at the beginning of a word: ro<u>ck.</u>

1.	z	g	b	w	v
2.	p	<u>qu</u>	t	n	z
3.	f	y	d	<u>ck</u>	t
4.	p	c	t	n	l
5.	g	m	s	b	j
6.	s̲	<u>ck</u>	l	z	s
7.	b	z	p	t	<u>ck</u>
8.	<u>qu</u>	r	n	<u>qu</u>	x
9.	v	j	s	n	l
10.	t	<u>ck</u>	d	r	c
11.	t	b	f	b	p

5

Short Sound of *a*

Short sound of *a* with consonants

1.	az	ad	af	ag	al
2.	ab	at	a<u>ck</u>	am	an
3.	ap	av	ax	a<u>s</u>	at
4.	av	an	az	ab	at
5.	ad	a<u>ck</u>	ag	af	ap
6.	am	an	ap	as	at
7.	av	az	ab	ap	a<u>ck</u>
8.	af	ag	af	al	ad
9.	ag	ax	a<u>ck</u>	az	ag
10.	an	av	at	as	af
11.	ag	ad	ap	ab	az
12.	al	av	ap	az	an
13.	at	ab	ad	ap	a<u>ck</u>
14.	am	an	ab	at	am
15.	an	az	at	af	ap
16.	av	ap	al	ab	av
17.	ap	am	an	ax	ad

6

Sounding Out Words

Sounding out a word refers to the process of decoding a word by identifying the sounds of each individual letter in the word and then blending those sounds together. A student sounds out a word when he does not know what the word is. There is a specific sequence to follow when using this sounding out procedure. When a student is sounding out a word, have him perform the following steps, and insist that this sequence of activities be systematically followed.

Step One: Always begin by identifying the vowel sound.

Step Two: After accurately identifying the vowel sound, you should ask your student to identify the consonant sound which immediately follows the vowel sound.

Step Three: Blend together the sound of the vowel with the consonant sound which follows. Use this same procedure to add any additional consonant sounds which might come after the vowel.

Step Four: After the vowel sound and all consonant sounds found after the vowel have been blended together, have the student identify the sound of the consonant letter which comes before the vowel.

Step Five: Blend together the initial consonant sound with the sound of the rest of the word. If two or three consonant letters come before the vowel, start with the consonant closest to the vowel. Add one letter's sound at a time.

Your student is being asked to learn two things simultaneously: 1) to associate a specific sound with a specific letter and 2) to blend smoothly one sound to another. Either of these two skills can individually be difficult for some. Blending for someone to whom this concept is foreign can be particularly challenging. However with persistence your student will learn to perform both skills.

7

Short Sound of *a*

Nonsense Words

1.	cav	lat	fas	han	lal
2.	maz	nav	paf	<u>qu</u>ad	rad
3.	sab	taz	vav	ga<u>ck</u>	yap
4.	zan	mag	hap	jaf	ba<u>s</u>
5.	zat	tat	maf	lan	rav
6.	tam	saf	yal	va<u>ck</u>	naz
7.	pag	fa<u>s</u>	fam	san	jat
8.	gav	dag	zam	bab	<u>qu</u>am

Real Words

9.	hack	rap	ha<u>s</u>	dab	lag
10.	jam	gag	nab	pat	sad
11.	tap	van	wag	yam	rag
12.	jab	sa<u>ck</u>	gab	ham	can
13.	sap	bag	pan	tad	pad
14.	tag	sag	nap	mat	bad
15.	vat	nag	zap	bat	cab
16.	dad	fat	rag	ra<u>ck</u>	ban

8

Short Sound of *e*

Short sound of *e* with consonants

1.	eb	ed	ef	e<u>ck</u>	ev
2.	em	el	em	en	ep
3.	e<u>ck</u>	ev	es	et	ev
4.	en	em	ez	ev	ed
5.	eb	el	ed	ef	eg
6.	em	eb	el	em	en
7.	ep	e<u>s</u>	et	e<u>ck</u>	ex
8.	ed	ez	ef	ep	ev

Short sounds of *a* and *e* with consonants

9.	el	az	en	ab	ex
10.	ez	ag	en	an	ef
11.	a<u>ck</u>	es	at	an	az
12.	en	ab	en	ad	eb
13.	ap	ev	ax	e<u>s</u>	am
14.	et	af	ep	az	em
15.	e<u>ck</u>	el	ad	ef	ag
16.	ef	ap	el	am	en

9

Short Sound of *e*

Nonsense Words

1.	dev	det	hes	jep	sez
2.	lem	mel	we<u>ck</u>	pel	<u>qu</u>ef
3.	res	seb	<u>qu</u>et	nem	fep
4.	ved	jeg	kep	lep	wem
5.	pef	<u>qu</u>ez	deg	sef	tet
6.	ven	wep	yem	del	zet
7.	heg	tef	se<u>s</u>	pem	zeg
8.	vev	jen	ded	mex	fet

Real Words

9.	egg	fed	set	hem	bet
10.	ten	ne<u>ck</u>	get	wed	Peg
11.	met	Ed	yet	wet	Les
12.	let	web	Ted	Zed	pen
13.	leg	reb	zen	keg	pep
14.	men	Len	vet	led	Rex
15.	beg	de<u>ck</u>	Jed	hex	jet
16.	hen	Ned	yen	red	bed

Always capitalize the first letter in a person's name: Dan, Ed, Ann.

Short Sounds of *a* and *e* Review

Nonsense Words

1.	reg	tav	pex	jat	neb
2.	las	mev	gan	lel	kez
3.	jad	jez	cal	hev	zab
4.	fef	mav	<u>qu</u>en	ra<u>s</u>	peb
5.	pax	nen	dav	rel	naz
6.	kes	bap	je<u>ck</u>	tas	fes
7.	vaz	zet	tes	hab	sep
8.	jav	res	nas	yav	teb

Real Words

8.	ram	zen	ta<u>ck</u>	wax	Ned
9.	Jeb	lap	beg	Wes	mad
10.	yes	Dan	net	am	den
11.	had	wed	Ja<u>ck</u>	fed	jet
12.	fan	pet	jam	get	lad
13.	Red	at	bet	fen	tab
14.	set	tax	vet	rat	web
15.	hem	man	leg	pal	Ed
16.	ba<u>ck</u>	hen	ran	gas	bed

Short Sound of *o*

Short sound of *o* with consonants

1.	ob	od	of	o<u>s</u>	ot
2.	ol	o m	op	oz	ob
3.	o v	ox	ol	o<u>ck</u>	ob
4.	od	og	of	ol	o m
5.	op	os	ot	o v	oz
6.	ob	od	og	op	ol

Short sounds of *a*, *e*, and *o* with consonants

7.	ez	o m	ap	ef	ot
8.	ag	ex	ob	az	e m
9.	od	o v	el	a<u>s</u>	omol
10.	eb	ag	oz	et	al
11.	af	eb	os	ab	el
12.	ot	a v	e m	ol	a<u>ck</u>

* The short sound of *i* is introduced only after all other short vowel sounds are introduced. The short sounds of *e* and *i* are the two most difficult short vowel sounds for many students to articulate. Therefore these two sounds have been separated sequentially as much as is possible in order to give students the opportunity to learn thoroughly the short *e* sound prior to working with the short *i* sound.

Short Sound of *o*

Nonsense Words

1.	boz	dov	fot	go<u>ck</u>	hod
2.	jon	loz	mot	mov	pog
3.	<u>qu</u>of	ros	sol	toz	vov
4.	wot	yos	zop	bon	foz
5.	cof	lod	pom	<u>qu</u>om	rop
6.	lop	tov	bot	hob	lom
7.	non	sof	zob	gop	jof
8.	mon	<u>qu</u>op	sot	fov	vo<u>ck</u>

Real Words

9.	job	nod	cob	do<u>ck</u>	fox
10.	sob	mom	lo<u>ck</u>	box	mod
11.	mob	pod	con	rod	Ron
12.	wok	pop	cop	Bob	mop
13.	dot	not	rob	m<u>ock</u>	hop
14.	bog	tot	gob	ox	cot
15.	top	bob	cog	fog	Tom

13

Short Sounds of *a*, *e*, and *o* Review

Nonsense Words

1. <u>qu</u>av   tes   jod   pav   sep
2. hof   rad   ren   tog   mab
3. <u>qu</u>em   fof   jax   fex   dos
4. vav   tem   bo<u>ck</u>   jag   m<u>es</u>
5. jep   wot   sas   hez   vov
6. das   fem   toz   cam   lef
7. sol   caf   zes   <u>qu</u>of   za<u>s</u>
8. tem   def   sax   pav   nen

Real Words

9. hog   nab   dot   map   den
10. hop   hat   led   fog   fab
11. Ken   dog   gap   Jed   bop
12. fab   hen   hot   dad   fed
13. men   sob   pa<u>ck</u>   rev   not
14. Sam   Ted   sog   tan   met
15. lab   net   job   cap   let

Short Sound of u

Short sound of u with consonants

1.	ub	u v	ud	uf	ug
2.	ud	ux	ul	u m	u n
3.	up	u<u>ck</u>	us	ut	u v
4.	ux	ul	uz	ub	u<u>s</u>
5.	ub	ud	uf	ug	u m
6.	u<u>ck</u>	ul	u m	u n	ut
7.	u v	uz	ub	u<u>ck</u>	uf
8.	ul	ud	uf	ul	u v

Short sounds of a, e, o, and u with consonants

9.	o<u>ck</u>	a m	e<u>s</u>	ut	ag
10.	ug	al	es	o m	ud
11.	e m	o v	ut	ap	ez
12.	op	u m	a<u>ck</u>	es	ot
13.	ux	al	ep	oz	u n
14.	ab	e<u>ck</u>	ot	u v	al
15.	eg	u m	ub	ad	on

Short Sound of *u*

Nonsense Words

1.	buv	lul	dut	fud	wug
2.	hus	jum	lud	muf	nug
3.	rux	sul	vug	mub	wu<u>ck</u>
4.	sut	lu<u>s</u>	mun	cul	gug
5.	juf	num	nup	pud	sus
6.	nuf	tup	dus	nuv	ruf
7.	tu<u>s</u>	gu<u>ck</u>	bup	duf	vut
8.	tup	luv	wup	nux	hud

Real Words

9.	but	gut	dud	up	du<u>ck</u>
10.	hug	jut	lu<u>ck</u>	mum	nut
11.	pun	sub	bus	tug	bug
12.	cub	dub	hub	gun	jug
13.	Gus	rub	rug	rut	sum
14.	run	lug	fun	tub	sun
15.	bum	dug	gum	cup	pup

Short Sounds of *a, e, o,* and *u* Review

Nonsense Words

1.	gad	rez	jod	hud	fap
2.	qued	hof	gug	zat	pem
3.	tog	fum	cal	nef	fob
4.	dut	baf	mem	col	sus
5.	kep	zock	zas	yat	jen
6.	yut	bop	vav	hes	yop
7.	zus	taz	feg	wot	vun
8.	mav	tep	nug	des	lom

Real Words

9.	Al	red	jot	hum	fad
10.	fat	hen	tot	hut	lab
11.	bed	rot	gum	bam	net
12.	cot	fun	lap	Mel	dot
13.	bad	men	got	bun	Sal
14.	get	sog	duck	rap	fed
15.	mad	ten	nut	lab	den

Short Sound of *i*

Short sound of *i* with consonants

1.	ib	id	if	is	il
2.	id	im	in	ip	ig
3.	ix	i<u>s</u>	it	iv	ip
4.	iv	iz	ib	id	if
5.	ib	id	i<u>ck</u>	ip	il
6.	im	iv	ip	iv	iz
7.	in	iz	ig	ib	il
8.	i<u>ck</u>	iz	im	iz	ig

Short sounds of *a, e, i, o,* and *u* with consonants

9.	ack	ep	od	e<u>ck</u>	il
10.	up	od	et	al	an
11.	av	eb	o<u>ck</u>	em	ub
12.	ep	uf	ip	av	an
13.	id	ep	el	o<u>ck</u>	et
14.	un	ad	ap	i<u>ck</u>	un
15.	ag	ez	oz	ul	op

Short Sound of *i*

Nonsense Words

1.	biz	div	nit	hiv	ji<u>ck</u>
2.	kim	lif	mil	niv	<u>qu</u>if
3.	rit	sib	tiz	vit	yin
4.	zid	bim	dif	fim	jiv
5.	nib	niz	piv	<u>qui</u>n	ri<u>s</u>
6.	sig	tib	vil	yit	zim
7.	tif	mim	pim	tid	riv
8.	wi<u>ck</u>	nin	fis	rin	bix

Real Words

9.	din	tip	rid	kin	fix
10.	mid	hip	pi<u>ck</u>	rim	rib
11.	bit	vim	yip	zit	bin
12.	<u>qu</u>ip	hit	dim	lip	fin
13.	rip	sit	kit	hi<u>s</u>	him
14.	dig	pit	sis	fig	bib
15.	wig	jig	fit	hid	rig

Short Sounds of *a, e ,i, o,* and *u* Review

Nonsense Words

1.	lam	tes	com	pud	vif
2.	cas	pol	das	cag	q<u>uo</u>m
3.	jom	jeg	tib	fom	zud
4.	hup	za<u>s</u>	yeb	zil	pov
5.	mip	juz	nup	tog	diz
6.	nen	bon	jal	mis	nas
7.	hob	fim	duv	yad	zed
8.	sug	bav	se<u>ck</u>	tol	vup

Real Words

9.	zap	yen	fax	pad	Ned
10.	fib	nab	den	zip	bun
11.	sob	cup	rub	top	vat
12.	hum	bed	fix	bug	tip
13.	bat	him	rod	bet	peg
14.	pet	dot	dad	lot	m<u>o</u><u>ck</u>
15.	kid	vet	pen	t<u>i</u><u>ck</u>	rag

  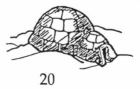  

More Short Sounds of *a, e, i, o,* and *u* Review

Nonsense Words

1.	pab	heg	rof	mun	vit
2.	cas	pol	das	cag	fod
3.	quo<u>c</u>k	bex	nin	zop	cux
4.	wup	pa<u>s</u>	lel	yim	fof
5.	ris	nuz	hux	quoz	viz
6.	beb	kon	saz	pim	sa<u>s</u>
7.	vob	mim	dup	yan	res
8.	cug	cas	<u>eck</u>	roz	wup

Real Words

9.	pop	six	hug	rob	ban
10.	mid	rat	net	kid	rub
11.	hog	bud	jug	lot	had
12.	gum	red	dip	hum	nip
13.	man	Tim	box	keg	pet
14.	set	not	back	sob	ro<u>ck</u>
15.	hi<u>s</u>	yet	den	li<u>ck</u>	Hal

Words Ending in *ff ll ss*

One-syllable words (words which contain only one vowel sound) with a single vowel which end in the letters *f*, *l*, and *s* usually double their final letter: puff, bell, toss.

Nonsense Words

1.	kell	deff	goll	noss	cass
2.	beff	rull	niss	kess	siff
3.	vull	doss	keff	caff	sall
4.	riss	coll	duff	sull	hess
5.	voff	fass	holl	liss	roff
6.	teff	vill	sess	daff	kess
7.	Bess	pill	jazz	buzz	moss

Real Words

8.	hiss	well	toss	huff	pass
9.	miss	huff	lass	well	doll
10.	toss	mass	cuff	yell	miff
11.	hull	mass	bell	ill	hoss
12.	fizz	tell	moss	bass	puff
13.	hull	toss	well	lass	quill
14.	kiss	puff	bass	dell	muss

22

Spelling with *c* and *k*

Use the letter *k* to represent the sound *k* when the *k* sound is immediately followed by the vowel letters *e, i, or y*. Use the letter *c* to represent the sound *k* when the *k* sound is immediately followed by the vowel letters *a, o,* or *u*: cat, cot, cut, Ken, kid, Kyle.

Use the letter team <u>*ck*</u> to represent the sound *k* when it comes immediately after a short vowel sound. The letter team <u>*ck*</u> is never used at the beginning of a syllable: ba<u>ck,</u> de<u>ck,</u> ti<u>ck,</u> ro<u>ck,</u> lu<u>ck.</u>

Nonsense Words

1.	kell	cav	kib	coss	cux
2.	coff	cug	kess	caz	kiv
3.	kem	ked	kiff	caff	cack
4.	cuv	coll	kiz	com	cag
5.	kex	coss	cov	kiv	cax
6.	caz	kuck	kib	coz	kell

Real Words

7.	kit	con	Cass	cab	cuff
8.	kick	Ken	cull	Kip	kid
9.	cab	cop	cud	cog	kit
10.	kiss	cob	Kim	cad	can
11.	cuff	kin	cap	kill	cot
12.	kid	cup	cat	keg	cub

Mastery Check and Review Charts

There are a total of twenty-one Mastery Check and Review Charts within this book. These charts are designed to accomplish several purposes.

1. The charts provide a systematic series of checkpoints for the teacher to use to determine whether or not the student has mastered the material most recently covered. This ability to determine how well the student has mastered any set of lessons is vital due to the sequential nature of this program. A student must demonstrate mastery at each step before being permitted to proceed to the next level. An important aspect of this book is that all of the words in all twenty-one charts have been carefully developed to include only those words which contain phonetic elements which have already been previously taught in the book. Thus a student is never confronted with a word containing phonetic elements which he has not yet been taught.

2. The charts isolate each sound and letter team that is introduced. Therefore the charts provide an excellent tool for the teacher to use when working with a student who is weak with any one particular letter or letter team. As an example if a student is having difficulty with the short *i* sound, the charts provide a way for the teacher to identify a list of words containing short *i*. If a student is having difficulty with the letter team *ch*, the teacher may then refer to the appropriate word list which will contain words which use exclusively the *ch* team. Once the appropriate word list is located, the teacher can ask the student to read the words found in that list and then reverse the process and ask the student to spell the words from that list. Thus the mastery lists enable the teacher to focus very specifically on any phonetic element with which the student is having difficulty.

At each Mastery Check and Review in Sections One and Two the teacher should ask the student to read the words under each heading within each chart. The teacher should then ask the student to spell words from the mastery chart as well. If a student is not able to pronounce accurately most of the words under any one heading within the chart or spell them correctly, then that the student is not yet sufficiently prepared to move on to the next set of lessons.

Mastery Check and Review
Number One: Short Vowels

Short *a*		Short *e*		Short *i*		Short *o*		Short *u*	
ad	lag	bed	let	bib	kill	bob	lot	bud	jug
add	lap	beg	men	bid	kin	bog	mob	buff	jut
am	lass	bell	mess	big	kiss	box	mop	bug	lug
an	lax	bet	met	bill	kit	cob	nod	bum	lull
as	mad	dell	net	bin	lid	cod	not	bun	mud
at	man	den	peg	bit	lip	cog	odd	bus	muff
ax	map	ebb	pen	did	lit	con	on	but	mug
bad	mass	egg	pep	dig	mid	dot	ox	buzz	mull
bag	mat	fed	pet	dim	mill	doll	pod	cub	mum
ban	nag	fell	red	din	miss	dot	pop	cud	muss
bass	nap	fen	sell	dip	mitt	fog	pot	cuff	null
bat	pad	fez	set	fib	mix	fox	rob	cull	nun
cab	pan	get	tell	fig	nip	got	rod	cup	nut
cad	pap	hell	ten	fill	pig	hog	rot	cut	puff
cam	pass	hem	vex	fin	pill	hop	sob	dub	pun
can	pat	hen	web	fit	pin	hot	sod	dud	pup
cap	rag	hex	wed	fix	pit	job	top	duff	rub
cat	ram	Jess	well	fizz	rib	jog	tot	dug	ruff
dab	ran	jet	wet	gig	rid	jot		dull	rug
dad	rap	keg	yell	gill	rig			fun	rum
dam	rat	Ken	yen	hid	rim			fuss	run
fad	sad	led	yes	him	rip			gull	rut
fan	sag	leg	yet	hip	sill			gum	sub
fat	Sal	less		his	sin			gun	sum
fax	sap			hiss	sip			gut	sun
gag	sat			hit	sit			huff	tub
gap	tab			if	six			hug	tug
gas	tag			ill	till			hull	up
had	tan			inn	tin			hum	us
hag	tap			is	tip			hut	
ham	tax			it	wig				
has	van			jib	will				
jab	wag			jig	win				
jag	wax			kid	wit				
jam	yam								
lad	yap								

25

Unit Two
Beginning Consonant Blends

A beginning consonant blend occurs before the vowel and consists of two or three consonant letters which are next to each other in the same syllable and do not form a consonant letter team. Instead each consonant letter retains its own sound and blends its sound together with the other consonant letters. Consonant blends are not underlined.

Beginning Consonant Blends are divided into three major groups.

L Blends

bl	cl	fl
gl	pl	sl

R Blends

br	cr	dr
fr	gr	pr
tr		

S Blends

sc	sk	sl
sm	sn	sp
st	sw	scr
spl	spr	str
squ		

Words Beginning with Consonant Blends

Nonsense Words

1.	dreb	scoz	blim	pleb	slell
2.	closs	trat	pless	skeff	snoss
3.	frav	droff	triz	frex	spig
4.	sliv	clim	sne<u>ck</u>	frob	frip
5.	cle<u>ck</u>	plob	dran	spux	trud
6.	sloff	trex	druss	claff	bluv
7.	plin	drig	spap	striss	snup
8.	blav	troz	blop	snill	plon
9.	snat	crav	slux	scun	blet

Real Words

10.	flex	glad	prom	snob	slid
11.	smo<u>ck</u>	clan	fret	brag	grit
12.	bran	cliff	sla<u>ck</u>	flop	swum
13.	sled	grub	slog	glen	grip
14.	grim	flick	cram	step	swell
15.	slab	skim	floss	slug	sta<u>ck</u>
16.	cra<u>ck</u>	brim	grab	drab	prim
17.	fled	smell	gruff	cram	spot
18.	stun	plus	swell	stop	press

More Words Beginning with Consonant Blends

Nonsense Words

1.	flaz	brex	skiv	scrut	ploss
2.	cren	skell	splup	flom	dreff
3.	slig	squit	sprob	glaz	frav
4.	smox	stret	pliss	grep	snun
5.	slem	proll	sput	trig	sted
6.	swuff	crub	braz	scrav	clet
7.	crim	scoss	slin	flid	drull
8.	squog	slell	spreff	glat	frob
9.	smaz	strax	plov	grot	snuss

Real Words

10.	trip	clot	drag	trick	Fred
11.	flop	drub	sled	scrap	sprig
12.	dress	frill	smack	strep	split
13.	gram	stack	slop	prop	span
14.	trot	stop	swam	bled	slug
15.	scrub	scrub	clap	scuff	splat
16.	flab	drug	slim	skip	flick
17.	slit	bred	spat	struck	bless
18.	grip	snip	slap	prod	track

Short *a*		Short *e*		Short *i*		Short *o*		Short *u*	
blab	grab	bled	glen	bliss	skin	blob	plot	bluff	scud
Brad	gram	bless	press	brig	skip	blot	prod	club	scuff
brag	grass	bred	sled	brim	slid	clod	prop	drub	scum
bran	plan	clef	sped	cliff	slim	clog	slop	drug	skull
brass	scab	cress	spell	clip	slip	drop	slot	drum	slug
brat	scan	dress	stem	crib	slit	flog	snob	fluff	slum
clad	scrap	dwell	step	drill	sniff	flop	spot	glum	smug
clam	slab	fled	stress	drip	snip	frog	stop	glut	snub
clan	slag	flex	swell	flip	spill	from	trod	grub	snuff
clap	slam	fret	trek	flit	spin	grog	trot	gruff	snug
class	slap			frill	spit			plug	spun
crab	slat			glib	split			plum	stub
crag	snag			grid	sprig			plus	stuff
cram	snap			grill	stiff			scrub	stun
drab	span			grim	still				
drag	spat			grin	strip				
dram	stab			grip	swill				
flag	staff			grit	swim				
flap	strap			prim	trill				
flat	swam			scrip	trim				
flax	tram			skid	trip				
glad	trap			skiff	twig				
glass				skill	twill				
				skim	twin				

Unit Three
Ending Consonant Blends

An ending consonant blend occurs after the vowel and consists of two or three consonant letters which are next to each other in the same syllable which do not form a consonant letter team. Instead each consonant letter retains its own sound and blends its sound together with the other consonant letters.

L Blends

lb	*ld*	*lf*
lk	*lm*	*lp*
lt		

S Blends

sk	*sp*	*st*

Other Blends

ct	*ft*	*mp*
nd	*nt*	*pt*
ps		

Vowels Ending With Consonant Blends

1.	aft	elt	ift	olb	und
2.	eft	ilt	oft	ulb	and
3.	ift	olt	uft	alb	end
4.	oft	ult	aft	elb	ind
5.	uft	alt	eft	ilb	ond
6.	ilk	esk	ilf	olm	ups
7.	eft	isk	olf	ulm	aps
8.	ilk	osk	ulf	olm	eps
9.	olk	usk	alf	elm	ips
10.	ulk	ask	elf	ilm	ops
11.	and	eld	int	omp	usk
12.	end	ild	ont	ump	ask
13.	ind	olf	unt	amp	esk
14.	ond	uld	and	emp	isk
15.	und	ald	ent	imp	osk
16.	apt	esp	ilp	oct	uft
17.	ept	isp	olp	uct	aft
18.	ipt	osp	ulp	act	eft
19.	opt	usp	alp	ect	ift
20.	upt	asp	elp	ict	oft

Words Ending With Consonant Blends

Nonsense Words

1.	baft	feld	sind	popt	tust
2.	dest	vilt	nolb	musp	laft
3.	galf	munt	mulp	balb	selm
4.	timp	fost	lund	rems	fisk
5.	zoft	teld	sont	tuct	somp
6.	pulk	rond	pupt	mest	nult
7.	lask	golt	filp	dift	bulf
8.	zint	tolp	rulb	semp	pilm
9	loct	mund	leps	dask	woft

Real Words

10.	held	gasp	cost	sent	went
11.	gust	mist	elm	dump	duct
12.	bond	lips	task	heft	hint
13.	bent	elf	lump	tint	rant
14.	kept	list	hilt	mask	melt
15.	rasp	aft	gulf	dent	Alps
16.	rust	helm	damp	fact	lend
17.	raft	band	rift	bust	gulp
18.	fast	limp	belt	fend	rapt
19.	tilt	bunt	golf	rest	fist

32

Mastery Check and Review
Number Three: Short Vowels with Ending Blends

Short *a*		Short *e*		Short *i*		Short *o*		Short *u*	
act	land	belt	mend	imp	lint	bond	pomp	bulk	husk
aft	last	bend	nest	its	lisp	fond	pond	bump	jump
and	mask	bent	next	dint	list	font	romp	bunt	just
ant	mast	best	pelt	disc	midst	golf		bust	lump
apt	pact	deft	pent	disk	milk			cult	lust
ask	pant	dent	pest	film	mint			cusp	musk
band	past	desk	rent	fist	mist			duct	must
bask	raft	elf	rest	gift	rift			dump	pulp
cask	ramp	elk	sect	gild	risk			dusk	pump
cast	rant	elm	self	gift	sift			dust	rump
daft	rasp	end	send	hilt	silk			fund	runt
damp	sand	felt	sent	hint	silt			gulf	rust
fact	tact	fend	tempt	jilt	tilt			gulp	suds
fast	talc	heft	tend	kiln	tint			gust	sulk
gasp	task	held	tent	kilt	wilt			hulk	tuft
hand	vamp	helm	test	lift	wind			hump	tusk
hasp	vast	help	text	lilt	wisp			hunt	
lamp		hemp	vent	limp	zinc				
		jest	vest						
		kelp	weld						
		kept	welt						
		left	wend						
		lend	went						
		lens	wept						
		lent	west						
		lest	yelp						
		melt	zest						

Unit Four
Words Beginning and Ending with Blends

Nonsense Words

1. blaft	brolk	scund	scrapt	clest
2. crosk	skelt	splald	flisp	cropt
3. slulf	squant	sprelb	glolp	frulm
4. smamp	strect	plind	greps	snask
5. sleft	prilk	spond	trups	stect
6. swimp	blolk	brund	scapt	scrist
7. clolt	drosk	skeld	splosp	flomp
8. drulf	slunt	squolp	sprilb	glulm
9. snasp	grift	plulf	strint	twoft

Real Words

10. graft	scrimp	scant	brunt	bland
11. crisp	plant	grunt	drift	slump
12. crept	trump	flint	swift	splint
13. trust	crimp	blast	trend	slant
14. frisk	brand	twist	brisk	slept
15. grant	spend	tramp	blunt	frond
16. squint	grist	clump	strand	grand
17. stunt	blend	blimp	print	frost
18. sprint	draft	crust	clamp	scalp

34

More Words Beginning and Ending with Blends

Nonsense Words

1.	blilb	brosk	stuct	prasp	greld
2.	snopt	flelm	prast	spimp	glolt
3.	trund	squeps	clent	croft	swulp
4.	slasp	drelf	scrilk	fresk	spland
5.	smelk	skist	sloft	scuct	glelm
6.	frild	stront	plulf	grapt	sprips
7.	flomp	prolp	clelt	blosk	splomp
8.	slulb	crusp	smoft	trind	scrulf
9.	brast	stent	swulk	skilm	snamp

Real Words

10.	tract	script	craft	grump	frond
11.	skimp	clasp	grunt	glint	plump
12.	dwelt	stump	strict	plant	spilt
13.	brunt	stint	spasm	spend	flask
14.	stint	stamp	stilt	frisk	crest
15.	grasp	swept	cramp	slump	blond
16.	blimp	crisp	trust	scamp	blest
17.	Clint	cleft	blunt	sprint	prompt
18.	twist	draft	crust	slant	smelt

35

Mastery Check and Review
Number Four: Short Vowels with Beginning and Ending Blends

Short *a*	Short *e*	Short *i*	Short *o*	Short *u*
bland	blend	brisk	blond	blunt
blast	blest	crimp	frond	brunt
brand	cleft	crisp	prompt	clump
clamp	crept	drift		crust
clasp	crest	flint		grump
craft	dwelt	frisk		grunt
cramp	slept	glint		plump
draft	smelt	grist		slump
flask	spend	print		stump
grand	spent	script		stunt
grasp	swept	skimp		trump
plant	trend	spilt		trust
scalp		splint		
scamp		sprint		
scant		stilt		
slant		stint		
		strict		
		swift		
		twist		

Consonant Teams

ch **church**	*tch* **match**
ck **rock**	*ng* **wing**
ph **phone**	*qu* **quit**
sh **shell**	*th* **thumb**
th **the**	*wh* **wheel**

Words With Consonant Teams
ch tch ck ng ph qu sh th <u>th</u> wh

Consonant letter teams are underlined to indicate that they represent one sound. Consonant letter teams remain together and represent a different sound from those of the individual letters which makeup the letter team. In contrast consonant letter blends are composed of individual letters which all retain their own individual sounds.

The letter team *tch* makes the sound *ch* and is used to represent that sound only when the *ch* sound follows directly after the short sound of a vowel: ca<u>tch</u>.

The letter team *ck* makes the sound *k* and is used to represent that sound only when the *k* sound follows directly after the short sound of a vowel: de<u>ck</u>.

The letter teams *tch*, *ck*, and *ng* are always preceded by a short vowel: m a<u>tch</u>, lo<u>ck</u>, bri<u>ng.</u>

It is very helpful and strongly recommended that students memorize these consonant teams. Notice that seven out of the ten consonant teams contain the letter *h*.

Nonsense Words

1.	vang	leck	hotch	shub	litch
2.	seng	thif	whuv	<u>th</u>os	thab
3.	tetch	shull	whaf	quis	ong
4.	<u>th</u>ip	whe<u>s</u>	chell	thos	chup
5.	gack	phep	shem	<u>th</u>od	meng

Real Words

6.	chum	fang	fetch	pick	quill
7.	shod	whiff	then	chat	wing
8.	quill	thin	whim	pang	notch
9.	quit	sham	chin	thus	sock
10.	shut	witch	mock	whet	thin

More Words With Consonant Teams
ch tch ck ng ph qu sh th th wh

Nonsense Words

1.	chaz	sheck	whoff	thung	quiff
2.	thetch	cha<u>s</u>	pung	<u>th</u>ox	whatch
3.	sheck	phutch	<u>th</u>ack	quing	thosh
4.	thim	phen	whetch	whog	shull
5.	chotch	phut	thiff	totch	eph
6.	whun	pham	wheck	quep	phan
7.	whe<u>s</u>	chin	shang	whib	thetch
8.	quetch	shax	<u>th</u>om	chut	shing
9.	whiv	sheng	chuth	<u>th</u>am	thung

Real Words

10.	chock	shed	thud	which	tang
11.	quiz	thick	ditch	Rick	thing
12.	shop	whack	puck	ketch	thing
13.	check	bang	quell	botch	etch
14.	ash	ding	with	mesh	pitch
15.	chick	itch	shuck	that	when
16.	luck	ring	chip	dash	buck
17.	which	peck	rang	chum	gash
18.	shock	shag	quick	ting	muck

Sounds of *ng* and <u>n</u>

The letters *n* and *g* form a consonant letter team when these two letters occur at the end of a syllable or word. The letter team *ng* represents the sound as heard in the word *ri<u>ng</u>*.

When a word is divided into syllables between the letters *n* and *g*, usually the letter *n* will make its second sound: bi<u>n</u>/go, co<u>n</u>/gress.

When the letter *n* is followed by the *k* or *g* sound, *n* makes its second sound. The second sound of *n* is the same sound as is made by the consonant team *ng*. The letter *n* will make its second sound when followed by the *k* or *g* sound even when the syllable division is made directly after the letter *n:* ba<u>n</u>k, twi<u>n</u>/kle, tra<u>n</u>/quill, i<u>n</u>/sti<u>n</u>ct, fi<u>n</u>/ger.

Nonsense Words

1.	ling	mang	wong	trung	snonk
2.	fenk	dronk	smunk	fing	lang
3.	rong	drung	tenk	twank	donk
4.	tunk	leng	drang	blong	mung
5.	teng	zang	bink	trenk	blunk
6.	bling	nung	brong	tung	senk

Real Words

7.	ping	Hank	fang	swung	crank
8.	bunk	sing	mink	drank	wing
9.	tong	link	blank	dunk	bring
10.	rang	long	rung	blink	rank
11.	slung	drink	dank	clunk	swing
12.	sang	prong	sung	mink	crank

40

Mastery Check and Review
Number Five: Short Vowels with Consonant Teams

Short *a*	Short *e*	Short *i*	Short *o*	Short *u*
ash	beck	itch	botch	buck
back	check	chick	chock	chuck
batch	chess	chill	chop	chug
cash	deck	chin	dock	chum
bang	fetch	chip	hock	duck
clang	ketch	ding	lock	hush
catch	mesh	dish	mock	hung
chaff	neck	ditch	notch	luck
chap	peck	fish	rock	lung
chat	quell	hick	shock	lush
dash	quest	hitch	shod	much
gash	shed	kick	shop	muck
hack	shell	king	shot	mush
hash	them	lick	sock	puck
jack	then	nick		rung
lash	when	pick		rush
latch	whet	pitch		shuck
mash		pith		shun
fang		quick		shut
pack		quid		such
quack		quill		suck
rack		quip		thud
rang		quit		thus
sack		shin		tuck
sang		ship		
sash		sick		
shad		sing		
hang		thick		
pang		thin		
shag		thing		
sham		this		
tack		tick		
tang		ting		
than		which		
that		whiff		
whack		whim		
		whip		
		whit		
		whiz		
		wick		
		wing		
		wish		
		witch		
		with		

41

Unit Six
Words With Blends and Consonant Teams
ch tch ck ng ph qu sh th <u>th</u> wh

Nonsense Words

1.	chaft	shelt	wholf	thust	quift
2.	pretch	chast	drung	<u>th</u>ont	cratch
3.	sheft	phust	chast	quind	thosk
4.	thimp	pleck	sletch	phopt	shulb
5.	choft	whult	thilk	smotch	sweng
6.	whusp	<u>th</u>amp	pleck	quemp	phand
7.	phest	chint	shast	whilb	thelk
8.	queps	shand	<u>th</u>olf	crung	shisp
9.	shapt	phend	shrup	steck	thruld

Real Words

10.	brunch	fleck	shrill	switch	branch
11.	chunk	quench	thrift	splash	stack
12.	drench	length	slosh	think	twang
13.	clack	whelp	munch	swing	slick
14.	blanch	smock	thresh	stretch	tenth
15.	throb	inch	string	shrunk	twelfth
16.	crutch	block	spring	shrug	truck
17.	shrink	whisk	smack	cling	quench
18.	sting	thump	thrush	clench	shred

42

More Words With Consonant Teams and Blends
ch tch ck ng ph qu sh th <u>th</u> wh

Nonsense Words

1.	slatch	<u>th</u>ilm	plick	quosk	phend
2.	whilp	chesp	shust	thamp	glong
3.	phant	scong	thelk	shupt	gritch
4.	chold	whuft	grick	<u>th</u>elt	qualb
5.	swetch	chalf	scrong	phips	chuct
6.	shulm	thisk	splack	shoft	<u>th</u>eld
7.	tritch	quent	whust	<u>th</u>alk	phept
8.	shalb	chosp	squeck	thund	sming
9.	pholp	shuct	fritch	breng	thaps

Real Words

10.	stitch	flock	thrust	fresh	pinch
11.	shrub	flinch	thrush	stock	clinch
12.	trench	crock	bring	crush	trick
13.	bench	sling	thrust	pluck	brush
14.	punch	blotch	stick	fling	slash
15.	clutch	stuck	slack	theft	speck
16.	hunch	finch	wench	sprang	flick
17.	chest	shelf	brick	shrimp	snack
18.	slush	thresh	lunch	thrill	crunch

Mastery Check and Review
Number Six: Short Vowels with Blends and Consonant Teams

Short *a*	Short *e*	Short *i*	Short *o*	Short *u*
blanch	bench	brick	block	blush
branch	chest	bring	blotch	brush
brash	clench	chink	clock	bunch
clack	depth	chintz	crock	chunk
clash	drench	click	flock	cluck
crack	fleck	clinch	frock	clung
crash	flesh	cling	smock	clutch
flash	fresh	fifth	stock	crunch
graph	length	filch	throb	crush
splash	quench	filth		crutch
ranch	shelf	finch		flung
shaft	shred	flick		flush
shrank	sketch	flinch		gulch
slack	speck	fling		hunch
slang	stench	pinch		lunch
slash	stretch	prick		mulch
smack	tenth	quilt		munch
smash	theft	shift		pluck
snack	thresh	shrill		plush
splash	trench	shrimp		punch
sprang	twelfth	shrink		shrub
stack	wench	sixth		shrug
thank	whelp	slick		shrunk
track		sling		slung
trash		sphinx		slush
twang		spring		stuck
		squid		stung
		squint		swung
		stick		thrush
		sting		thrust
		stitch		thump
		string		truck
		swing		
		swish		
		switch		
		think		
		thrift		
		thrill		
		trick		
		twitch		
		whisk		
		winch		

Mastery Check and Review
Number Seven: Consonant Teams

ck	ch	tch	
			shack
back	champ	batch	sick
beck	chant	blotch	slack
black	chap	botch	slick
block	chat	Butch	smack
brick	chest	catch	smock
check	chick	clutch	snack
chick	chill	crutch	sock
chock	chin	ditch	speck
chuck	chip	etch	stack
clack	chock	fetch	stick
click	chop	hatch	stock
clock	chuck	hitch	struck
cluck	chug	itch	stuck
crack	chum	match	thick
crock	chunk	notch	tick
deck	bench	patch	track
dock	blanch	pitch	trick
duck	clench	scotch	truck
flick	bunch	scratch	tuck
flock	clinch	sketch	whack
frock	crunch	snatch	wick
hack	drench	stitch	
heck	filch	stretch	*n*
jack	finch	switch	(*n* is not a team)
kick	flinch	thatch	bank
lack	gulch	twitch	blank
lick	hunch	witch	blink
lock	inch		brink
luck	lunch		bunk
mock	much		chink
muck	mulch		chunk
neck	munch		clank
nick	pinch		clink
pack	punch		crank
pick	ranch		dank
pluck	stench		drank
quick	wench		drink
rack	which		drunk
rock			flank
sack			

45

Mastery Check and Review
Number Seven: Consonant Teams

n (*n* is not a team)	*ng*	*sh*	*th*
Hank	bang	shack	thrash
honk	bring	shad	thresh
ink	clang	shaft	thrift
junk	cling	shag	throb
kink	ding	shall	throng
lank	fang	sham	thrush
link	fling	shank	thrust
mink	flung	shelf	thump
monk	gang	shell	thwack
pink	gong	shift	bath
plank	hang	ship	cloth
prank	hung	shock	depth
punk	king	shod	fifth
rank	long	shop	filth
sank	lung	shrank	froth
shank	pang	shred	length
shrank	prong	shrill	month
shrink	rang	shrimp	moth
shrunk	sang	shrub	sixth
sink	sing	shrug	sloth
slink	slang	shrunk	smith
slunk	sling	shuck	tenth
spank	slung	shunt	width
stank	sprang	shut	
stink	spring	bash	*th*
sunk	sprung	ash	than
tank	sting	blush	that
thank	string	crush	them
think	strong	flesh	then
trunk	strung	fresh	this
wink	stung	hush	thus
yank	swing	lush	with
	swung	mesh	
	tang	plush	*wh*
	thing	slash	whack
	thong	slush	whelp
	throng	splash	which
	twang	thrash	whiff
	wing	thrush	whisk

46

Section Two

At this point students should be reasonably competent at sounding out one-syllable words when the vowels all make their short sounds; however, all vowels make more than one sound. The long sound of a vowel is one in which the vowel makes the sound of its own name as in the *e* sound in the word *be*.

Once a student learns the long sound for each vowel, the next step for him is to learn in which situations the vowel will make its short sound and in which situations the vowel will make its long sound. There are six major vowel rules which determine the sound a vowel will make. Once a student learns these six basic vowel rules, then it becomes a relatively easy task for him to identify what sound the vowel will likely make in any given situation.

In Section Two each of the six major vowel rules is explained. In addition a system for marking the vowels to indicate the sounds they will make is introduced. This system of marking vowels, coupled with the already-introduced technique of underlining consonant teams, will along with other techniques that will be introduced in future lessons provide a comprehensive and sequential marking procedure to enable anyone to decode virtually any word in the language.

This marking system is a most effective tool to insure that a student has thoroughly mastered the various component steps involved in decoding. Through the repetitive process of analyzing and then marking each of thousands of words, a student is provided with an adequate supply of material to internalize the principles being taught. Finally this system of analyzing and marking words is also ideally suited for the student faced with the task of overcoming an intermediate or even a severe level of a spelling deficiency.

From this point onward students are to mark, using the marking system that is now being introduced, all words in the particular list from which they are working. (Words from the Mastery Check and Review Lists are not marked by the student.)

Sequence of instruction to follow for introducing each new lesson:

1. Introduce to the student the new concept or new letter teams which are being introduced in the lesson.

2. Write words on the board or on paper which contain the concepts or new letter teams being introduced. The Mastery Check and Review Lists, which are correlated to each new set of letter teams introduced, are an excellent source for the teacher to use to identify words containing new letter teams. Most of the twenty-one learning units in this book begin with a list of new letter teams to be memorized by the student and end with a Mastery Check and Review of those same teams. Between those two points are located lists of words which contain the new letter teams and which the student is to mark and read. Marking so many words within each unit enables the student to learn and integrate thoroughly each new set of teams before moving to the next unit.

3. The student marks the words found in each individual lesson and reads each word out loud as he completes marking that word. The student does not apply the marking system to the words found in the Mastery Check and Review Lists.

A Word About Spelling

Up until this point in the program the teacher has been asked to spend approximately half of each instructional lesson dictating words for spelling. However starting on page fifty-seven for the first time in this program, the student will be introduced to two and sometimes three vowel teams which will each make the same identical sound. As an example the sound *ee* is represented by three teams: *ea, ee,* and *ey.* Therefore the dictation procedure must be altered somewhat to avoid causing confusion on the student's part.

Starting from page fifty-eight onwards, dictate only from the Mastery Check and Review Charts; most specifically do not use nonsense words for dictation any longer. When dictating words which contain letter teams which share a common sound with other letter teams such as *ai/ay, ea/ee/ey,* or *oa/oe/ow,* identify for your student which team will be used in the words about to be dictated. As an example you might say to your students, "The next group of words which I am about to dictate will all contain the vowel team *ay.*" In this way your student is able to continue to practice the important skill of listening to sounds in order to spell them accurately without encountering the attendant confusion which occurs if the student is asked to choose from several equally plausible spelling possibilities. Later in the program the student will be asked to spell words without advance notice as to what teams will be encountered in the word. An answer key is provided starting on page 135 to enable a student working independently to be able to check the accuracy of his work. This answer key may be used starting from page 49 through to the end of Section Three found on page 134.

Unit Seven
Vowel Rules One and Two

Vowel Rule One - When there is only one vowel in a syllable and it is followed by a consonant, the vowel will usually make its short sound. Vowels in this category are marked by writing the number *one* directly under the vowel.

tint	sled	twist	<u>ch</u>imp
1	1	1	1

Vowel Rule Two - When there is only one vowel in a syllable and that vowel is the final letter in the syllable, the vowel will usually make its long sound. Vowels in this category are marked by writing the number *two* directly under the vowel.

<u>sh</u>e	hi	m e	be
2	2	2	2

In the words below notice how the vowel sound changes from long to short when a consonant is added to follow the vowel.

Nonsense Words

1. bla - blaft	fli - flim	bre - brelt	cha - chasp
2. pro - prolf	cle - clelb	glo - glomp	scro - scromp
3. ble - blent	shi - shind	cle - clelk	slo -slost
4. cra - crask	gre - greft	tro - tront	spla - splask
5. pli - plict	whi - whist	cre - crent	bli - blift
6. sta - stap	ble - bleck	chi - chist	tha - thaf

Real Words

7. sla - slack	bla - black	dro - drop	fla - flab
8. spe - spend	sha - shack	fla - flash	cho - chop
9. twi - twist	fla - flash	sho - shop	gri - grip
10. ki - kin	sho - shot	flo - flop	tro - trod
11. spri - sprint	che - chest	ble - blend	thro - throb
12. gri - grist	glo - glob	bri - bring	she - shed

More Practice Vowel Rules One and Two

**In the words below notice how the vowel sound changes from
long to short when a consonant is added to follow the vowel.**

Nonsense Words

1. fle - flench	wha - whap	thri - thrip	tro - tront
2. ja - jav	pre - preng	bli - blit	shro - shrop
3. ba - bant	clo - clonk	dre - drelt	smi - smint
4. yo - yob	sha - shang	pre - prempt	fri - fritch
5. spro - sprosh	gle - glenk	whi - whiv	tra - tranch
6. sme - smest	quo - quond	tha - thamp	shri - shrint
7. fla - flant	te - telch	pli - plink	sko - skop
8. phi - phitch	twe - tweld	scri - scrinch	dro - droft
9. tro- troft	the - thest	cha - chank	spli - splipt

Real Words

10. bla - blast	ski - skimp	pa - pang	tha - thatch
11. cli - clink	cho - chock	fa - fang	cra - cramp
12. shi - shift	fle - fleck	whi - which	sta - stamp
13. cri - crimp	sla - slang	twi - twitch	spe - spent
14. spla - splash	sho - shock	si - sixth	ya - yank
15. thro - throng	shra - shrank	spri - spring	scri - script
16. hi - hitch	po- pomp	gli - glint	che - chest
17. ki - kilt	te - tempt	tha - thatch	whi - whisk

Vowel Rules One and Three

Vowel Rule Three - When two vowels in the same short word or syllable are separated by one or more consonants and the second vowel is the letter *e* and is also the final letter in the syllable, then the first vowel usually makes its long sound, and the *e* is silent. In syllables governed by vowel rule three, the number *three* is written directly under the vowel which makes its long sound, and one line is placed directly under the silent letter *e* to indicate that the *e* is silent. The silent letter *e* is a signal that the first vowel says its name.

smil<u>e</u>	<u>chase</u>	slop<u>e</u>	wh<u>ale</u>
3	3	3	3

In the words below notice how the vowel sound changes from short to long when a silent *e* is added at the end of the word.

Nonsense Words

1. bam - bame	sop - sope	bev - beve	pim - pime
2. quev - queve	cof - cofe	dif - dife	rax - raxe
3. han - hane	sez - seze	yad - yade	jem - jeme
3. tab - tabe	lil - lile	vad - vade	pif - pife
4. gop - gope	whop - whope	chan - chane	fim - fime
5. prot - prote	sab - sabe	tiv - tive	zop - zope

Real Words

6. quack - quake	slat - slate	fill - file	pick - pike
7. shin - shine	fat - fate	pop - pope	grim - grime
8. slim - slime	them - theme	van - vane	snip - snipe
9. ban - bane	spit - spite	cloth - clothe	grip - gripe
10. din - dine	cap - cape	chock - choke	slop - slope
11. slid - slide	glad - glade	twin - twine	rob - robe
12. stock - stoke	win - wine	Ross - rose	cop - cope

51

More Practice Vowel Rules One and Three

In the words below notice how the vowel sound changes from short to long when a silent *e* is added at the end of the word.

Nonsense Words

1. glap - glape	smick - smike	twest - tweste	rab - rabe
2. dod - dode	grem - greme	fid - fide	veb -vebe
3. riv - rive	gop -gope	snep - snepe	op - ope
4. rev - reve	pon - pone	maf - mafe	quet - quete
5. grod - grode	slin - sline	prat - prate	hin - hine
6. lel -lele	chack - chake	dod - dode	whem - wheme
7. tem - teme	miv - mive	bam - bame	stot - stote
8. grod - grode	lill - lile	losh - loshe	creb - crebe

Real Words

9. mop - mope	whiff - wife	shack - shake	cut - cute
10. quack - quake	prim - prime	mat - mate	glob - globe
11. rack - rake	bod - bode	spin - spine	plan - plane
12. luck - Luke	whip - wipe	tack - take	bill - bile
13. sham - shame	spit - spite	Ross - rose	sack - sake
14. past - paste	strip - stripe	Brock - broke	rid - ride
15. snack - snake	fin - fine	slack - slake	rip - ripe
16. mad - made	Tim - time	mull - mule	lack - lake
17. Jack - Jake	kit - kite	pock - poke	bid - bide

The Long Sound of Vowel *u*

The letter *u* is unique among vowels because it makes two different long sounds: the sound *yoo* as in the word *mule* and the sound *oo* as in the word *dude*. Both of these two sounds are classified as long *u*, but because long *u* makes two different sounds, it must be marked in one of two ways. The letter *u* when making the sound *yoo* as in *mule* is marked as any other long vowel would be marked.

m ul<u>e</u>   cub<u>e</u>   fum<u>e</u>   cut<u>e</u>
3   3   3   3

The letter *u* when making the sound *oo* as in *dude* is double underlined to indicate the different sound it makes.

du̲d<u>e</u>   ru̲d<u>e</u>   du̲/ty   cru̲d<u>e</u>
3   3   2   3

The letter *u* is the only one of the five major vowels which has not one but two long sounds. Refer to these two separate long sounds that *u* makes as the first long sound and the second long sound of the letter *u*.

First Long Sound of *u* - u̲s<u>e</u>   **Second Long Sound of *u* - ru̲l<u>e</u>**
                      3   3

1.	prune	use	rule	dude
2.	jute	brute	dupe	pure
3.	fluke	rule	cube	fume
3.	mute	rude	Yule	dune
4.	tube	plume	muse	duke
5.	cute	prude	dupe	flume
6.	ruse	tune	fuse	nude
7.	mule	lute	rule	prude
8.	dude	crude	use	fluke
9.	cube	nuke	brute	lube

53

Mastery Check and Review
Number Eight: Vowel Plus the Silent Letter e

a *e*	shade	kite	tithe	probe
ale	shame	life	tribe	prose
ate	taste	like	trite	quote
bake	vase	lime	twine	rope
base	waste	line	vile	rose
bathe	wave	mile	vine	scone
blame	whale	mine	while	scope
brake		nine	whine	slope
case	*e* *e*	pike	wife	smoke
crane	eke	pine	wine	smote
crape	eve	pipe	wipe	spoke
crave	mete	pride	wire	stoke
dame	theme	prime	wise	stole
daze	these	prize		stove
drape		quite	*o* *e*	strode
fade	*i* *e*	ride	ode	stroke
fame	bide	ripe	bode	strove
fate	bile	rise	broke	those
flake	bite	rite	choke	throne
flame	bribe	scribe	chose	whole
frame	bride	shine	close	wove
gaze	brine	shrine	close	yoke
glade	chide	side	clothe	
glaze	chime	size	cope	*u* *e*/ *u* *e*
grade	chive	slide	crone	use
graze	clime	slime	dose	cube
haste	crime	smile	drone	cute
haze	dime	snipe	drove	dude
jade	dine	spike	globe	duke
lake	dive	spine	grope	dupe
lame	drive	spite	grove	fume
lane	file	squire	hole	fuse
made	fine	stride	home	Luke
male	glide	strife	hose	mule
mane	grime	strike	lone	mute
mate	gripe	stripe	mope	nude
pave	hide	strive	nose	pure
phase	hike	swine	poke	rule
phrase	hire	thrive	pole	tube
plate	hive	tide	pose	tune
quake		tile		

Review of Vowel Rules One, Two, and Three

Nonsense Words

1.	bluft	fli	sprope	pro	fli
2.	chesp	plip	jave	jope	dro
3.	cax	flusk	jop	flom	hif
4.	juse	pra	mone	bax	spint
5.	blat	bri	lale	throp	cobe
6.	dop	fote	trent	squisp	chilp
7.	bape	eft	bo	wabe	lefe
8.	mune	ti	plosp	keze	twise
9.	cresk	shast	mun	jeme	chome

Real Words

10.	chafe	crash	fist	mule	splint
11.	twist	just	quack	joke	pine
12.	crib	punt	flat	swipe	shrine
13.	so	lip	crank	swell	dope
14.	fuse	will	go	shut	block
15.	file	drift	trip	shade	fluke
16.	splash	she	white	close	runt
17.	whack	drag	cane	game	hi

More Review of Vowel Rules One, Two, and Three

Nonsense Words

1.	twile	cletch	prempt	clo	phabe
2.	whulp	pline	stre	prack	chone
3.	theln	slonst	wode	chi	bebe
4.	strinch	qui	spamp	clile	fatch
5.	prist	shope	sle	flust	shand
6.	quetch	fo	phalp	chust	flish
7.	mo	ench	clibe	phum	ave
8.	whilst	chone	brene	flusp	thro

Real Words

9.	clutch	throne	spend	shrink	grope
10.	hose	tenth	slung	whelp	me
11.	filch	shrug	tune	batch	these
12.	squelch	fling	crunch	throne	rule
13.	shrimp	chose	shake	clench	cube
14.	she	sprang	clothe	drape	clench
15.	scratch	shelf	choke	blotch	bathe
16.	frock	tithe	twist	scone	stench
17.	phone	thank	scribe	haste	pluck

Vowel Rule Four Teams

ai r<u>ai</u>n	*ay* pr<u>ay</u>
ea <u>ea</u>t	*ee* s<u>ee</u>
ey k<u>ey</u>	*oa* <u>oa</u>k
oe t<u>oe</u>	*ow* l<u>ow</u>
ue d<u>ue</u>	*ui* fr<u>ui</u>t

Vowel Rule Four Teams

Vowel Rule Four - When certain vowels come together, they form teams where the first vowel makes its long sound, and the second vowel is silent. Vowels in this category are marked by underlining the vowel team and writing the number *four* under the team. It is very helpful and strongly recommended that students memorize these ten vowel teams. Consult the preceding page for examples.

The letter *w* can function as either a vowel or as a consonant in a word. Usually *w* becomes part of a vowel team when preceded by the letters *a*, *e*, or *o*. When *w* acts as a vowel, it is silent.

The major vowel rule four teams
*ai ay ea ee ey oa oe ow *u e *u i*

Nonsense Words

1.	baiz	deev	fay	geas	jow
2.	koem	leal	mue	neep	tay
3.	queaf	rey	soab	toez	veav
4.	weet	yais	zow	beas	keef
5.	vay	fluid	noak	quaim	reep
6.	saip	tees	zay	weaz	yoab

Real Words

7.	toad	dream	meek	boat	sheet
8.	paint	squeal	gloat	brain	leaf
9.	seen	mow	tray	road	bowl
10.	team	suit	bloat	foe	lain
11.	rail	sheep	spray	heat	beach
12.	blue	toe	sprain	fruit	pray

* The vowel teams *u e* and *u i* are double underlined because these teams normally make the second long sound of the letter *u*: blue, fruit.

Review of the Major Vowel Rule Four Teams
ai ay ea ee ey oa oe ow u_e ui

Nonsense Words

1.	prain	eenst	sleach	cloe	floant
2.	frow	theam	whoap	shay	fleek
3.	pruip	noan	stroe	thow	scray
4.	queast	tue	queep	chaip	thoab
5.	droe	saish	boav	streand	tuid
6.	quaich	drow	preesh	tay	cload
7.	owb	eef	cleab	phain	troe
8.	gleav	vay	cleeb	whoap	thraip

Real Words

9.	braid	wheel	stream	throw	roach
10.	blue	hoe	beech	maize	tweed
11.	preach	stray	throat	shown	fruit
12.	oath	praise	woe	key	faith
13.	tweed	leash	bowl	roam	drain
14.	doe	spray	sown	speech	wheat
15.	shoal	quaint	three	growth	true
16.	bruise	sheath	sow	cheek	pray
17.	quail	seed	hoax	eel	breach

ai		ea	
aid	snail		peach
ail	sprain	each	peak
aim	stain	east	peal
bail	strain	eat	peat
bait	tail	bead	plead
braid	taint	beak	preach
brain	trail	beam	reach
chain	train	bean	read
claim	trait	beast	ream
drain	vain	beat	reap
fail	wail	bleach	seal
faint	waist	bleak	seam
faith	wait	bleat	seat
flail	maize	breach	sheath
frail	praise	cheap	sneak
gain	raise	cheat	speak
gait		clean	squeak
grail		cleat	squeal
grain	**ay**	creak	steal
hail	way	cream	steam
jail	bay	deal	streak
laid	bray	dean	stream
lain	clay	feast	teach
maid	day	feat	team
mail	flay	freak	treat
maim	fray	gleam	veal
nail	gray	glean	weak
paid	hay	heal	wheat
pail	jay	heap	yeast
pain	lay	heat	zeal
paint	may	jean	pea
plain	nay	leach	plea
plait	pay	lead	sea
quail	play	leaf	tea
quaint	pray	leak	
raid	ray	lean	**ee**
rail	say	leap	eel
rail	slay	leash	beech
rain	splay	least	beef
sail	spray	meal	beet
	stay	mean	bleed
	stray		

60

Mastery Check and Review
Number Nine: Vowel Rule Four Teams

ee		oa	ow
cheek	sheen	oak	own
cheep	sheep	oat	bowl
creed	sheet	oath	flown
creek	sleek	bloat	shown
creel	sleep	board	sown
creep	sleet	boat	thrown
deem	speech	cloak	blow
deep	speed	coast	bow
feed	spleen	coat	crow
feel	steed	croak	flow
feet	steel	float	glow
fleet	steep	gloat	grow
greed	street	goad	low
green	sweep	goat	mow
greet	sweet	groan	row
heed	teem	hoax	show
heel	teens	load	slow
jeep	teeth	loan	snow
keel	tweed	moan	sow
keen	weed	moat	stow
keep	week	poach	throw
leech	weep	roach	tow
leek	wheel	road	
meek	bee	roam	
meet	fee	roar	ue
need	flee	roast	blue
peek	glee	shoal	clue
peel	see	soak	flue
peep	tee	soap	glue
preen	thee	soar	rue
queen	three	throat	true
reed	wee	toad	
reef			ui
reek	ey	oe	fruit
reel	key	doe	bruise
screech		foe	cruise
screen	*Almost all ey	hoe	
seed	teams are found in	roe	
seek	multiple syllable	toe	
seem	words.	woe	

61

Review of Vowel Rules One, Two, Three, and Four
Nonsense Words

1.	keef	fome	quep	meaf	sav
2.	noak	drack	whilt	drope	reen
3.	lunt	twise	ti	heze	yoab
4.	deat	mune	squisp	wabe	jeen
5.	thraft	scri	seab	bede	vay
6.	dro	neen	dite	shamp	doal
7.	blant	hafe	twep	spra	toeg
8.	hile	fle	spop	heef	swost
9.	keze	splisk	blo	noab	lade

Real Words

10.	jade	ho	smash	beet	blunt
11.	fresh	globe	boat	brash	five
12.	flap	film	tow	no	bride
13.	plum	joke	splash	treat	lost
14.	plane	trim	speed	say	slide
15.	strap	stain	trot	clap	stand
16.	shaft	swipe	crate	drank	me
17.	cheap	trash	spoke	toad	mule
18.	blend	fist	so	plank	pray

More Review of Vowel Rules One, Two, Three, and Four
Nonsense Words

1.	crenk	jaste	maint	quete	chonk
2.	quoll	bithe	cleack	grimp	tro
3.	bletch	whone	bloech	chack	smike
4.	cree ch	twone	clunch	skank	scray
5.	brinch	heste	prumpt	thown	sha
6.	cleme	troan	vene	splas	clithe
7.	fla	stroct	cranch	freen	scrent
8.	quev	oax	spape	muve	swinch
9.	frund	smick	squere	twaize	sloke

Real Words

10.	chide	quench	shown	me	clump
11.	tee	flinch	chose	trench	fume
12.	bruise	those	shrunk	blond	phase
13.	twang	foe	fuse	woe	squid
14.	shrine	stretch	preen	she	whale
15.	gait	brisk	shrimp	quote	munch
16.	dwelt	scone	preach	sketch	oath
17.	duke	be	depth	tithe	shrank
18.	glue	sown	gulch	chime	clamp

Vowel Rule Five Teams

ar c<u>ar</u>	*er* h<u>er</u>
ir b<u>ir</u>d	*or* c<u>or</u>n
ur h<u>ur</u>l	*ear* h<u>ear</u>d

Vowel Rule Five Teams
ar er ir ur or ear

Vowel Rule Five - When a vowel is followed by the letter *r* at the end of a word or when a vowel is followed by the letter *r* and immediately followed by a consonant sound, the vowel and the letter *r* combine to form a vowel team. Vowels in this category are marked by underlining the vowel team and writing the number *five* directly under the team. It is very helpful and strongly recommended that students memorize these six vowel teams. Consult the preceding page for examples.

When <u>ear</u> is followed by a consonant sound, <u>ear</u> usually forms a group five vowel team. When <u>ear</u> is followed by a vowel sound or ends a word, *ea* usually forms a team, and the *r* makes its own sound: n<u>ear</u>, h<u>ear</u>d.

| | | | 4 | 5 |

Nonsense Words

1.	dard	ler	surt	nort	tirk
2.	bern	furd	larm	seark	blerk
3.	squird	burl	slort	tarst	clerd
4.	harn	churd	scorb	dirk	twur
5.	blorn	scurp	snarn	nerch	sporsh
6.	skirp	harst	stearch	lork	twur

Real Words

7.	cart	thorn	burn	earth	squirm
8.	fort	shirk	stark	hurt	fork
9.	charm	earn	stork	storm	burst
10.	verb	dirt	mirth	horn	jerk
11.	shirt	arm	turn	blur	first
12.	learn	lurch	dark	churn	cord

65

More Review of Vowel Rule Five Teams
ar   er   ear   ir   or   ur

1.	slerk	sarck	mearl	dard	dorn
2.	nurst	charf	slirl	mern	dearch
3.	quirl	varsh	chorb	sparm	quirb
4.	chirt	swerb	verf	larst	shirp
5.	clorb	slirk	morft	parm	sherst
6.	plerp	querb	lerd	turst	ferl
7.	berck	dorf	horst	wurnt	flird
8.	swer	farb	lorx	twearn	hurm
9.	zirst	blerv	shorst	dearl	larp

Real Words

10.	stern	birch	surf	charm	earl
11.	burnt	parch	berth	squirt	torch
12.	whirl	dearth	lurk	pert	harsh
13.	yarn	scorch	heard	cork	church
14.	yearn	term	hurl	horn	garb
15.	serf	lord	flirt	slur	marsh
16.	blurt	park	morn	perk	smirk
17.	pearl	scarf	birth	north	spark
18.	scorn	chirp	arch	curb	search

66

Mastery Check and Review
Number Ten: Vowel Rule Five

ar		ear	or	ur
arc	mart	earl	born	blur
arch	par	earn	cord	blurt
ark	parch	earth	cork	burn
arm	park	dearth	corn	burnt
art	part	heard	for	burp
bar	scar	learn	fork	burr
barb	scarf	pearl	fort	burst
bard	shark	search	horn	church
bark	sharp	yearn	lord	churl
barn	smart		morn	churn
car	snarl	**ir**	nor	curb
card	spar		north	curd
cart	spark	birch	or	curl
char	star	bird	orb	curt
charm	starch	birth	scorch	fur
chard	stark	chirp	scorn	furl
chart	start	dirt	snort	hurl
dark	tar	fir	sort	hurt
darn	tart	firm	stork	lurch
dart	yard	first	storm	lurk
far	yarn	flirt	thorn	purr
farm		girl	torch	slur
garb	**er**	girth		spur
hard		mirth		spurn
hark	berth	quirk		spurt
harm	clerk	shirk		surf
harp	her	shirt		turf
harsh	herd	sir		turn
jar	jerk	skirt		urn
lard	per	smirk		
lark	perch	squirm		
mar	perk	squirt		
march	pert	stir		
mark	serf	swirl		
marsh	stern	third		
	term	thirst		
	verb	twirl		
		whir		
		whirl		

67

Review of Vowel Rules One, Two, Three, Four, and Five

Nonsense Words

1.	snar	shate	bli	fey	smer
2.	jeen	lunt	naik	drack	glor
3.	mune	squisp	quor	whift	twide
4.	ti	wabe	swesh	kur	reen
5.	spop	toeg	bir	thraft	yor
6.	shamp	ster	twep	doal	fle
7.	scri	plor	flaft	neem	dar
8.	quode	dite	spep	bede	swir
9.	mupe	chift	fave	blar	peet

Real Words

10.	splint	sport	speech	seal	fresh
11.	fern	flint	bloke	lark	hi
12.	squirt	shaft	swipe	slate	charm
13.	drank	me	cheap	spark	trash
14.	spoke	boat	lord	mule	trend
15.	fist	ho	heat	plank	birch
16.	stove	shell	burst	while	no
17.	joke	bland	smoke	thirst	squeak
18.	split	green	farm	meek	foe

More Review of Vowel Rules One, Two, Three, Four, and Five

Nonsense Words

1.	leent	darch	shrenk	glave	cro
2.	milch	yake	cromp	roash	blart
3.	grome	dearch	brint	blay	smish
4.	quilch	brebe	prait	shirth	chiph
5.	sloach	twe	merd	shosh	wunch
6.	whaip	glosh	pretch	blund	proe
7.	blinch	vunk	eed	phect	twebe
8.	foaz	twearch	draze	zo	bonch
9.	blonk	phape	greck	snersh	chetch

Real Words

10.	sweep	close	clench	grasp	shark
11.	tube	stripe	earl	sprain	stench
12.	graph	birch	creak	swept	pose
13.	crust	strain	phrase	starch	vote
14.	thrive	throb	chuck	throw	churn
15.	botch	rule	yearn	creep	length
16.	throw	lurch	cruise	ale	which
17.	flock	bray	scope	crutch	perch
18.	cleat	prime	chirp	shale	speck

Vowel Rule Six Teams

au <u>Au</u>gust	*aw* s<u>aw</u>
oi <u>oi</u>l	*oy* b<u>oy</u>
oo b<u>oo</u>t	<u>*oo*</u> f<u>oo</u>t
ou <u>ou</u>t	*ow* c<u>ow</u>
ew st<u>ew</u>	

Vowel Rule Six Teams
au aw oi oy oo o͟o

Vowel Rule Six - When certain vowels combine to form a team, the first vowel will not say its name, and the team instead makes another sound. Vowels in this category are marked by underlining the team and writing the number *six* directly under the team. The letter team o͟o represents two different sounds; the less frequently encountered second sound is indicated by underlining the letter team twice. It is very helpful and strongly recommended that students memorize these nine vowel teams. Notice that six of these vowel teams begin with the letter o. Consult the preceding page for examples.

Nonsense Words

1.	foog	bloob	droos	joop	toop
2.	moond	loopt	noomp	groot	voy
3.	sploy	zoip	swood	spoog	troif
4.	smoom	sloon	sproop	scroomp	toov
5.	baw	caud	daw	faub	gaw
6.	foib	taw	sloy	doot	slawp

Real Words

7.	coil	broil	joy	point	ploy
8.	smooth	drool	broom	soon	moon
9.	loom	coop	tooth	booth	hood
10.	look	book	stood	took	foot
11.	cook	hoof	crook	brook	shook
12.	launch	bawl	haul	crawl	fault

71

Vowel Rule Six Teams
ew ou ow

Nonsense Words

1.	boun	cowt	doub	fouf	gouk
2.	howm	joug	kout	lewp	mowm
3.	noust	pousk	roubs	vew	youns
4.	zowts	bloub	cloump	floum	glowsp
5.	plowz	scount	slout	smew	snoup
6.	spoun	stous	swoul	sploun	brout
7.	drowd	frouck	groub	prowm	sproub
8.	trowk	shrowl	tewk	whous	shoump

Real Words

9.	owl	crowd	trout	wow	slouch
10.	how	crouch	brown	now	mount
11.	bow	growl	grouch	chew	mound
12.	found	ouch	sound	drew	cloud
13.	clown	loud	round	scout	mouth
14.	chow	proud	fowl	out	grew
15.	cow	gown	town	pound	bound
16.	stout	drown	clew	scowl	down
17.	foul	oust	hound	tout	slew

Review of Vowel Rule Six Teams
au aw ew oi oy oo <u>oo</u> ou ow

Nonsense Words

1.	loy	doop	traw	plaw	haut
2.	boun	mausp	br<u>oo</u>p	foy	moust
3.	drauk	fawl	moof	moim	doy
4.	bew	mauk	boust	foik	hool
5.	bowp	moy	drouft	shoip	nout
6.	hoin	baum	shaw	whoot	splaw
7.	crouf	thauk	choy	clewb	moun
8.	bloy	brout	moip	hoopt	doul

Real Words

9.	cloy	flaunt	brawl	crowd	hawk
10.	brew	fault	oink	oil	broil
11.	shout	soon	coy	yawn	hook
12.	sound	thaw	loin	ploy	dawn
13.	point	new	mouth	joint	too
14.	gown	roost	join	south	hood
15.	pound	Floyd	stew	troop	spoil
16.	maul	soil	doom	fawn	drown
17.	moist	shook	sprawl	how	coin

73

Mastery Check and Review
Number Eleven: Vowel Rule Six Teams

au	raw	oy	spool	hound
daunt	saw	noise	spoon	loud
faun	squ aw	poise	stoop	lout
flaunt	straw	boy	swoon	mound
fraud	thaw	cloy	swoop	mount
gaunt		coy	tool	mouth
haul	**ew**	joy	toot	noun
haunch	blew	toy	too th	pouch
haunt	brew	Troy	troop	pound
jaunt	chew		whoop	pout
laud	crew	**oo**	zoo	proud
launch	dew			round
maul	drew	bloom	**oo**	scour
paunch	flew	boom		scout
taunt	grew	boon	book	shout
taut	news	boost	brook	shroud
vault	new	boot	cook	slouch
vaunt	shrew	boo th	crook	sound
cause	slew	brood	foot	sour
	stew	broom	good	south
aw	threw	cool	hood	spout
bawl		coop	hook	stout
brawl	**oi**	croon	look	trout
brawn		doom	nook	vouch
crawl	oil	droop	rook	
dawn	boil	food	shook	**ow**
drawl	broil	fool	soot	
drawn	coif	gloom	stood	owl
fawn	coil	groom	took	brown
hawk	coin	hoof	wood	crowd
lawn	foist	hoop	wool	crown
pawn	groin	hoot		down
prawn	join	loom		drown
scrawl	joint	loon		fowl
shawl	joist	loop		gown
spawn	loin	loot	**ou**	growl
sprawl	moist	mood	our	howl
squawk	point	moon	oust	prowl
yawn	soil	moot	out	scowl
caw	spoil	noon	bound	town
claw	toil	proof	bout	bow
draw	void	roof	cloud	brow
flaw		room	clout	ch ow
haw		root	couch	cow
jaw		scoop	flour	how
law		shoot	flout	now
paw		smooth	foul	plow
		snoop	found	scow
			gout	vow

74

Review of Vowel Rules One, Two, Three, Four, Five, and Six

Nonsense Words

1.	claft	groad	skube	phorst	crosk
2.	frean	browt	chausk	traze	stri
3.	blilp	shaust	splees	whoze	splirst
4.	hese	ploift	throost	blarf	scretch
5.	bleab	scoifs	shract	whait	prape
6.	clarn	scroem	skells	shive	floff
7.	sperd	chouck	braub	slipe	quisp
8.	swersk	pleept	drine	thrend	smoamp
9.	zipe	ya	wesk	veanst	chine

Real Words

10.	hurl	gulp	say	bite	hard
11.	grouch	trash	doe	daunt	birch
12.	barn	boom	fame	seal	spent
13.	hook	fern	Pete	pray	prompt
14.	bird	couch	key	foe	split
15.	north	brown	pose	bloat	scrimp
16.	burst	blow	boil	fume	rail
17.	stomp	toy	dark	drape	teek
18.	strand	taut	eke	her	branch

More Review of Vowel Rules One, Two, Three, Four, Five, and Six

Nonsense Words

1.	smesk	thrape	dreask	shurst	swi
2.	frand	slaik	brime	chilt	sparf
3.	floam	grefe	skern	scra	phouft
4.	progs	whape	shroe	scirl	blafe
5.	smarp	draimp	plafe	snook	cratch
6.	sweend	birst	shrime	sprooft	straul
7.	shremp	troasp	thrine	chond	whirp
8.	gloe	fruft	slede	flarmp	griffs
9.	ploask	splome	stresh	blonsk	turst

Real Words

10.	strive	hoe	trust	flee	hoist
11.	grow	hay	twist	gloom	tray
12.	greet	draft	skirt	fume	groan
13.	shank	furl	shoot	champ	bone
14.	rain	look	noun	cheek	shine
15.	squint	charm	crow	toil	thine
16.	whiff	trail	imp	shave	chant
17.	eel	fame	brisk	blast	strike
18.	sheep	brine	room	point	cook

Section Three

The instructional procedure changes at this point. No more nonsense words are used. Another important change is that no spelling dictation is done in Section Three of the book. Instead the focus is now entirely directed towards mastering the marking system for decoding. In Section Four we will turn our focus exclusively to spelling. The marking system is very important because a student must understand the phonetic principles involved with any given word in order to be able to mark accurately that word with the system used in this book. Until now only one-syllable words have been used. In this next section students will learn how to divide words into syllables through the application of three syllable rules. As in the previous sections, ample practice will be provided so that each rule can be thoroughly learned.

There is a specific sequence to follow when decoding a word. Follow this precise sequence. Do not skip steps. Always work from left to right as that is the direction in which English is read.

Step One - Underline all vowel and consonant teams. (Later in the program the second sounds of *c* and *g* are introduced; mark those letters when appropriate.)

Step Two - If a word ends with a silent letter *e*, underline the letter *e* once to indicate it is silent.

Step Three - Place dots under all vowels which make sounds. Place one centered dot under each vowel team.

Step Four - If necessary, divide the word into syllables, listing the correct syllable rule number above the word or even with the letters in the word. (Identify consonant blends which must be protected. See page eighty-two.)

Step Five - Determine the vowel group number for each vowel sound in the word, and write that number directly under the vowel or vowel team. When encountering a word containing a vowel rule *three* configuration, always write the vowel rule number under the vowel which makes the sound. Numbers written under syllables always indicate vowel sounds. Each syllable must have one and only one vowel sound.

Step Six - Blend the syllable sounds together in multiple syllable words. Proceeding from left to right only, isolate the sound of the first syllable and then that of the second syllable. Blend those two sounds together. Next determine the sound of the third syllable if there is one, and blend that sound with the sound of the combined first and second syllables. Continue in this sequence until the entire word syllable by syllable is sounded out and then blended together. Note that the student should first divide into syllables and then mark each word before reading that word out loud.

77

Consonant Blends and Letter Teams Review Page
Beginning Consonant Blends
L Blends

bl	*cl*	*fl*
gl	*pl*	*sl*

R Blends

br	*cr*	*dr*
fr	*gr*	*pr/tr*

S Blends

sc	*sk*	*sl*
sm	*sn*	*sp*
st	*sw*	*scr*
spl	*spr*	*str/squ*

Ending Consonant Blends
L Blends

lb	*ld*	*lf*
lk	*lm*	*lp/lt*

S Blends

sk	*sp*	*st*

Other Ending Blends

ct	*ft*	*mp*
nd	*nt*	*pt/ps*

Major Consonant Teams

ch	*tch*	*ck*
ng	*ph*	*qu*
sh	*th / th*	*wh*

Major Vowel Teams
Vowel Rule Four Teams

ai	*ay*	*ea*
ee	*ey*	*oa*
oe	*ow*	*ue/ ue*

Vowel Rule Five Teams

ar	*er*	*ear*
ir	*ur*	*or*

Vowel Rule Six Teams

au	*aw*	*ew*
oi	*oy*	*oo*
oo	*ou*	*ow*

• This page is a quick reference guide to the blends and letter teams learned thus far in the program.

Unit Eleven
Syllable Rules

Syllable rules indicate where words divide into syllables. Each syllable must have one and only one vowel sound; each vowel sound in a word must have its own syllable. We will learn the three syllable rules which govern syllable division for any word in English. Syllable rules one and two are introduced at this point in the program; syllable rule three will be introduced at a later point in the program.

Syllable Rule One - When two vowel sounds are separated by one consonant, syllable division is usually before the consonant.

All syllable rules are set off by dashes. Write the number *one*, and then set that number off by dashes to divide between syllables when syllable rule one is in effect. When dividing a word already printed out where it is not possible to insert dashes between syllables, draw instead a line between the letters where division occurs. Start the line above the letters, and continue the line below the letters so as to avoid confusing the division line for another letter. In this instance syllable rule numbers go above the letters and vowel rule numbers go below the letters. Place the syllable rule number directly above the syllable division line or to the side of the line if there is not enough room directly above it.

	1	1	1	← Syllable Rule Numbers
	si|lent	ta|ble	pho|to	
	2 1	2 7	2 2	← Vowel Rule Numbers

Vowel - Consonant - Vowel

1.	result	nomad	student	bonus
2.	iris	resist	deter	elect
3.	rodent	token	sequel	bequest
4.	zero	season	silent	begin
5.	adult	focus	began	select
6.	resent	brazen	human	remit
7.	demand	amen	joker	making
8.	refund	mucus	defect	present
9.	using	emit	prefix	tidings

Syllable Rule Two

Syllable Rule Two - When two vowel sounds are separated by two or more consonants, the syllable is usually divided between the first and second of those consonant letters. When syllable rule two is in effect, write the number *two* set off by dashes to divide between the two syllables: rab-2-bit, fil-2-ter, pic-2-nic, jel-2-lo.

   1   1 1   5 1   1 1   2

Vowel - Consonant - Consonant - Vowel

1.	conduct	tonsil	cannon	tennis
2.	gossip	victim	seldom	subject
3.	whiplash	kidnap	blanket	classic
4.	gallop	lesson	publish	contact
5.	afford	fossil	basket	district
6.	enrich	inquest	piston	hamlet
7.	cactus	nutshell	congress	convict
8.	fragment	conquest	better	instinct
9.	tinsel	downtown	ransack	muffin
10.	pamphlet	bandit	buzzard	flutter
11.	segment	distant	hammock	napkin
12.	vendor	kindred	public	embark
13.	monster	nostril	unpack	hollow
14	skeptic	attempt	snapper	zigzag
15.	flipper	common	luster	standard
16.	object	bellow	dictate	rustic
17.	confuse	jabber	drummer	gutter

Review of Syllable Rules One and Two

1.	shrunken	prevail	impose	idol
2.	bogus	hunger	miser	eastern
3.	cremate	whimper	gospel	predict
4.	chapter	laurel	gusto	maggot
5.	dolphin	addict	winnow	framer
6.	August	specter	splinter	viper
7.	icon	humdrum	barber	obtrude
8.	mellow	presto	bonnet	retire
9.	often	voter	author	trinket
10.	devise	assume	jumbo	incline
11.	furnish	teepee	latent	dispute
12.	shimmer	lawyer	footprint	edict
13.	pretend	amend	torment	fluster
14.	doctor	female	igloo	beset
15.	founder	victor	diner	clutter
16.	orbit	elbow	emote	vapor
17.	jester	hello	await	junket
18.	tempo	detail	motel	acute
19.	ego	slipper	vulgar	funnel
20.	pollen	ruler	distinct	meter

Applying Syllable Rules One and Two
with Consonant Blends

L Blends

bl	cl	fl	gl	pl	sl

R Blends

br	cr	dr	fr	gr	pr	tr

S Blends

sc	sk	sl	sm	sn	sp	st
sw	scr	spl	spr	str	squ	

Consonant teams and consonant blends are counted as one letter when counting the number of consonants between vowels to determine where to divide a word into syllables. As an example in the word *respond* the consonant blend *sp* counts as one letter; thus syllable rule one is in effect when dividing *respond* into syllables: re-1-spond. In the word *mushroom* the team *sh* is counted as one letter: mush-2-room.

Letter teams are always underlined; however, consonant blends are never marked unless a consonant blend occurring between two vowel sounds would be split up when applying either syllable rule one or two. In this instance and only in this instance join the consonant blend letters together in a half circle to show that these letters remain together in the same syllable because they form a blend.
a-1-cross re-1-spect

Note that while consonant teams never separate, consonant letters which form blends in some words will in other words separate and divide into different syllables: re-1-flect, tef-2-lon, chest-2-nut, Ches-2-ter.

1.	teaspoon	deflate	urchin	matrix
2.	program	retreat	spendthrift	hangman
3.	bestow	gopher	protrude	detract
4.	orphan	secret	bumpkin	respond
5.	outshine	deplete	betray	sackcloth
6.	rancher	regret	reprint	neglect
7.	sportsman	nitric	playground	egret

Unit Twelve
Vowel Rule Seven

Vowel Rule 7- When a word ends in a consonant followed by the letters *le*, that consonant and *le* form the final syllable. When, however, a word ends in *ckle*, the letters *le* generally stand alone as the final syllable. In either case *le* is a vowel team with no vowel sound. Final syllables which end in *le* are with few exceptions the only syllables in English which have no vowel sound: bat <u>tle</u>, pick <u>le</u>.
    7   7

When a syllable does not divide according to the appropriate syllable rule and instead divides at some other point within the word, write the syllable rule number that normally would apply wherever the syllables actually divide, and then underline that syllable rule number. The underlined number indicates that an exception to the normal division rule is occurring. This situation often occurs in words where a short vowel is followed by the consonant letter *x* or the consonant teams *ck*, *ng*, or *tch* which must remain with the short vowel: ti<u>ck</u>-<u>1</u>-<u>le</u>, box-<u>1</u>-er.

Vowel Rule Seven

1.	babble	paddle	bubble	chuckle
2.	jumble	puzzle	ankle	tickle
3.	kettle	shackle	gurgle	title
4.	middle	heckle	table	scribble
5.	fickle	cuddle	dazzle	wobble
6.	smuggle	jingle	trickle	swindle
7.	dimple	buckle	crackle	battle
8.	fiddle	sparkle	mangle	speckle
9.	dwindle	fumble	settle	little
10.	muddle	noodle	gamble	stumble
11.	foible	thimble	sickle	mettle
12.	haggle	riddle	twinkle	tackle

83

le			
able	goggle	puzzle	tinkle
amble	grapple	rabble	title
ample	grumble	ramble	toddle
angle	gurgle	rankle	topple
ankle	guzzle	rattle	tousle
apple	haggle	riddle	treble
axle	handle	rifle	tremble
battle	hobble	ruffle	trifle
beagle	huddle	rumble	triple
beetle	humble	rumple	trundle
bible	hurdle	sable	tumble
bottle	hurtle	saddle	turtle
bramble	idle	sample	tussle
bridle	jangle	scramble	twinkle
bubble	jiggle	scribble	uncle
bugle	jingle	scruple	waddle
cable	joggle	scuttle	waffle
candle	juggle	settle	wiggle
chortle	jumble	shamble	wobble
cobble	jungle	shingle	
coddle	kettle	shuffle	
cradle	kindle	shuttle	*ckle*
crinkle	ladle	simple	buckle
cripple	mangle	single	cackle
crumble	mantle	smuggle	chuckle
cuddle	maple	snuggle	crackle
dangle	marble	spangle	fickle
dapple	meddle	sparkle	hackle
dazzle	mettle	spindle	heckle
dimple	middle	sprinkle	pickle
doodle	mingle	stable	shackle
dribble	muffle	staple	sickle
drizzle	mumble	startle	speckle
eagle	muzzle	steeple	tackle
fable	needle	stifle	tickle
feeble	nibble	straddle	trickle
fiddle	nimble	straggle	
foible	noble	strangle	
fondle	noodle	struggle	
fumble	nuzzle	stubble	
gable	paddle	stumble	
gamble	pebble	swindle	
garble	peddle	table	
gargle	pimple	tangle	
giggle	poodle	temple	
gobble	prattle	thimble	
	puddle	tingle	
	purple		

84

Two-Syllable Words
Vowel Rule Four Teams: *ai ay ea ee ey oa oe ow ue*

1. abbey	constrain	maiden	canteen
2. donkey	approach	heedless	beaten
3. entail	villain	medley	sheepskin
4. kidney	contain	treatment	waitress
5. chimney	inlay	alley	midway
6. trolley	complaint	increase	mislead
7. Yankee	monkey	valley	upkeep
8. squeamish	obtain	impeach	unload
9. railing	mislay	indeed	upstream
10. esteem	constraint	galley	treason
11. payment	attain	jockey	blackmail
12. complain	mainland	peacock	fifteen
13. disclaim	raisin	motley	toadstool
14. rescue	fellow	volley	steamship
15. explain	acquaint	appeal	plaintiff
16. value	sustain	mayhem	crayfish
17. abstain	display	assail	disdain
18. exclaim	ingrain	midday	bowling
19. discreet	mistake	essay	raindrop
20. captain	playpen	inroad	seamstress

Two-Syllable Words
Vowel Rule Five Teams: *ar er ir or ur*
Vowel Rule Six Teams: *au aw ew oi oy oo oo ou ow*

1. harness	assert	unhurt	outwit
2. perfect	carpet	thousand	exploit
3. perhaps	anoint	foolish	augment
4. subvert	escort	stubborn	balloon
5. verdict	hermit	persist	enjoy
6. forget	morbid	checker	appoint
7. convert	import	target	alloy
8. permit	artist	hardship	disjoint
9. invert	squirrel	manner	employ
10. market	support	filter	account
11. correct	banner	garden	annoy
12. expert	garment	transport	surpass
13. monsoon	varnish	merchant	convoy
14. ferment	platform	raccoon	mushroom
15. faster	contort	tabloid	under
16. cornet	lantern	embroil	dewdrop
17. perplex	sarcasm	enjoin	awning
18. insert	distort	mawkish	bitter
19. hornet	pattern	buffoon	turban

Two-Syllable Words

Vowel Rule Four Teams: *ai ay ea ee ey oa oe ow*
Vowel Rule FiveTeams: *ar er ir or ur*
Vowel Rule Six Teams: *au aw ew oi oy oo oo ou ow*

1. abate	refer	bemoan	belay
2. halo	between	humor	odor
3. declaim	aloof	rejoin	shaven
4. betray	proclaim	polite	trigger
5. profound	razor	destroy	vacate
6. milkweed	restrain	elope	ahoy
7. relay	bewail	promote	devout
8. obese	remote	radar	toothbrush
9. demote	tiger	hallow	overt
10. atone	relate	tumor	defeat
11. minor	despoil	denote	wafer
12. sober	demean	domain	refrain
13. retail	taker	reclaim	dilute
14. disturb	ago	rumor	detain
15. canine	reproof	devour	amount
16. avail	regain	delay	prepare
17. solo	strident	saber	retain
18. spider	labor	vibrate	decay

Two-Syllable Words
Vowel Rule Four Teams: *ai ay ea ee ey oa oe ow*
Vowel Rule Five Teams: *ar er ir or ur*
Vowel Rule Six Teams: *au aw ew oi oy oo oo ou ow*

1. bloomer	outside	outgrowth	pointer
2. arcade	rainbow	forebode	perfume
3. beeline	sailboat	forsake	storeroom
4. airmail	perspire	outburst	speaker
5. cartoon	scooter	namesake	boyhood
6. bridegroom	trooper	outlay	verbose
7. curtail	owner	cloudburst	boomer
8. cooler	sideboard	ornate	launder
9. foretaste	sailor	portray	boarder
10. harpoon	cookbook	flounder	weaver
11. gainsay	sideways	partake	oyster
12. moonshine	waistline	broiler	roadside
13. forgave	lookout	pervade	trawler
14. milestone	grapevine	cleaver	toaster
15. mainsail	partook	homemade	ouster
16. roommate	daydream	stateroom	surmount
17. nineteenth	seeker	rosewood	saunter
18. railroad	cloister	meanwhile	barter
19. rooster	corrode	moisture	porter

88

Unit Fourteen
Vowel Rule Eight

Vowel Rule Eight - The vowels *a, o,* and *u* each have an extra sound in addition to their short and long sounds. Write the number *8* under the letters *a, o,* and *u* whenever any one of them make its extra sound.

The letter *a* will often make its extra sound when followed by the letter *l* at the end of a word or when *a* is followed by *l* plus another consonant even when the consonant after *l* is located in the next syllable. The letter *a* also will make its extra sound when *a* is the very last letter in a word or when *a* is preceded by the *w* sound. When *a* makes its extra sound, write the number *8* under the *a:* halt, wall, extra, wasp, equal.

The extra sound for *o* is *oo* as in *do*. The extra sound for *u* is <u>oo</u> as in *put*. There is usually no way to determine from *o* or *u*'s position in a word when these vowels will make their extra sound; however, words containing the extra sound of *o* and *u* tend to be very common one-syllable words. The letter *u* makes its extra sound in words ending in *ful*: joyful, painful.

1.	watch	full	soda	Anna
2.	proven	stall	zebra	squander
3.	to	bald	stalk	wander
4.	ambush	waltz	bullet	Cuba
5.	small	who	comma	squabble
6.	bull	was	also	thrall
7.	swaddle	push	whom	tuna
8.	squall	squadron	falter	do
9.	hula	bushel	careful	wallet
10.	China	mouthful	extra	put
11.	gall	balk	water	Walter

Mastery Check and Review
Number Thirteen: Extra Sound of *a, o,* and *u*

a		u
almost	swadd<u>le</u>	ambu<u>sh</u>
appall	talk	<u>ar</u>mful
bald	tall	<u>ar</u>tful
balk	<u>th</u>rall	<u>aw</u>ful
ball	tuna	ba<u>sh</u>ful
befall	walk	blissful
caldron	wall	bull
calk	wallet	bullet
call	walnut	bu<u>sh</u>
call<u>er</u>	walrus	bu<u>sh</u>el
<u>ch</u>alk	waltz	car<u>e</u>ful
<u>Ch</u>ina	wand<u>er</u>	<u>ch</u>eerful
comma	wasp	fa<u>ith</u>ful
Cuba	wat<u>er</u>	f<u>ea</u>rful
extra	zebra	full
fall		handful
fallen		h<u>ar</u>mful
falt<u>er</u>		helpful
gall	***o***	j<u>oy</u>ful
hall	do	lawful
halt	into	m<u>ou</u><u>th</u>ful
halt<u>er</u>	lo<u>s</u>er	n<u>ee</u>dful
hula	proven	p<u>ai</u>nful
install	to	pl<u>ay</u>ful
mall	<u>wh</u>o	puddi<u>ng</u>
malt	<u>wh</u>om	pull
pall		pu<u>sh</u>
recall		put
salt		sc<u>or</u>nful
scald		<u>sh</u>a<u>me</u>ful
small		sinful
soda		sp<u>oo</u>nful
squabb<u>le</u>		<u>th</u>ankful
squadron		us<u>e</u>ful
squall		
squand<u>er</u>		
stall		

Unit Fifteen
Exceptions to Vowel Rules One, Two, and Three

Exceptions to Vowel Rule One - Sometimes because of its position, in a syllable, a vowel according to vowel rule number one should make its short sound but instead makes its long sound. In this instance underline the number *one* under the vowel. *The underlined vowel rule number indicates that an exception to vowel rule one is occurring.* Exceptions to vowel rule one most commonly occur in one-syllable words containing the vowels *i* or *o* when they are followed by two consonants: child, colt.

1   1

Exceptions to Vowel Rules Two and Three - Sometimes because of its position in a syllable, a vowel according to vowel rule number two or vowel rule number three should make its long sound but will instead make its short sound. In this instance underline the numbers *two* or *three*. *When vowel rule numbers two or three are underlined, the underlined numbers indicate that an exception to vowel rules two or three is occurring.* di vide, gone.

2   3

* Exceptions to vowel rule numbers one, two, and three often cannot be identified prior to sounding out the word. In those such instances trial and error is the only method by which a student will know when an exception to the first three vowel rules is occurring.

1.	bass	cadet	grind	tribute
2.	scold	honey	chamber	credit
3.	famish	wild	holster	salute
4.	mind	decade	scroll	color
5.	gross	pint	divine	sedate
6.	polish	devil	mold	climate
7.	dozen	binder	stroll	host
8.	poll	behold	kind	debit
9.	divide	told	disease	toll

Letters *ar er ir or ur* Followed by a Vowel Sound

When a vowel comes before the letter *r* at the end of a syllable or when a vowel is followed by the letter *r* and another consonant, the vowel plus the *r* form a vowel rule five team. When the vowels *a, e, i, o,* and *u* plus *r* are followed immediately by another vowel, then the first vowel and the letter *r* often each make a separate sound and do not combine to form a team. When a vowel is immediately followed by two *r* letters, the vowel plus the first letter *r* will usually not form a team: i-1-rate, mir-2-ror.

	2	3	1	5
1.	bare	sphere	boredom	Harold
2.	dire	mirror	compare	marrow
3.	lure	burrow	adhere	erode
4.	bore	admire	bereft	sparrow
5.	blare	terror	mire	carrot
6.	fire	spirit	baron	fanfare
7.	pure	barrel	aspire	parish
8.	fore	quagmire	surround	acquire
9.	care	parrot	conspire	ferret
10.	hire	irate	farewell	perish
11.	secure	ensnare	surreal	horror
12.	hero	duress	erupt	transpire
13.	Huron	spire	during	siren
14.	narrate	Carol	merit	sparing
15.	peril	Iran	Karen	error

Two-Syllable Words: Cumulative Review

Vowel Rule Four Teams - *ai ay ea ee ey oa oe ow*
Vowel Rule Five Teams - *ar er ir or ur*
Vowel Rule Six Teams: *au aw ew oi oy oo oo ou ow*

1.	rabbit	pillow	Joseph	splendid
2.	impress	pudding	mermaid	lilac
3.	pastel	sirloin	torpor	venom
4.	London	imbibe	extent	fester
5.	startle	chowder	phonics	shelter
6.	patter	limit	sharpen	caldron
7.	redeem	expose	donate	moonbeam
8.	cluster	ruffle	coddle	stagger
9.	ditto	uproar	alpha	timid
10.	address	halter	item	profane
11.	flagrant	sector	music	stampede
12.	lobster	mishap	miscount	mundane
13.	shameful	walnut	traffic	muzzle
14.	reflect	waxen	preclude	major
15.	picnic	lampoon	frazzle	tender
16.	awful	mottle	sluggish	medal
17.	open	photo	confess	shamble
18.	other	because	accrue	snuggle
19.	goggle	plastic	decline	scald

93

Two-Syllable Words: Cumulative Review
Vowel Rule Four Teams - *ai ay ea ee ey oa oe ow*
Vowel Rule Five Teams - *ar er ir or ur*
Vowel Rule Six Teams: *au aw ew oi oy oo oo ou ow*

1. disrupt	serpent	splendor	below
2. excuse	convent	confound	maintain
3. default	recall	harbor	pistol
4. audit	banquet	witness	pellet
5. tattoo	trample	concoct	scornful
6. appall	poison	polka	goblin
7. context	darling	reckon	patrol
8. outlaw	virtue	pester	tactics
9. weasel	ostrich	temper	methane
10. painless	either	ticklish	walrus
11. farther	bicker	oppress	Friday
12. auburn	whittle	weevil	label
13. condone	whisper	welcome	expel
14. turkey	pitcher	stagnate	seaboard
15. befall	exhale	loser	finish
16. condor	meager	acquit	mistook
17. serum	inform	quibble	attach
18. magnet	order	eject	into

Sounds for c̲ and g̲
Consonant Teams *ce ge dge*

c̲	g̲
c̲ent	g̲em
ce	*ge*
dan**c̲e**	char**g̲e**
dge	
e**d̲ge**	

Sounds c̲ ce

When *c* is followed by the letters *e*, *i*, or *y*, it will usually make its second sound. There are very few exceptions to this rule. Use a double underline to indicate when *c* is not part of a team yet makes its second sound: fac̲e̲, c̲ell, i-1-c̲ing, pen-2-c̲il, voic̲e̲.
        3   1 2   1   1   1 6

The letter team *ce* is a consonant team when the letter *e*'s sole purpose in following the *c* is to enable the *c* to make its second sound and has no other function in the word. The *e* which follows the *c* in this instance is silent: princ̲e̲, danc̲e̲, ro-1-manc̲e̲, si-1-lenc̲e̲.
              1   1   2   1   2 1

1.	rancid	wince	spice	censor
2.	farce	concern	nuisance	ounce
3.	commerce	spruce	ceiling	entrance
4.	cinch	stencil	princess	office
5.	cigar	succeed	fleece	license
6.	trance	force	biceps	process
7.	peace	concert	accent	announce
8.	sentence	device	invoice	racism
9.	cease	icing	balance	sauce
10.	pounce	substance	advanc̲e̲	pincers
11.	conceal	furnace	notice	space
12.	sincere	decide	romance	chance
13.	divorce	acid	practice	rejoice
14.	bounce	cancel	embrace	choice
15.	pencil	success	glance	truce

96

c			*ce*	
accent	decease	produce	absence	pounce
accept	decent	race	advance	practice
access	decide	racism	announce	prance
ace	deduce	rancid	balance	prince
acid	deface	recede	bounce	rejoice
advice	device	recent	cadence	renounce
biceps	dice	recess	chalice	riddance
brace	disgrace	recite	chance	romance
bracelet	embrace	reduce	choice	sauce
bracing	entice	replace	clearance	sentence
cancel	face	rice	commence	service
cancer	forceps	saucer	commerce	silence
cease	grace	scarce	crevice	since
cedar	grocer	secede	dance	solstice
cede	ice	sincere	denounce	stance
cell	icing	slice	divorce	substance
cement	incense	space	dunce	trance
censor	incite	spice	entrance	wince
census	lace	splice	essence	
cent	lice	spruce	farce	
cesspool	license	stencil	fence	
cider	mace	succeed	fleece	
cigar	mice	success	force	
cinch	misplace	thrice	furnace	
cinder	nice	trace	glance	
cipher	pace	truce	hence	
circle	parcel	twice	instance	
cite	pencil	vice	invoice	
citrus	pincers	voice	juice	
civil	place		justice	
conceal	precede		lance	
concede	precept		lettuce	
concept	precinct		mince	
concern	precise		notice	
concert	price		novice	
concise	princess		nuisance	
dancer	proceed		office	
	process		ounce	
			peace	
			penance	

97

Unit Seventeen
Sounds _g_ _ge_ _dge_

When _g_ is followed by the letters _e_, _i_, or _y_, it will usually make its second sound. There are a number of exceptions to this rule with the letter _g_. Use a double underline to indicate when _g_ is not part of a team yet makes its second sound: stage, gent.
3   1

The letter team _ge_ is a consonant team when the letter _e's_ sole purpose in following the _g_ is to enable the _g_ to make its second sound. The _e_ which follows the _g_ in this instance is silent: plunge, charge.
1   5

Letter combination _dge_ is a team when it occurs at the end of a syllable. The letter team _dge_ represents the sound _j_ and is used only when it directly follows the short sound of a vowel: edge.
1

1.	bridge	merger	agent	emerge
2.	bulge	badge	disgorge	hedge
3.	enlarge	plunger	nudge	staging
4.	budge	wedge	urgent	indulge
5.	strange	lounge	wager	begrudge
6.	digest	fringe	sludge	manger
7.	trudge	vigil	exchange	forge
8.	ranger	huge	diverge	dodge
9.	outrage	ledge	gender	plunge
10.	submerge	gouge	college	sledge
11.	smudge	barge	cringe	ginger
12.	engage	discharge	pledge	range
13.	ingest	ridge	merge	angel

g		ge	dge
age	huge	barge	badge
agent	ingest	bilge	begrudge
angel	legend	bulge	bridge
cage	logic	charge	budge
change	magic	college	dislodge
congeal	manger	cringe	dodge
congest	merger	dirge	drudge
digest	outrage	discharge	edge
digit	page	disgorge	fudge
engage	plunger	diverge	grudge
enrage	rage	divulge	hedge
exchange	range	emerge	judge
fragile	ranger	enlarge	ledge
frigid	refuge	expunge	lodge
gee	regent	forge	nudge
gem	rigid	fringe	pledge
gender	sage	gorge	ridge
gene	stage	gouge	sedge
gent	staging	hinge	sledge
gentile	strange	impinge	sludge
germ	tangent	indulge	smudge
germane	tragic	infringe	trudge
gin	turgid	large	wedge
ginger	urgent	lounge	
gist	vigil	lunge	
	wage	merge	
	wager	orange	
		plunge	
		purge	
		serge	
		singe	
		sponge	
		submerge	
		surge	
		tinge	
		twinge	
		urge	
		verge	

The Letter Y

y yard	g**y**m 1
b**y** 2	ba-1-b**y** 2
styl**e** 3	*ay* 4 pr**ay**
ey 4 k**ey**	*oy* 6 t**oy**

The Letter *y*

The letter *y* can function as either a vowel or consonant in a word. The letter *y* as a vowel within a word is marked as any other vowel normally would be. In English *y* as a vowel has no sound of its own and instead normally represents the short and long sounds of the vowel *i*. Keep in mind, however, that the vowel *y* has two long sounds. When *y* makes the sound *ee* as in baby, double underline the *y* to indicate that the vowel *y* is making its second long sound. Unlike the vowel *u* which is the only other vowel to make two long sounds, the vowel *y* makes its second long sound only in the vowel rule two position. The vowel *u* may make its second long sound in both the vowel rule two and three positions. The letter *y* is a vowel in every position in a word other than the first letter in the syllable. When the letter *y* is the first letter in a syllable, it then is a consonant, and no mark is made to it.

The six functions of *y*

1. The letter *y* is a consonant at the beginning of any syllable as in *yard*.

2. The letter *y* makes the short sound of *i* when it is the only vowel in a syllable and is followed by a consonant as in the word *gym:* gym.

1

3. When the letter *y* is at the end of a one-syllable word and *y* is the only vowel in the syllable, it makes the long sound of *i* as in the word by: by.

2

4. The letter *y* occurring by itself at the end of any syllable after the first syllable in a word generally makes the long sound of *e* as in *baby*. There are some exceptions to this rule where the letter *y* in this position will make the long sound of *i* as in *lullaby*.

First Long Sound of *y* - by \ lul la by   **Second Long Sound of *y*** - ba by

2   2   2

5. When two vowels in one syllable are separated by one or more consonants, and the first vowel is the letter *y* and the second vowel is a silent letter *e*, then the letter y makes the long sound of *i*, and the letter *e* is silent as in the word *style*: styl<u>e</u>.

3

6. The letter *y* is part of the vowel teams <u>ay</u> and <u>ey</u> and <u>oy</u> in which the letter *y* is silent: p<u>ay</u>, k<u>ey</u>, b<u>oy</u>.

4   4   6

101

Sounds of *y*
Short and Long Sound of *i*

1.	hymnal	supply	python	pylon
2.	rely	vinyl	by	hereby
3.	thereby	pry	hydrant	thy
4.	sky	system	sylvan	ally
5.	crystal	typhus	gyrate	shy
6.	physics	hyphen	sly	cynic
7.	cyclist	defy	thyroid	mystic
8.	cymbal	abyss	apply	cyclone
9.	dry	lymph	cycle	gypsum

Long Sound of *e*

10.	entry	angry	rowdy	mushy
11.	navy	scurry	rangy	tardy
12.	holly	dizzy	pantry	cozy
13.	dowdy	only	ruby	lowly
14.	puny	marry	noisy	moody
15.	dingy	murky	whisky	gently
16.	hurry	hooky	gloomy	frisky
17.	sloppy	hardly	balmy	pony
18.	daisy	easy	duty	lofty
19.	breezy	early	bulky	queasy

Letter Y Consonant and Vowel Review

1.	cry	yams	play	bay
2.	stay	fancy	fly	bounty
3.	crypt	yammer	gym	type
4.	okay	imply	tray	city
5.	deny	ply	baggy	yet
6.	army	cyst	lay	decry
7.	poppy	bony	syrup	sly
8.	yen	manly	lousy	pray
9.	spy	clay	lynch	myth
10.	body	gravy	pry	yellow
11.	yard	shy	reply	wavy
12.	hybrid	dummy	typhoid	may
13.	greedy	why	comply	husky
14.	key	pay	fussy	fry
15.	my	stodgy	envy	gyp
16.	filthy	outcry	Yukon	belly
17.	defy	hay	chilly	Lynn
18.	oily	faulty	lynx	paltry
19.	mercy	dry	candy	very
20.	fray	baby	booty	empty

Mastery Check and Review
Number Sixteen: *y* as a Vowel

y as short *i* sound	*y* as long *i* sound		*y* as long *e* sound	
abyss	ally	thyroid	easy	pantry
crypt	apply	try	empty	penny
cryptic	by	trying	entry	pity
crystal	cry	type	envy	pony
cymbal	cycle	typhoid	fancy	poppy
cynic	cyclist	typhus	faulty	pretty
cyst	cyclone	tyrant	fifty	puny
gym	cypress	why	filthy	putty
gyp	defy		flaky	pygmy
gypsum	deny	**y as long e sound**	foggy	qu easy
gypsy	dry	angry	frisky	rang y
hymnal	fly	army	funny	really
lymph	fry	baby	fuzzy	rowdy
lynch	gyrate	baggy	gently	ruby
lynx	hereby	balmy	gloomy	rusty
lyric	hybrid	body	gravy	sandy
mystic	hydrant	bony	greasy	scurry
myth	hyphen	bounty	greedy	shady
physics	imply	breezy	gully	shaggy
pygmy	lyre	bulky	handy	skinny
sylvan	my	bully	hardly	snowy
symbol	ply	burly	hobby	speedy
symptom	pry	bushy	hooky	steely
syntax	pylon	carry	husky	stodgy
syrup	python	clammy	jury	sunny
system	rely	clergy	lady	tardy
vinyl	reply	cloudy	leaky	tidy
	shy	copy	lobby	twenty
	sky	coz y	lofty	trusty
	sly	crazy	lowly	truly
	spry	daddy	marry	ugly
	spy	dairy	milky	very
	style	dais y	misty	wary
	supply	dewy	moody	wildly
	thereby	ding y	mummy	windy
	thy	dirty	musty	woody
		dizzy	nasty	worldly
		dowdy	navy	worry
		dusty	nois y	worth y
		duty	oily	

Comprehensive Review

1.	clearance	symptom	grocer	murder
2.	cable	fabric	style	decent
3.	congeal	fable	steely	symbol
4.	respect	corner	install	cackle
5.	crony	cryptic	humane	dislodge
6.	gorge	surprise	needful	miner
7.	bully	congest	lyric	insane
8.	access	chatter	legend	obscure
9.	fertile	burly	deduce	propping
10.	mummy	enrage	copy	table
11.	cheaply	recess	sponge	cattle
12.	syntax	gentile	regent	profile
13.	stroller	gist	excess	tyrant
14.	produce	bottle	contest	circle
15.	precinct	afraid	folly	fortress
16.	change	entice	hackle	purple
17.	instance	rooster	vagrant	effort
18.	tangent	chamber	survive	citrus
19.	really	juice	essence	molest
20.	charcoal	bracelet	tragic	divulge

More Comprehensive Review

1. recede	contrite	clergy	repel
2. magic	solstice	escape	woody
3. uncle	rubbish	nanny	English
4. drudge	noble	surge	freedom
5. bracing	accept	crumble	ballot
6. infringe	digit	blister	marble
7. clammy	refuge	penny	recent
8. renounce	austere	budge	impinge
9. event	recite	traitor	mature
10. slimy	moment	replace	jersey
11. console	commence	fragile	badger
12. Chinese	octave	sleazy	apron
13. disgrace	across	ignite	gypsy
14. germane	musket	Roman	pollute
15. concede	tangle	reduce	carbon
16. forceps	fifty	muster	absence
17. cinder	disown	logic	denounce
18. bargain	cement	transcribe	lettuce
19. pacer	service	decease	panther
20. unit	advice	cloudy	precise

Letter Team *ed*

The letter team *ed* is a letter team when used at the end of a word to indicate past tense. The letter team *ed* makes a vowel sound and forms its own syllable when it follows directly after the letters *d* or *t*. In this instance divide the syllable containing the *ed* team using syllable rules one or two. When *ed* forms its own syllable along with the preceding *t* or *d* letter, underline the *ed* team and place a one directly under the letter *e* to indicate that while *ed* functions as a team, the letter *e* will make its short sound: no-1-t<u>ed</u>, nod-2-d<u>ed</u>.

1   1

The letter team *ed* as a letter team does not form its own syllable when it is not preceded by the letters *d* or *t*. In this instance, the first vowel in the syllable will make the syllable's vowel sound. Note that when the *ed* team does not form its own syllable and is preceded by two or more consonants, the first vowel in that syllable will make its short sound. In the instance where the *ed* is separated from the first vowel in the syllable by only one consonant, the letter *e* in the *ed* team will often serve as a signal to the first vowel to make its long sound: pinn<u>ed</u>, bak<u>ed</u>.

1   3

1.	shaped	jammed	batted	rested
2.	wined	dimmed	rotted	tipped
3.	polished	matted	scraped	baked
4.	blessed	shouted	nodded	seemed
5.	hoped	traded	toasted	dusted
6.	landed	stopped	returned	happened
7.	picked	ravished	founded	faked
8.	rested	raked	pleaded	hummed
9.	wheeled	fitted	resumed	prepared
10.	planted	hugged	danced	rated
11.	flattened	added	pointed	marked

Three-Syllable Words

1.	organic	industry	badminton	compensate
2.	ancestry	gingerly	narcotic	consonant
3.	encounter	communist	December	terminus
4.	constancy	ancestor	encumber	prosecute
5.	imitate	adventure	magnetism	porcupine
6.	utensil	daffodil	engagement	important
7.	raspberry	luxury	advertise	incident
8.	counselor	Olympics	retirement	uncommon
9.	discover	octagon	finalize	delinquent
10.	balcony	remainder	tranquilize	potato
11.	decipher	officer	sanctity	merchandise
12.	molasses	currency	blasphemy	disinfect
13.	buffalo	embassy	expedite	syllable
14.	density	detergent	tormentor	furniture
15.	projector	enamel	synopsis	stabilize
16.	acrobat	vinegar	summary	alphabet
17.	insolvent	disorder	adequate	informant
18.	hypocrite	overlook	innocent	enterprise
19.	marmalade	captivate	disengage	bursitis
20.	dependent	abnormal	eccentric	ratify

More Three-Syllable Words

1.	impetus	bachelor	substitute	impolite
2.	agreement	fascinate	deployment	formulate
3.	appetite	passenger	computer	universe
4.	excellent	undermine	turbulent	abdomen
5.	edible	magnetize	wonderland	emphasize
6.	tomato	intercept	paradise	indirect
7.	popular	intellect	document	majestic
8.	remember	assessment	replenish	October
9.	alcohol	excitement	challenger	volcano
10.	perpetrate	equipment	apprehend	prototype
11.	another	tornado	diminish	editor
12.	hydrogen	tuxedo	satellite	embroider
13.	marketing	comprehend	permanent	decompose
14.	assistant	director	frequently	tendency
15.	torpedo	accomplish	obsolete	infancy
16.	appendix	lunatic	amusement	estimate
17.	confident	amberjack	attitude	energy
18.	astonish	bulletin	publisher	consultant
19.	organize	consumer	typesetter	reporter
20.	centipede	entertain	policy	financing

Syllable Rule Three

Syllable Rule Three - Whenever two vowels come together and do not form a vowel team, divide the syllable between those two vowels.
li-3-on   di-3-et   flu-3-ent   boy-3-ish   flow-3-er   co-3-ed

1. oasis	mower	violin	fiery
2. forest	rodeo	peony	orange
3. bayonet	manual	poet	hyena
4. violent	vowel	nauseate	create
5. video	graduate	towel	flamboyant
6. voyage	meteor	coward	funeral
7. defiant	glory	reactor	artery
8. brewery	mosaic	lying	coerce
9. royal	hyacinth	pliable	heroism
10. denial	prowess	stoic	podium
11. Creole	genuine	mediate	misery
12. cameo	giant	violet	mayor
13. punctuate	vial	audio	operate
14. prayer	poetry	sewer	howitzer
15. iodine	mackerel	celery	gory
16. cereal	flier	neon	idiot
17. diagnose	foyer	glorify	reunite
18. violence	history	fuel	plowing
19. ruin	dialect	react	piety

Consonant Teams

ci spe-1-<u>ci</u>al	*si* pen-2-<u>si</u>on
si vi-1-<u>si</u>on	*ti* na-1-<u>ti</u>on
qu con-2-<u>qu</u>er	*ve* val<u>ve</u>
wr <u>wr</u>ap	

Consonant Teams
ci si si̲ ti ve qu̲ wr

The letter teams *ci*, *si*, and *ti* are consonant teams which make the *s h* sound at the beginning of any syllable except the first syllable of a word: spe-1-<u>ci</u>al, pen-2-<u>si</u>on, suc-2-<u>ti</u>on.

The letter team <u>si</u> is a consonant team which makes the sound *zh* at the beginning of any syllable except the first syllable of a word: vi-1-<u>si</u>o n

No English word ends in the letter *v*. The letters *v* and *e* form a consonant team at the end of the word when the silent *e* has no other function except to prevent the *v* from being the last letter in the word: val<u>ve</u>.

1.	sanction	crucial	confession	partial
2.	wrack	conclusion	magician	extension
3.	pension	affection	wrap	involve
4.	reserve	wreck	position	invasion
5.	emission	facial	wretch	vindictive
6.	fraction	mention	collection	marquee
7.	passion	wrench	deserve	transfusion
8.	social	explosion	wrapper	mosquito
9.	percussion	successive	desertion	regression
10.	wreath	clique	official	collision
11.	traction	condition	seclusion	extensive
12.	physician	adhesive	delve	mansion
13.	wren	liquor	corruption	revolve
13.	grotesque	cursive	taxation	abrasion

112

More Review of Consonant Teams
ci si si ti ve qu wr

1.	compassion	duration	magician	plaque
2.	wringer	additive	quotation	incision
3.	obsession	conquer	correction	extinction
4.	division	expression	heave	solution
5.	turquoise	ignition	wrinkle	writer
6.	exclusive	initial	excursion	tension
7.	perfection	mortician	repulsive	commotion
8.	wriggle	erosion	statuesque	protective
9.	absorption	creation	glacial	receptive
10.	perspective	nerve	illusion	torque
11.	musician	probation	revulsion	wrest
12.	precision	wrath	lucrative	profession
13.	festive	exclusion	productive	eruption
14.	deceptive	native	promotion	inclusion
15.	fantasia	concession	racial	approve
16.	mosque	citation	wrong	prevention
17.	suspicion	mannequin	vision	incentive
18.	impulsive	impression	remove	nutrition
19.	confusion	groove	descriptive	special

si	*si*	*ti*	
admission	abrasion	abortion	initial
commission	artesian	absorption	injunction
compassion	aversion	action	junction
compulsion	cohesion	addition	lotion
concession	collision	adoption	mention
confession	conclusion	affection	nation
convulsion	confusion	ambition	notion
depression	decision	attention	nutrition
digression	delusion	attraction	objection
emission	derision	auction	option
expansion	diffusion	caption	ovation
expression	division	caution	par tial
expulsion	erosion	citation	partition
extension	evasion	collection	perception
impassion	exclusion	commotion	perfection
impression	excursion	compunction	petition
intercession	explosion	condition	portion
intermission	fantasia	correction	position
mansion	fusion	creation	potion
mission	illusion	deception	prevention
obsession	implosion	deduction	probation
omission	incision	desertion	production
passion	inclusion	detection	projection
passionate	incursion	diction	promotion
pension	infusion	direction	protection
percussion	intrusion	discretion	quotation
permission	invasion	disruption	ration
possession	lesion	donation	reaction
pretension	occasion	duration	reception
procession	precision	edition	reduction
profession	profusion	election	reflection
progression	provision	eruption	rejection
recession	revision	extinction	relation
regression	seclu sion	fiction	resumption
remission	transfusion	fixation	retention
session	vision	fraction	rotation
submission		fruition	sanction
succession		gradation	section
suppression		ignition	seduction
tension		impartial	sensation
transgression		inaction	solu tion
transmission		inflation	station

114

suction
taxation
temptation
traction
transition
translation
tuition
vacation
vibration
vocation

ci

crucial
facial
glacial
racial
social
magician
mortician
musician
official
physician
special
suspicion

ve

absolve
abusive
active
additive
adhesive
approve
attentive
behoove
captive
carve
cleave
curve
cursive
deceptive
decisive
defective
defensive
delve

descriptive
elective
evasive
evolve
exclusive
expansive
explosive
expressive
extensive
festive
give
glove
groove
have
heave
illusive
impassive
impressive
improve
impulsive
incentive
incisive
inclusive
intensive
involve
live
love
lucrative
massive
motive
move
native
negative
nerve
objective
offensive
oppressive
perspective
positive
possessive
preserve
preventive
primitive
productive

progressive
protective
prove
receptive
relative
remove
repulsive
resolve
responsive
revolve
seductive
selective
sensitive
serve
shelve
solve
starve
subjective
successive
talkative
twelve
valve
vindictive

qu

antique
burlesque
clique
conquer
critique
croquet
etiquette
grotesque
lacquer
liquor
mannequin
marquee
mosque
mosquito
oblique
physique
picturesque
plaque

statuesque
torque
turquoise
unique

wr

wrack
wrangle
wrap
wrapper
wrath
wreak
wreath
wreck
wren
wrench
wrest
wrestle
wretch
wriggle
wring
wringer
wrinkle
wrist
writ
write
writer
writhe
wrong
wrote
wroth
wrung
wry

115

ei 4 c<u>ei</u>ling	*ei* 6 th<u>ei</u>r
ey 4 k<u>ey</u>	*ey* 6 gr<u>ey</u>
ie 4 p<u>ie</u>	*ie* 6 f<u>ie</u>ld
ue 4 c<u>ue</u>	*ue* 4 bl<u>ue</u>

Vowel Teams
ei ei ey ey ie ie ue u̲e̲
4   6   4   6   4   6   4   4

When a vowel team says the name of its first vowel, it is classified under vowel rule four. When a vowel team does not say the name of its first vowel, it is classified under vowel rule six except when the letter *r* is part of the vowel team which then places the vowel team under vowel rule five.

To indicate that a letter is silent, put a wave sign under that letter: half
                                                                        ~

1.	collie	unveil	grieve	bluebird
2.	ceiling	wield	greyhound	tie
3.	prairie	deceive	blarney	yield
4.	prey	receive	belief	reindeer
5.	pulley	shield	cashier	virtue
6.	genie	clue	receipt	fondue
7.	vein	survey	caddie	besiege
8.	argue	thieves	turnkey	donkey
9.	calorie	either	believe	due
10.	true	brief	shriek	their
11.	osprey	chief	conceit	relief
12.	belie	reverie	thief	obey
13.	laddie	beige	priest	statue
14.	deceit	achieve	conveyance	grief

More Review of Vowel Teams

ei ei ey ey ie ie ue u e
 4   6   4   6   4   6   4   4

1. brownie	cruise	trolley	heir
2. qualified	barbecue	disbelief	money
3. convey	abbey	rein	dignified
4. hygiene	weird	subdue	value
5. certified	hockey	disobey	barley
6. heiress	imbue	blue	niece
7. honey	fiend	gruesome	leisure
8. kidney	avenue	lassie	whey
9. juice	continue	applied	sue
10. seizure	retrieve	volley	pie
11. monkey	they	purvey	glue
12. dried	chimney	relieve	accrue
13. jersey	rescue	perceive	turkey
14. grievance	feint	hey	notified
15. bruise	piece	lackey	parley
16. allied	neither	parsley	pursue
17. surveillance	revenue	cried	jockey
18. medley	cue	aggrieve	falsified
19. siege	galley	seize	fried

118

ei 4	*ey* 4	*ey* 6	*ie* 6	*ue* 4
ceiling	abbey	convey	achieve	argue
conceit	alley	disobey	aggrieve	barbecue
conceive	barley	greyhound	belief	continue
deceit	blarney	hey	believe	cue
deceive	chimney	obey	besiege	hue
either	cockney	prey	brief	imbue
leisure	donkey	purvey	brownie	issue
neither	galley	survey	caddie	rescue
perceive	hackney	they	calorie	revue
receipt	hockey	whey	chief	statue
receive	honey		collie	tissue
seize	jersey	*ie* 4	coolie	value
seizure	jockey		disbelief	virtue
weird	key	allied	fief	
	kidney	applied	field	*ue* 4
ei 6	lackey	belie	fiend	
	medley	certified	frieze	accrue
beige	money	cried	genie	avenue
feint	monkey	die	grief	blue
heir	motley	dignified	grievance	bruise
heiress	osprey	dried	grieve	clue
heirloom	palfrey	fried	hygiene	construe
rein	parley	lie	laddie	cruise
reindeer	parsley	pie	lassie	due
seine	pulley	qualified	niece	flue
sheik	trolley	tie	piece	fondue
skein	turkey	tried	prairie	fruit
surveillance	valley	vie	priest	glue
their	volley		relief	gruesome
veil			relieve	juice
vein			retrieve	pursue
			reverie	revenue
			shield	rue
			shriek	sluice
			siege	subdue
			thief	sue
			wield	true
			yield	

augh 6 <u>cau</u>ght	*eigh* 6 <u>eigh</u>t
ea 6 br<u>ea</u>d	*igh* 4 hi<u>gh</u>
<u>*ou*</u> 6 fa-1-m<u>ou</u>s	<u>*ar*</u> 5 w<u>ar</u>m
<u>*or*</u> 5 w<u>or</u>k	

Vowel Teams

augh eigh ea <u>ou</u> igh w<u>ar</u> w<u>or</u>
  6   6   6   6   4   5   5

When the team *ar* is preceded by the letter *w*, *ar* usually makes the *o r* sound and is double underlined to indicate the second sound for *ar*: w<u>ar</u>m.
$\overline{\overline{5}}$

When the team *or* is preceded by the letter *w*, *or* usually makes the *er* sound and is double underlined to indicate the second sound for *or*: w<u>or</u>k.
$\overline{\overline{5}}$

The letter team *ea* makes the sound *ay* in three words: great, break, and steak. Mark these words by underlining *ea* and placing an *x* directly under the *ea* team. An *x* written under a letter or letter team indicates that the sound being made by the letter or letters is a totally different sound than it normally makes: br<u>ea</u>k.

1.	neighbor	pugnacious	jealous	nervous
2.	taught	famous	heather	steady
3.	dealt	leather	worm	youngster
4.	pleasant	trouble	high	weapon
5.	reward	dread	hazardous	bear
6.	serious	healthy	fraught	meadow
7.	plight	country	world	stealth
8.	couple	realm	eight	pious
9.	double	wart	frivolous	sweat
10.	slaughter	read	flight	wealth
11.	lead	quart	vicious	threat
12.	bread	night	curious	dead

More Review of Vowel Teams

augh eigh ea <u>o u</u> igh w<u>ar</u> w<u>or</u>
  6   6   6   6   4   5   5

1. cleanse	thigh	eighteen	warp
2. distraught	worthy	pheasant	delicious
3. lighter	thwart	malicious	breakfast
4. precious	caught	weighty	warble
5. treachery	envious	airtight	word
6. swarthy	quartz	zealot	tenacious
7. freight	dangerous	daughter	sprightly
8. worth	instead	spacious	previous
9. glamorous	almighty	weather	infectious
10. onslaught	wharf	joyous	momentous
11. feather	weight	work	readily
12. enormous	gracious	swarm	cousin
13. worship	sweater	delight	haughty
14. prosperous	warden	sleigh	auspicious
15. thread	aught	horrendous	young
16. fabulous	slight	worst	ahead
17. ambitious	eighty	dwarf	tedious
18. naughty	worse	mighty	breath
19. various	heavy	worry	weigh

augh 6	ea 6		ou 6	
aught	ahead	sweater	ambitious	tedious
caught	behead	thread	auspicious	tenacious
distraught	bread	threat	barbarous	touch
fraught	breadth	treachery	cautious	treacherous
taught	breakfast	tread	country	trouble
onslaught	breast	treasure	couple	various
daughter	breath	treasurer	cousin	vicious
haughty	cleanse	treasury	curious	young
naughty	dead	wealth	dangerous	zealous
slaughter	deaf	weapon	delicious	
	dealt	weather	devious	
eigh 6	death	zealot	double	*war/wor* 5 5
	dread		dubious	
eight	feather	*igh* 4	enormous	dwarf
eighteen	head		envious	quart
eighty	health	airtight	fabulous	quartz
freight	heather	alight	famous	reward
inveigh	heaven	almighty	frivolous	stalwart
neighbor	heavy	blight	glamorous	swarm
sleigh	instead	bright	gracious	swarthy
weigh	lead	delight	grievous	thwart
weight	leapt	fight	hazardous	war
weighty	leather	flight	horrendous	warble
	leaven	fright	infectious	ward
	meadow	high	jealous	warden
	meant	light	joyous	warm
	measure	lighter	malicious	warn
	peasant	might	nervous	warp
	pheasant	mighty	precious	wart
	pleasant	night	previous	wharf
	pleasure	plight	prosperous	world
	read	right	rigorous	worm
	readily	sigh	serious	worry
	ready	sight	spacious	worse
	spread	slight	studious	worship
	stead	sprightly		worst
	steady	thigh		worth
	stealth	tight		worthy
	sweat			

Consonant Teams

ch s**ch**ool	*ch* **ch**ef
gh **gh**ost	*gn* **gn**at
gu **gu**itar	*kn* **kn**ot
rh **rh**yme	*sc* **sc**ene

Consonant Teams
<u>ch</u> <u>ch</u> *gh gn gu kn rh sc*

The letter team *gu* is a team when *u's* only job is to prevent *g* from making its second sound.

Draw a dotted underline to indicate when *ch* makes its third sound: <u>chef</u>.

1.	chaperone	guide	ascend	tech
2.	orchid	knack	ghost	chrome
3.	science	Rhodes	schwa	ache
4.	chemist	resign	rogue	choral
5.	rhino	chronic	rescind	machine
6.	design	anchor	leprechaun	knead
7.	brochure	scent	Christ	monarchy
8.	kneel	harpsichord	assign	guitar
9.	obscene	ghetto	charlatan	Rhine
10.	league	benign	knit	orchestra
11.	chevron	knife	transcend	Cher
12.	assignment	ricochet	rhubarb	Christmas
13.	schedule	catalogue	chute	knob
14.	chef	chasm	scissors	arraign
15.	sorghum	chemistry	knot	crochet
16.	knuckle	rhetoric	sign	chloride
17.	architect	crescent	chivalry	stomach
18.	campaign	character	guise	lichen

More Review of Consonant Teams
ch ch gh gn gu kn rh sc

1. condescend	Anchorage	rhythm	vanguard
2. spaghetti	mustache	plague	knoll
3. scholar	schooner	champagne	muscle
4. parachute	guidance	knock	fatigue
5. technique	align	cologne	guile
6. travelogue	scenery	echo	rhapsody
7. chronicle	foreign	echelon	christen
8. chemical	chlorophyll	synagogue	known
9. scientist	ghastly	archangel	intrigue
10. epilogue	knives	machinist	scheme
11. chloroform	disguise	abscess	reign
12. ascent	rhinestone	school	trachea
13. chaos	chagrin	guardian	bronchitis
14. ensign	archive	knight	descent
15. chiffon	strychnine	aghast	morgue
16. disciple	dialogue	nonchalance	consign
17. rhyme	knee	technical	chromium
18. guarantee	gnash	cholera	chivalrous
19. chlorine	scenic	gnaw	chorus

ch	ch	gh		rh
ache	orchestral	aghast	guarantee	rhapsody
anarchy	orchid	ghastly	guard	rhetoric
anchor	pachyderm	ghetto	guidance	rheumatism
Anchorage	schedule	ghost	guide	rhinestone
archaic	schematic	spaghetti	guile	rhino
archangel	scheme	sorghum	guise	rhubarb
archetype	schism		guitar	rhyme
architect	scholar	**gn**	intrigue	rhythm
archive	scholastic	align	league	
bronchitis	school	arraign	monologue	**sc**
chaos	schooner	assign	morgue	abscess
character	stomach	benign	pedagogue	ascend
chasm	strychnine	campaign	plague	ascent
chemical	technical	champagne	prologue	ascetic
chemist	technique	cologne	rogue	condescend
chemistry	trachea	consign	synagogue	crescent
chloride		deign	travelogue	descend
chlorine	**ch**	design	vague	descent
chlorophyll	brochure	ensign	vanguard	disciple
cholera	cache	feign	vogue	discipline
choral	chagrin	foreign		nascent
chord	chaise	gnash	**kn**	obscene
chorus	champagne	gnat	acknowledge	plebiscite
christen	chaperon	gnaw	knack	quiescent
chrome	charlatan	gnome	knave	rescind
chronic	chauffeur	reign	knead	scene
chronicle	chef	resign	knee	scenery
echo	chevron	sign	kneel	scenic
epoch	chiffon	sovereign	knelt	scent
harpsichord	chivalrous		knew	science
leprechaun	chivalry	**gu**	knife	scientist
lichen	chute	beguile	knight	scion
matriarch	crochet	brogue	knit	scissors
mechanic	echelon	catalogue	knives	transcend
monarchy	machine	colleague	knob	
orchestra	mustache	demagogue	knock	
	nonchalance	dialogue	knoll	
	parachute	disguise	knot	
	ricochet	epilogue	knowledge	
		fatigue	known	
		fugue	knuckle	
			knurl	

Unit Twenty-Four
Four-Syllable Words

1. explanation	aluminum	economic
2. appropriate	intersection	astronomers
3. peninsula	secretary	additional
4. comparison	fortunately	authority
5. illustration	colonial	punctuation
6. remarkable	divisible	January
7. everyday	majority	automatic
8. contributed	helicopter	parenthesis
9. variations	February	mechanical
10. expedition	economy	perimeter
11. horizontal	altogether	complicated
12. radiation	emotional	professional
13. uranium	interrupted	underwater
14. Colorado	development	continental
15. unexpected	operation	American
16. usually	political	material
17. beautiful	equivalent	everything
18. temperature	combination	interesting
19. locomotive	oriental	sincerity
20. invisible	industrial	differential

More Review of Four-Syllable Words

1. estimation	society	comprehension
2. gradually	diameter	consolidate
3. actually	industrial	retribution
4. community	valuable	population
5. vegetables	territory	variety
6. observation	secondary	operation
7. reverberate	discontinue	supersonic
8. temperature	dishonesty	comfortable
9. deodorant	considerate	favorable
10. interruption	particular	inaccurate
11. violinist	satisfaction	experience
12. circulation	readjustment	intimidate
13. generation	inattention	disadvantage
14. impossible	universal	original
15. reservation	irregular	intermission
16. prehistoric	periodic	jurisdiction
17. incarnation	experiment	necessary
18. corporation	tributary	photography
19. calculating	inspiration	vigorously
20. difficulty	mysterious	democracy

ou 4 s<u>ou</u>l	<u>ou</u> 6 s<u>ou</u>p
our 5 j<u>our</u>nal	*ough* 4 d<u>ough</u>
ough 6 This team has many different sounds.	

Vowel Teams *ou* <u>ou</u> *ough ough our*
4   6   4   6   5

Draw a dotted underline to indicate when *ou* makes its third sound: so̤ṳp̤.

The letter team *our* usually forms a vowel rule five team when followed by a consonant.

The letter team *ough* has many different sounds. Do not try and learn the separate sounds for this team. Instead from the sounds of the consonants in the word and from the context of the word in the sentence, try and determine the correct sound. Note that by far the most common sound that this team makes is o (the long o sound): d<u>ough</u>
4

1.	boulevard	soul	cough	courage
2.	cantaloupe	mourn	sojourn	discourse
3.	encourage	group	troupe	uncouth
4.	rough	soup	glamour	acoustics
5.	journey	wound	throughout	concourse
6.	four	youth	roulette	discourteous
7.	caribou	course	tough	flourish
8.	shoulder	journal	doughnut	fought
9.	nourish	coupon	wrought	youthful
10.	thorough	scourge	nourishment	though
11.	roughen	adjourn	courtesy	you
12.	souvenir	courteous	furlough	courtyard
13.	resource	cougar	thought	gourd
14.	drought	enough	boulder	although
15.	routine	thoroughbred	brought	through
16.	route	discourage	source	bayou

131

ou 4	*ou* 6	*our* 5	*ough* 4
boulder	accouterment	adjourn	although
bourn	acoustics	courage	borough
cantaloupe	bayou	courteous	dough
concourse	boulevard	courtesy	doughnut
course	bouquet	discourage	furlough
court	caribou	discourteous	thorough
courtly	cougar	encourage	thoroughbred
courtyard	coulee	flourish	thoroughfare
discourse	coupon	glamour	thoroughgoing
downpour	ghoul	journal	though
four	goulash	journey	
fourth	group	nourish	*ough* 6
gourd	rouge	nourishment	
mould	roulette	sojourn	afterthought
mourn	route	scourge	besought
pompadour	routine		bethought
pour	soup		bought
resource	souvenir		brought
shoulder	troubadour		cough
soul	troupe		drought
source	uncouth		enough
	wound		forethought
	you		fought
	youth		nought
	youthful		ought
			overwrought
			rough
			roughen
			sought
			thought
			thoughtful
			thoughtless
			through
			throughout
			tough
			wrought

Four-Five-Six Syllable Words

1. reverberation	quartermaster	reincarnation
2. congratulations	communication	individual
3. administration	association	civilization
4. intoxication	generalization	qualification
5. instantaneous	preposterous	superstitious
6. inexperience	commissioner	unnecessarily
7. professorship	irresponsible	superiority
8. retardation	personality	experimentation
9. unfortunate	desirable	proportionately
10. contamination	disproportion	dissatisfaction
11. disintegration	unaccountable	masculinity
12. hallucination	reinforcement	professional
13. disappearance	correspondent	interdependence
14. assassination	denomination	excommunication
15. mathematical	matrimonial	tonsillectomy
16. intellectual	congregation	counterrevolution
17. illegitimate	rehabilitation	consideration
18. metropolitan	multiplication	flexibility
19. stabilization	miraculous	perpendicular
20. arbitrarily	bibliography	tuberculosis

133

More Review of Four-Five-Six Syllable Words

1. hypothetical	preoccupy	depersonalize
2. chiropractic	absolution	utilitarian
3. biographical	virtuosity	metamorphosis
4. solicitous	choreographer	ubiquitous
5. derogative	unprecedented	effervescent
6. tribulation	flabbergasted	unimpeachable
7. glorification	reverberating	inflammable
8. questionable	laboratory	preponderance
9. obsequious	Neolithic	miscellaneous
10. liquidation	pandemonium	memorabilia
11. nitroglycerin	incredulous	reactionary
12. homogeneous	semiannual	fertilization
13. sagacity	monosyllable	predecessor
14. deficiency	irresponsible	photosynthesize
15. triangular	Jerusalem	paraphernalia
16. industrialize	incomprehension	electricity
17. introversion	acquiescence	monolithic
18. unseasonable	sanitarium	expediency
19. dandelion	passionately	extraordinary
20. stereotype	unserviceable	hypoglycemia

Page 49

1. bla - blaft 2 1	fli - flim 2 1	bre - brelt 2 1	cha - chasp 2 1
2. pro - prolf 2 1	cle - clelb 2 1	glo - glomp 2 1	scro - scromp 2 1
3. ble - blent 2 1	shi - shind 2 1	cle - clelk 2 1	slo - slost 2 1
4. cra - crask 2 1	gre - greft 2 1	tro - tront 2 1	spla - splask 2 1
5. pli - plict 2 1	whi - whist 2 1	cre - crent 2 1	bli - blift 2 1
6. sta - stap 2 1	ble - bleck 2 1	chi - chist 2 1	tha - thaf 2 1
7. sla - slack 2 1	bla - black 2 1	dro - drop 2 1	fla - flab 2 1
8. spe - spend 2 1	sha - shack 2 1	fla - flash 2 1	cho - chop 2 1
9. twi - twist 2 1	fla - flash 2 1	sho - shop 2 1	gri - grip 2 1
10. ki - kin 2 1	sho - shot 2 1	flo - flop 2 1	tro - trod 2 1

11. spri - sprint
  2 1
	che - chest
	2 1
		ble - blend
		2 1
			thro - throb
			  2 1

12. gri - grist 2 1	glo - glob 2 1	bri - bring 2 1	she - shed 2 1

Page 50

1. fle - flench 2 1	wha - whap 2 1	thri - thrip 2 1	tro - tront 2 1
2. ja - jav 2 1	pre - preng 2 1	bli - blit 2 1	shro - shrop 2 1
3. ba - bant 2 1	clo - clonk 2 1	dre - drelt 2 1	smi - smint 2 1
4. yo - yob 2 1	sha - shang 2 1	pre - prempt 2 1	fri - fritch 2 1
5. spro - sprosh 2 1	gle - glenk 2 1	whi - whiv 2 1	tra - tranch 2 1
6. sme - smest 2 1	quo - quond 2 1	tha - thamp 2 1	shri - shrint 2 1
7. fla - flant 2 1	te - telch 2 1	pli - plink 2 1	sko - skop 2 1
8. phi - phitch 2 1	twe - tweld 2 1	scri - scrinch 2 1	dro - droft 2 1
9. tro- troft 2 1	the - thest 2 1	cha - chank 2 1	spli - splipt 2 1
10. bla - blast 2 1	ski - skimp 2 1	pa - pang 2 1	tha - thatch 2 1

11. cli - clin̲k̲
  2   1
	cho̲ - c̲hoc̲k̲
	  2 1
		fa - fan̲g̲
		  2 1
			cra - cram̲p̲
			  2 1

12. s̲hi - s̲hif̲t̲
  2   1
	fle - flec̲k̲
	  2 1
		w̲hi - w̲hic̲h̲
		  2 1
			sta - stam̲p̲
			  2 1

13. cri - crim̲p̲
  2   1
	sla - slan̲g̲
	  2 1
		twi - twit̲c̲h̲
		  2 1
			spe - spen̲t̲
			  2 1

14. spla - splas̲h̲
  2   1
	s̲ho - s̲hoc̲k̲
	  2 1
		si - sixt̲h̲
		  2 1
			ya - yan̲k̲
			  2 1

15. t̲hro - t̲hron̲g̲
  2   1
	s̲hra - s̲hran̲k̲
	  2 1
		spri - sprin̲g̲
		  2 1
			scri - scrip̲t̲
			  2 1

16. hi - hit̲c̲h̲
  2   1
	po- pom̲p̲
	  2 1
		gli - glin̲t̲
		  2 1
			c̲he - c̲hes̲t̲
			  2 1

17. ki - kil̲t̲
  2   1
	te - tem̲p̲t̲
	  2 1
		t̲ha - t̲hat̲c̲h̲
		  2 1
			w̲hi - w̲his̲k̲
			  2 1

Page 51

1. bam - bam̲e̲
  1   3
	sop - sop̲e̲
	  1 3
		bev - bev̲e̲
		  1 3
			pim - pim̲e̲
			  1 3

2. q̲uev - q̲uev̲e̲
  1   3
	cof - cof̲e̲
	  1 3
		dif - dif̲e̲
		  1 3
			rax - rax̲e̲
			  1 3

3. han - han̲e̲
  1   3
	sez - sez̲e̲
	  1 3
		yad - yad̲e̲
		  1 3
			jem - jem̲e̲
			  1 3

3. tab - tab̲e̲
  1   3
	lil - lil̲e̲
	  1 3
		vad - vad̲e̲
		  1 3
			pif - pif̲e̲
			  1 3

4. gop - gop̲e̲
  1   3
	w̲hop - w̲hop̲e̲
	  1 3
		c̲han - c̲han̲e̲
		  1 3
			fim - fim̲e̲
			  1 3

5. prot - prot̲e̲
  1   3
	sab - sab̲e̲
	  1 3
		tiv - tiv̲e̲
		  1 3
			zop - zop̲e̲
			  1 3

6. q̲uac̲k̲ - q̲uak̲e̲
  1   3
	slat - slat̲e̲
	  1 3
		fill - fil̲e̲
		  1 3
			pic̲k̲ - pik̲e̲
			  1 3

7. s̲hin - s̲hin̲e̲
  1   3
	fat - fat̲e̲
	  1 3
		pop - pop̲e̲
		  1 3
			grim - grim̲e̲
			  1 3

8. slim - slim̲e̲
  1   3
	t̲hem - t̲hem̲e̲
	  1 3
		van - van̲e̲
		  1 3
			snip - snip̲e̲
			  1 3

9. ban - ban̲e̲
  1   3
	spit - spit̲e̲
	  1 3
		clot̲h̲ - clot̲h̲e̲
		  1 3
			grip - grip̲e̲
			  1 3

10. din - din̲e̲
  1   3
	cap - cap̲e̲
	  1 3
		c̲hoc̲k̲ - c̲hok̲e̲
		  1 3
			slop - slop̲e̲
			  1 3

11. slid - slid̲e̲
  1   3
	glad - glad̲e̲
	  1 3
		twin - twin̲e̲
		  1 3
			rob - rob̲e̲
			  1 3

12. stoc̲k̲ - stok̲e̲
  1   3
	win - win̲e̲
	  1 3
		Ross - ros̲e̲
		  1 3
			cop - cop̲e̲
			  1 3

Page 52

1. glap - glap̲e̲
  1   3
	smic̲k̲ - smik̲e̲
	  1 3
		twest - twest̲e̲
		  1 3
			rab - rab̲e̲
			  1 3

2. dod - dode	grem - greme	fid - fide	veb -vebe
1 3	1 3	1 3	1 3
3. riv - rive	gop - gope	snep - snepe	op - ope
1 3	1 3	1 3	1 3
4. rev - reve	pon - pone	maf - mafe	quet - quete
1 3	1 3	1 3	1 3
5. grod - grode	slin - sline	prat - prate	hin - hine
1 3	1 3	1 3	1 3
6. lel -lele	chack - chake	dod - dode	whem - wheme
1 3	1 3	1 3	1 3
7. tem - teme	miv - mive	bam - bame	stot - stote
1 3	1 3	1 3	1 3
8. grod - grode	lill - lile	losh - loshe	creb - crebe
1 3	1 3	1 3	1 3
9. mop - mope	whiff - wife	shack - shake	cut - cute
1 3	1 3	1 3	1 3
10. quack - quake	prim - prime	mat - mate	glob - globe
1 3	1 3	1 3	1 3
11. rack - rake	bod - bode	spin - spine	plan - plane
1 3	1 3	1 3	1 3
12. luck - Luke	whip - wipe	tack - take	bill - bile
1 3	1 3	1 3	1 3
13. sham - shame	spit - spite	Ross - rose	sack - sake
1 3	1 3	1 3	1 3
14. past - paste	strip - stripe	Brock - broke	rid - ride
1 3	1 3	1 3	1 3
15. snack - snake	fin - fine	slack - slake	rip - ripe
1 3	1 3	1 3	1 3
16. mad - made	Tim - time	mull - mule	lack - lake
1 3	1 3	1 3	1 3
17. Jack - Jake	kit - kite	pock - poke	bid - bide
1 3	1 3	1 3	1 3

Page 53

1.	prune	use	rule	dude
	3	3	3	3
2.	jute	brute	dupe	pure
	3	3	3	3
3.	fluke	rule	cube	fume
	3	3	3	3
3.	mute	rude	Yule	dune
	3	3	3	3
4.	tube	plume	muse	duke
	3	3	3	3
5.	cute	prude	dupe	flume
	3	3	3	3

137

6. ruse /ru se   tune   fuse   nude
    3   3   3   3   3

7. mule   lute   rule   prude
    3   3   3   3

8. dude   crude   use   fluke
    3   3   3   3

9. cube   nuke   brute   lube
    3   3   3   3

Page 55

#					
1.	bluft 1	fli 2	sprope 3	pro 2	fli 2
2.	chesp 1	plip 1	jave 3	jope 3	dro 2
3.	cax 1	flusk 1	jop 1	flom 1	hif 1
4.	juse 3	pra 2	mone 3	bax 1	spint 1
5.	blat 1	bri 2	lale 3	throp 1	cobe 3
6.	dop 1	fote 3	trent 1	squisp 1	chilp 1
7.	bape 3	eft 1	bo 2	wabe 3	lefe 3
8.	mune 3	ti 2	plosp 1	keze 3	twise 3
9.	cresk 1	shast 1	mun 1	jeme 3	chome 3
10.	chafe 3	crash 1	fist 1	mule 3	splint 1
11.	twist 1	just 1	quack 1	joke 3	pine 3
12.	crib 1	punt 1	flat 1	swipe 3	shrine 3
13.	so 2	lip 1	crank 1	swell 1	dope 3
14.	fuse 3	will 1	go 2	shut 1	block 1
15.	file 3	drift 1	trip 1	shade 3	fluke 3
16.	splash 1	she 2	white 3	close/close 3 3	runt 1
17.	whack 1	drag 1	cane 3	game 3	hi 2

Page 56

1.	twil<u>e</u> 3	cle<u>tch</u> 1	prempt 1	clo 2	<u>ph</u>ab<u>e</u> 3
2.	<u>wh</u>ulp 1	plin<u>e</u> 3	stre 2	pra<u>ck</u> 1	<u>ch</u>o ne 3
3.	<u>th</u>eln 1	slonst 1	wod<u>e</u> 3	<u>ch</u>i 2	beb<u>e</u> 3
4.	strin<u>ch</u> 1	<u>qu</u>i 2	spamp 1	clil<u>e</u> 3	fa<u>tch</u> 1
5.	prist 1	<u>sh</u>op<u>e</u> 3	sle 2	flust 1	<u>sh</u>and 1
6.	<u>qu</u>e<u>tch</u> 1	fo 2	<u>ph</u>alp 1	<u>ch</u>ust 1	fli<u>sh</u> 1
7.	m o 2	en<u>ch</u> 1	clib<u>e</u> 3	<u>ph</u>u m 1	av<u>e</u> 3
8.	<u>wh</u>ilst 1	<u>ch</u>o ne 3	brene 3	flusp 1	<u>th</u>ro 2
9.	clu<u>tch</u> 1	<u>th</u>ron<u>e</u> 3	spend 1	<u>sh</u>ri<u>n</u>k 1	grop<u>e</u> 3
10.	h o<u>se</u> 3	ten<u>th</u> 1	slung 1	<u>wh</u>elp 1	m e 2
11.	fil<u>ch</u> 1	<u>sh</u>rug 1	t<u>une</u> 3	ba<u>tch</u> 1	<u>these</u> 3
12.	s<u>qu</u>el<u>ch</u> 1	fli<u>ng</u> 1	crun<u>ch</u> 1	<u>th</u>ron<u>e</u> 3	r<u>ule</u> 3
13.	<u>sh</u>rimp 1	<u>ch</u>o<u>se</u> 3	<u>sh</u>ak<u>e</u> 3	clen<u>ch</u> 1	cub<u>e</u> 3
14.	<u>sh</u>e 2	spra<u>ng</u> 1	clo<u>the</u> 3	drap<u>e</u> 3	clen<u>ch</u> 1
15.	scra<u>tch</u> 1	<u>sh</u>elf 1	<u>ch</u>ok<u>e</u> 3	blo<u>tch</u> 1	ba<u>the</u> 3
16.	fro<u>ck</u> 1	ti<u>the</u> 3	twist 1	scon<u>e</u> 3	sten<u>ch</u> 1
17.	<u>ph</u>on<u>e</u> 3	<u>th</u>a<u>n</u>k 1	scrib<u>e</u> 3	hast<u>e</u> 3	plu<u>ck</u> 1

Page 58

1.	b<u>ai</u>z 4	d<u>ee</u>v 4	f<u>ay</u> 4	g<u>ea</u>s 4	j<u>ow</u> 4
2.	k<u>oe</u>m 4	l<u>ea</u>l 4	m <u>ue</u> 4	n<u>ee</u>p 4	t<u>ay</u> 4
3.	<u>qu</u><u>ea</u>f 4	r<u>ey</u> 4	s<u>oa</u>b 4	t<u>oe</u>z 4	v<u>ea</u>v 4
4.	w<u>ee</u>t 4	y<u>ai</u>s 4	z<u>ow</u> 4	b<u>ea</u>s 4	k<u>ee</u>f 4

5. vay / 4   fluid / 4   noak / 4   quaim / 4   reep / 4

6. saip / 4   tees / 4   zay / 4   weaz / 4   yoab / 4

7. toad / 4   dream / 4   meek / 4   boat / 4   sheet / 4

8. paint / 4   squeal / 4   gloat / 4   brain / 4   leaf / 4

9. seen / 4   mow / 4   tray / 4   road / 4   bowl / 4

10. team / 4   suit / 4   bloat / 4   foe / 4   lain / 4

11. rail / 4   sheep / 4   spray / 4   heat / 4   beach / 4

12. blue / 4   toe / 4   sprain / 4   fruit / 4   pray / 4

Page 59

1. prain / 4   eenst / 4   sleach / 4   cloe / 4   floant / 4

2. frow / 4   theam / 4   whoap / 4   shay / 4   fleek / 4

3. pruip / 4   noan / 4   stroe / 4   thow / 4   scray / 4

4. queast / 4   tue / 4   queep / 4   chaip / 4   thoab / 4

5. droe / 4   saish / 4   boav / 4   streand / 4   tuid / 4

6. quaich / 4   drow / 4   preesh / 4   tay / 4   cload / 4

7. owb / 4   eef / 4   cleab / 4   phain / 4   troe / 4

8. gleav / 4   vay / 4   cleeb / 4   whoap / 4   thraip / 4

9. braid / 4   wheel / 4   stream / 4   throw / 4   roach / 4

10. blue / 4   hoe / 4   beech / 4   maize / 4   tweed / 4

11. preach / 4   stray / 4   throat / 4   shown / 4   fruit / 4

12. oath / 4   praise / 4   woe / 4   key / 4   faith / 4

13. tweed / 4   leash / 4   bowl / 4   roam / 4   drain / 4

14. doe / 4   spray / 4   sown / 4   speech / 4   wheat / 4

Answer Key for Sections One Through Three

15.	sho<u>a</u>l	<u>qu</u>ain<u>t</u>	<u>three</u>	gro<u>w</u>th	tr<u>ue</u>
	4	4	4	4	4
16.	br<u>ui</u>se	<u>shea</u>th	s<u>ow</u>	<u>ch</u>eek	pr<u>ay</u>
	4	4	4	4	4
17.	<u>qu</u>ail	seed	h<u>oa</u>x	<u>ee</u>l	brea<u>ch</u>
	4	4	4	4	4

Page 62

1.	k<u>ee</u>f	fom<u>e</u>	<u>qu</u>ep	m<u>ea</u>f	sav
	4	3	1	4	1
2.	n<u>oa</u>k	dra<u>ck</u>	<u>wh</u>ilt	drop<u>e</u>	r<u>ee</u>n
	4	1	1	3	4
3.	lunt	twis<u>e</u>	ti	hez<u>e</u>	y<u>oa</u>b
	1	3	2	3	4
4.	d<u>ea</u>t	m u n<u>e</u>	<u>squ</u>isp	wab<u>e</u>	j<u>ee</u>n
	4	3	1	3	4
5.	<u>thr</u>aft	scri	s<u>ea</u>b	bed<u>e</u>	v<u>ay</u>
	1	2	4	3	4
6.	dro	n<u>ee</u>n	dit<u>e</u>	<u>sh</u>amp	d<u>oa</u>l
	2	4	3	1	4
7.	blant	haf<u>e</u>	twep	spra	t<u>oe</u>g
	1	3	1	2	4
8.	hil<u>e</u>	fle	spop	h<u>ee</u>f	swost
	3	2	1	4	1
9.	kez<u>e</u>	splisk	blo	n<u>oa</u>b	lad<u>e</u>
	3	1	2	4	3
10.	jad<u>e</u>	ho	sma<u>sh</u>	b<u>ee</u>t	blunt
	3	2	1	4	1
11.	fre<u>sh</u>	glob<u>e</u>	b<u>oa</u>t	bra<u>sh</u>	fiv<u>e</u>
	1	3	4	1	3
12.	flap	film	t<u>ow</u>	no	brid<u>e</u>
	1	1	4	2	3
13.	plum	jok<u>e</u>	spla<u>sh</u>	tr<u>ea</u>t	lost
	4	3	1	4	1
14.	plan<u>e</u>	trim	sp<u>ee</u>d	s<u>ay</u>	slid<u>e</u>
	3	1	4	4	3
15.	strap	st<u>ai</u>n	trot	clap	stand
	1	4	1	1	1
16.	<u>sh</u>aft	swip<u>e</u>	crat<u>e</u>	dra<u>nk</u>	me
	1	3	3	1	2
17.	<u>ch</u><u>ea</u>p	tra<u>sh</u>	spok<u>e</u>	t<u>oa</u>d	mul<u>e</u>
	4	1	3	4	3
18.	blend	fist	so	pla<u>nk</u>	pr<u>ay</u>
	1	1	2	1	4

Answer Key for Sections One Through Three

Page 63

1.	cre<u>n</u>k 1	jast<u>e</u> 3	m<u>ai</u>nt 4	<u>qu</u>et<u>e</u> 3	<u>ch</u>o<u>n</u>k 1
2.	<u>qu</u>oll 1	bi<u>the</u> 3	cle<u>a</u><u>ck</u> 4	grimp 1	tro 2
3.	ble<u>tch</u> 1	<u>wh</u>on<u>e</u> 3	bl<u>oe</u><u>ch</u> 4	<u>ch</u>a<u>ck</u> 1	smik<u>e</u> 3
4.	cr<u>ee</u><u>ch</u> 4	twon<u>e</u> 3	clu<u>n</u><u>ch</u> 1	ska<u>n</u>k 1	scra<u>y</u> 4
5.	brin<u>ch</u> 1	hest<u>e</u> 3	prumpt 1	<u>th</u>o<u>w</u>n 4	<u>sh</u>a 2
6.	clem<u>e</u> 3	tr<u>oa</u>n 4	ven<u>e</u> 3	splas 1	cli<u>the</u> 3
7.	fla 2	stroct 1	cra<u>n</u><u>ch</u> 1	fr<u>ee</u>n 4	scrent 1
8.	<u>qu</u>ev 1	<u>oa</u>x 4	spap<u>e</u> 3	mu<u>v</u><u>e</u> 3	swi<u>n</u><u>ch</u> 1
9.	frund 1	smi<u>ck</u> 1	s<u>qu</u>er<u>e</u> 3	tw<u>ai</u>z<u>e</u> 4	slok<u>e</u> 3
10.	<u>ch</u>id<u>e</u> 3	<u>qu</u>e<u>n</u><u>ch</u> 1	<u>sh</u>o<u>w</u>n 4	me 2	clump 1
11.	te<u>e</u> 4	fli<u>n</u><u>ch</u> 1	<u>ch</u>os<u>e</u> 3	tren<u>ch</u> 1	fum<u>e</u> 3
12.	br<u>ui</u>s<u>e</u> 4	<u>th</u>os<u>e</u> 3	<u>sh</u>ru<u>n</u>k 1	blond 1	<u>ph</u>as<u>e</u> 3
13.	twa<u>ng</u> 1	f<u>oe</u> 4	fus<u>e</u> 3	w<u>oe</u> 4	s<u>qu</u>id 1
14.	<u>shr</u>in<u>e</u> 3	stre<u>tch</u> 1	pr<u>ee</u>n 4	<u>sh</u>e 2	<u>wh</u>al<u>e</u> 3
15.	<u>g</u><u>ai</u>t 4	brisk 1	<u>shr</u>imp 1	<u>qu</u>ot<u>e</u> 3	mu<u>n</u><u>ch</u> 1
16.	dwelt 1	scon<u>e</u> 3	pr<u>ea</u><u>ch</u> 4	sketch 1	<u>oa</u><u>th</u> 4
17.	du<u>k</u><u>e</u> 3	be 2	dep<u>th</u> 1	ti<u>the</u> 3	<u>sh</u>ra<u>n</u>k 1
18.	gl<u>ue</u> 4	s<u>ow</u>n 4	gul<u>ch</u> 1	<u>ch</u>i m<u>e</u> 3	clamp 1

Page 65

1.	d<u>ar</u>d 5	l<u>er</u> 5	s<u>ur</u>t 5	n<u>or</u>t 5	t<u>ir</u>k 5
2.	b<u>er</u>n 5	f<u>ur</u>d 5	l<u>ar</u>m 5	s<u>ear</u>k 5	bl<u>er</u>k 5
3.	s<u>qu</u><u>ir</u>d 5	b<u>ur</u>l 5	sl<u>or</u>t 5	t<u>ar</u>st 5	cl<u>er</u>d 5

4.	h<u>ar</u>n 5	ch<u>ur</u>d 5	sc<u>or</u>b 5	d<u>ir</u>k 5	tw<u>ur</u> 5
5.	bl<u>or</u>n 5	sc<u>ur</u>p 5	sn<u>ar</u>n 5	n<u>er</u>ch 5	sp<u>or</u>sh 5
6.	sk<u>ir</u>p 5	h<u>ar</u>st 5	st<u>ear</u>ch 5	l<u>or</u>k 5	tw<u>ur</u> 5
7.	c<u>ar</u>t 5	th<u>or</u>n 5	b<u>ur</u>n 5	<u>ear</u>th 5	squ<u>ir</u>m 5
8.	f<u>or</u>t 5	sh<u>ir</u>k 5	st<u>ar</u>k 5	h<u>ur</u>t 5	f<u>or</u>k 5
9.	ch<u>ar</u>m 5	<u>ear</u>n 5	st<u>or</u>k 5	st<u>or</u>m 5	b<u>ur</u>st 5
10.	v<u>er</u>b 5	d<u>ir</u>t 5	m<u>ir</u>th 5	h<u>or</u>n 5	j<u>er</u>k 5
11.	sh<u>ir</u>t 5	<u>ar</u>m 5	t<u>ur</u>n 5	bl<u>ur</u> 5	f<u>ir</u>st 5
12.	l<u>ear</u>n 5	l<u>ur</u>ch 5	d<u>ar</u>k 5	ch<u>ur</u>n 5	c<u>or</u>d 5

Page 66

1.	sl<u>er</u>k 5	s<u>ar</u>ck 5	m<u>ear</u>l 5	d<u>ar</u>d 5	d<u>or</u>n 5
2.	n<u>ur</u>st 5	ch<u>ar</u>f 5	sl<u>ir</u>l 5	m<u>er</u>n 5	d<u>ear</u>ch 5
3.	qu<u>ir</u>l 5	v<u>ar</u>sh 5	ch<u>or</u>b 5	sp<u>ar</u>m 5	qu<u>ir</u>b 5
4.	ch<u>ir</u>t 5	sw<u>er</u>b 5	v<u>er</u>f 5	l<u>ar</u>st 5	sh<u>ir</u>p 5
5.	cl<u>or</u>b 5	sl<u>ir</u>k 5	m<u>or</u>ft 5	p<u>ar</u>m 5	sh<u>er</u>st 5
6.	pl<u>er</u>p 5	qu<u>er</u>b 5	l<u>er</u>d 5	t<u>ur</u>st 5	f<u>er</u>l 5
7.	b<u>er</u>ck 5	d<u>or</u>f 5	h<u>or</u>st 5	w<u>ur</u>nt 5	fl<u>ir</u>d 5
8.	sw<u>er</u> 5	f<u>ar</u>b 5	l<u>or</u>x 5	tw<u>ear</u>n 5	h<u>ur</u>m 5
9.	z<u>ir</u>st 5	bl<u>er</u>v 5	sh<u>or</u>st 5	d<u>ear</u>l 5	l<u>ar</u>p 5
10.	st<u>er</u>n 5	b<u>ir</u>ch 5	s<u>ur</u>f 5	ch<u>ar</u>m 5	<u>ear</u>l 5
11.	b<u>ur</u>nt 5	p<u>ar</u>ch 5	b<u>er</u>th 5	squ<u>ir</u>t 5	t<u>or</u>ch 5
12.	wh<u>ir</u>l 5	d<u>ear</u>th 5	l<u>ur</u>k 5	p<u>er</u>t 5	h<u>ar</u>sh 5
13.	y<u>ar</u>n 5	sc<u>or</u>ch 5	h<u>ear</u>d 5	c<u>or</u>k 5	ch<u>ur</u>ch 5

14.	yearn 5	term 5	hurl 5	horn 5	garb 5
15.	serf 5	lord 5	flirt 5	slur 5	marsh 5
16.	blurt 5	park 5	morn 5	perk 5	smirk 5
17.	pearl 5	scarf 5	birth 5	north 5	spark 5
18.	scorn 5	chirp 5	arch 5	curb 5	search 5

Page 68

1.	snar 5	shate 3	bli 2	fey 4	smer 5
2.	jeen 5	lunt 1	naik 4	drack 1	glor 5
3.	mune 3	squisp 1	quor 5	whift 1	twide 3
4.	ti 2	wabe 3	swesh 1	kur 5	reen 4
5.	spop 1	toeg 4	bir 5	thraft 1	yor 5
6.	shamp 1	ster 5	twep 1	doal 4	fle 2
7.	scri 2	plor 5	flaft 1	neem 4	dar 5
8.	quode 3	dite 3	spep 1	bede 3	swir 5
9.	mupe 3	chift 1	fave 3	blar 5	peet 4
10.	splint 1	sport 5	speech 4	seal 4	fresh 1
11.	fern 5	flint 1	bloke 3	lark 5	hi 2
12.	squirt 5	shaft 1	swipe 3	slate 3	charm 5
13.	drank 1	me 2	cheap 4	spark 5	trash 1
14.	spoke 3	boat 1	lord 5	mule 3	trend 1
15.	fist 1	ho 2	heat 4	plank 1	birch 5
16.	stove 3	shell 1	burst 5	while 3	no 2
17.	joke 3	bland 1	smoke 3	thirst 5	squeak 4

18. split   gr<u>ee</u>n   <u>f</u>arm   m<u>ee</u>k   <u>f</u><u>oe</u>
     1   4   5   4   4

Page 69

#					
1.	l<u>ee</u>nt	d<u>ar</u>ch	<u>sh</u>re<u>n</u>k	glav<u>e</u>	cro
	4	5	1	3	2
2.	mil<u>ch</u>	yak<u>e</u>	cromp	r<u>oa</u><u>sh</u>	bl<u>ar</u>t
	1	3	1	4	5
3.	grom<u>e</u>	d<u>ear</u>ch	brint	bl<u>ay</u>	smi<u>sh</u>
	3	5	1	4	1
4.	<u>qu</u>ilch	breb<u>e</u>	pr<u>ai</u>t	<u>sh</u>ir<u>th</u>	<u>ch</u>i<u>ph</u>
	1	3	4	5	1
5.	sl<u>oa</u><u>ch</u>	twe	m<u>er</u>d	<u>sh</u>o<u>sh</u>	wun<u>ch</u>
	4	2	5	1	1
6.	<u>wh</u><u>ai</u>p	glo<u>sh</u>	pre<u>tch</u>	blund	pr<u>oe</u>
	4	1	1	1	4
7.	blin<u>ch</u>	v u<u>n</u>k	<u>ee</u>d	<u>ph</u>ect	tweb<u>e</u>
	1	1	4	1	3
8.	<u>f</u><u>oa</u>z	tw<u>ear</u>ch	draz<u>e</u>	zo	bon<u>ch</u>
	4	5	3	2	1
9.	blo<u>n</u>k	<u>ph</u>ap<u>e</u>	gre<u>ck</u>	sn<u>er</u><u>sh</u>	<u>ch</u>e<u>tch</u>
	1	3	1	5	1
10.	sw<u>ee</u>p	clo<u>se</u>	clen<u>ch</u>	grasp	sh <u>ar</u>k
	4	3	1	1	5
11.	t<u>u</u><u>be</u>	strip<u>e</u>	<u>ear</u>l	spr<u>ai</u>n	sten<u>ch</u>
	3	3	5	4	1
12.	gra<u>ph</u>	bi<u>r</u>ch	cr<u>ea</u>k	swept	po<u>se</u>
	1	5	4	1	3
13.	crust	str<u>ai</u>n	<u>ph</u>ra<u>se</u>	star <u>ch</u>	vot<u>e</u>
	1	4	3	5	3
14.	<u>th</u>ri<u>ve</u>	<u>th</u>rob	<u>ch</u>u<u>ck</u>	<u>th</u>r<u>ow</u>	<u>ch</u>u<u>r</u>n
	3	1	1	4	5
15.	bo<u>tch</u>	r<u>u</u><u>le</u>	<u>y</u>earn	cr<u>ee</u>p	le<u>ng</u><u>th</u>
	1	3	5	4	1
16.	<u>th</u>r<u>ow</u>	lu<u>r</u>ch	cr<u>u</u><u>ise</u>	al<u>e</u>	<u>wh</u>i<u>ch</u>
	4	5	4	3	1
17.	flo<u>ck</u>	br<u>ay</u>	scop<u>e</u>	cru<u>tch</u>	pe<u>r</u> <u>ch</u>
	1	4	3	1	5
18.	cl<u>ea</u>t	prim<u>e</u>	<u>ch</u>i<u>r</u>p	shal<u>e</u>	spe<u>ck</u>
	4	3	5	3	1

Page 71

#					
1.	<u>f</u><u>oo</u>g	bl<u>oo</u>b	dr<u>oo</u>s	<u>j</u>oop	t<u>oo</u>p
	6	6	6	6	6
2.	m<u>oo</u>nd	l<u>oo</u>pt	n<u>oo</u>mp	gr<u>oo</u>t	v<u>oy</u>
	6	6	6	6	6

145

3.	sploy	zoip	swood	spoog	troif
	6	6	6	6	6
4.	smoom	sloon	sproop	scroomp	toov
	6	6	6	6	6
5.	baw	caud	daw	faub	gaw
	6	6	6	6	6
6.	foib	taw	sloy	doot	slawp
	6	6	6	6	6
7.	coil	broil	joy	point	ploy
	6	6	6	6	6
8.	smooth	drool	broom	soon	moon
	6	6	6	6	6
9.	loom	coop	tooth	booth	hood
	6	6	6	6	6
10.	look	book	stood	took	foot
	6	6	6	6	6
11.	cook	hoof	crook	brook	shook
	6	6	6	6	6
12.	launch	bawl	haul	crawl	fault
	6	6	6	6	6

Page 72

1.	boun	cowt	doub	fouf	gouk
	6	6	6	6	6
2.	howm	joug	kout	lewp	mowm
	6	6	6	6	6
3.	noust	pousk	roubs	vew	youns
	6	6	6	6	6
4.	zowts	bloub	cloump	floum	glowsp
	6	6	6	6	6
5.	plowz	scount	slout	smew	snoup
	6	6	6	6	6
6.	spoun	stous	swoul	sploun	brout
	6	6	6	6	6
7.	drowd	frouck	groub	prowm	sproub
	6	6	6	6	6
8.	trowk	shrowl	tewk	whous	shoump
	6	6	6	6	6
9.	owl	crowd	trout	wow	slouch
	6	6	6	6	6
10.	how	crouch	brown	now	mount
	6	6	6	6	6
11.	bow	growl	grouch	chew	mound
	6	6	6	6	6
12.	found	ouch	sound	drew	cloud
	6	6	6	6	6

13.	cl<u>ow</u>n	l<u>ou</u>d	r<u>ou</u>nd	sc<u>ou</u>t	m<u>ou</u>th
	6	6	6	6	6
14.	<u>ch</u>ow	pr<u>ou</u>d	f<u>ow</u>l	<u>ou</u>t	gr<u>ew</u>
	6	6	6	6	6
15.	c<u>ow</u>	g<u>ow</u>n	t<u>ow</u>n	p<u>ou</u>nd	b<u>ou</u>nd
	6	6	6	6	6
16.	st<u>ou</u>t	dr<u>ow</u>n	cl<u>ew</u>	sc<u>ow</u>l	d<u>ow</u>n
	6	6	6	6	6
17.	f<u>ou</u>l	<u>ou</u>st	h<u>ou</u>nd	t<u>ou</u>t	sl<u>ew</u>
	6	6	6	6	6

Page 73

1.	l<u>oy</u>	d<u>oo</u>p	tr<u>aw</u>	pl<u>aw</u>	h<u>au</u>t
	6	6	6	6	6
2.	b<u>ou</u>n	m<u>au</u>sp	br<u>oo</u>p	f<u>oy</u>	m<u>ou</u>st
	6	6	6	6	6
3.	dr<u>au</u>k	f<u>aw</u>l	m<u>oo</u>f	m<u>oi</u>m	d<u>oy</u>
	6	6	6	6	6
4.	b<u>ew</u>	m<u>au</u>k	b<u>ou</u>st	f<u>oi</u>k	h<u>oo</u>l
	6	6	6	6	6
5.	b<u>ow</u>p	m<u>oy</u>	dr<u>ou</u>ft	<u>sh</u>oip	n<u>ou</u>t
	6	6	6	6	6
6.	h<u>oi</u>n	b<u>au</u>m	<u>sh</u>aw	<u>wh</u>oot	spl<u>aw</u>
	6	6	6	6	6
7.	cr<u>ou</u>f	<u>th</u>auk	<u>ch</u>oy	clewb	m<u>ou</u>n
	6	6	6	6	6
8.	bl<u>oy</u>	br<u>ou</u>t	m<u>oi</u>p	h<u>oo</u>pt	d<u>ou</u>l
	6	6	6	6	6
9.	cl<u>oy</u>	fl<u>au</u>nt	br<u>aw</u>l	cr<u>ow</u>d	h<u>aw</u>k
	6	6	6	6	6
10.	br<u>ew</u>	f<u>au</u>lt	<u>oi</u>nk	<u>oi</u>l	br<u>oi</u>l
	6	6	6	6	6
11.	<u>sh</u>out	s<u>oo</u>n	c<u>oy</u>	y<u>aw</u>n	h<u>oo</u>k
	6	6	6	6	6
12.	s<u>ou</u>nd	<u>th</u>aw	l<u>oi</u>n	pl<u>oy</u>	d<u>aw</u>n
	6	6	6	6	6
13.	p<u>oi</u>nt	n<u>ew</u>	m<u>ou</u>th	j<u>oi</u>nt	t<u>oo</u>
	6	6	6	6	6
14.	g<u>ow</u>n	r<u>oo</u>st	j<u>oi</u>n	s<u>ou</u>th	h<u>oo</u>d
	6	6	6	6	6
15.	p<u>ou</u>nd	Flo<u>y</u>d	st<u>ew</u>	tr<u>oo</u>p	sp<u>oi</u>l
	6	6	6	6	6
16.	m<u>au</u>l	s<u>oi</u>l	d<u>oo</u>m	f<u>aw</u>n	dr<u>ow</u>n
	6	6	6	6	6
17.	m<u>oi</u>st	<u>sh</u><u>oo</u>k	spr<u>aw</u>l	h<u>ow</u>	c<u>oi</u>n
	6	6	6	6	6

Answer Key for Sections One Through Three

Page 75

1.	claft 1	gr<u>oa</u>d 4	skube 3	<u>ph</u>orst 5	crosk 1
2.	fr<u>ea</u>n 4	br<u>ow</u>t 6	<u>ch</u>ausk 6	traz<u>e</u> 3	stri 2
3.	blilp 1	<u>sh</u>aust 6	spl<u>ee</u>s 4	<u>wh</u>oz<u>e</u> 3	spl<u>ir</u>st 5
4.	hes<u>e</u> 3	pl<u>oi</u>ft 6	<u>thr</u>oost 6	blarf 5	scre<u>tch</u> 1
5.	bl<u>ea</u>b 4	sc<u>oi</u>fs 6	<u>sh</u>ract 1	<u>wh</u>a<u>i</u>t 4	prap<u>e</u> 3
6.	cl<u>ar</u>n 5	scr<u>oe</u>m 4	skells 1	<u>sh</u>i v<u>e</u> 3	floff 1
7.	sp<u>er</u>d 5	<u>ch</u>o<u>u</u>ck 6	br<u>au</u>b 6	slip<u>e</u> 3	quisp 1
8.	sw<u>er</u>sk 5	pl<u>ee</u>pt 4	drin<u>e</u> 3	<u>th</u>rend 1	sm<u>oa</u>mp 4
9.	zip<u>e</u> 3	ya 2	wesk 1	v<u>ea</u>nst 4	<u>ch</u>i n<u>e</u> 3
10.	h<u>ur</u>l 5	gulp 1	s<u>ay</u> 4	bit<u>e</u> 3	h<u>ar</u>d 5
11.	gr<u>ou</u>ch 6	tra<u>sh</u> 1	d<u>oe</u> 4	d<u>au</u>nt 6	b<u>ir</u><u>ch</u> 5
12.	b<u>ar</u>n 5	b<u>oo</u>m 6	fam<u>e</u> 3	s<u>ea</u>l 4	spent 1
13.	h<u>oo</u>k 6	f<u>er</u>n 5	Pet<u>e</u> 3	pr<u>ay</u> 4	prompt 1
14.	b<u>ir</u>d 5	c<u>ou</u><u>ch</u> 6	k<u>ey</u> 4	f<u>oe</u> 4	split 1
15.	n<u>or</u><u>th</u> 5	br<u>ow</u>n 6	pos<u>e</u> 3	bl<u>oa</u>t 4	scrimp 1
16.	b<u>ur</u>st 5	bl<u>ow</u> 4	b<u>oi</u>l 6	fum<u>e</u> 3	r<u>ai</u>l 4
17.	stomp 1	t<u>oy</u> 6	d<u>ar</u>k 5	drap<u>e</u> 3	t<u>ee</u>k 4
18.	strand 1	t<u>au</u>t 6	ek<u>e</u> 3	h<u>er</u> 5	bran<u>ch</u> 1

Page 76

1.	smesk 1	<u>thr</u>ap<u>e</u> 3	dr<u>ea</u>sk 4	<u>sh</u><u>ur</u>st 5	swi 2
2.	frand 1	sl<u>ai</u>k 4	brim<u>e</u> 3	<u>ch</u>ilt 1	sp<u>ar</u>f 5
3.	fl<u>oa</u>m 4	gref<u>e</u> 3	sk<u>er</u>n 5	scra 2	<u>ph</u>o<u>u</u>ft 6
4.	progs 1	<u>wh</u>ap<u>e</u> 3	<u>sh</u>r<u>oe</u> 4	sc<u>ir</u>l 5	blaf<u>e</u> 3

148

5.   s<u>mar</u>p   dr<u>aim</u>p   plaf<u>e</u>   sn<u>oo</u>k   cra<u>tch</u>
               5   4   3   6   1

6.   sw<u>ee</u>nd   b<u>ir</u>st   shrim<u>e</u>   spr<u>oo</u>ft   str<u>au</u>l
               4   5   3   6   6

7.   <u>sh</u>remp   tr<u>oa</u>sp   <u>thr</u>ine   <u>ch</u>ond   <u>wh</u>i<u>r</u>p
               1   4   3   1   5

8.   <u>gloe</u>   fruft   sled<u>e</u>   fl<u>ar</u>mp   griffs
               4   1   3   5   1

9.   <u>pl</u>o<u>a</u>sk   splom<u>e</u>   stre<u>sh</u>   blonsk   tu<u>r</u>st
               4   3   1   1   5

10.   striv<u>e</u>   h<u>oe</u>   trust   fl<u>ee</u>   h<u>oi</u>st
               3   4   1   4   6

11.   gr<u>ow</u>   h<u>ay</u>   twist   gl<u>oo</u>m   tr<u>ay</u>
               4   4   1   6   4

12.   gr<u>ee</u>t   draft   sk<u>ir</u>t   fum<u>e</u>   gr<u>oa</u>n
               4   1   5   3   4

13.   <u>shank</u>   <u>fur</u>l   <u>sh</u>oot   <u>ch</u>amp   bon<u>e</u>
               1   5   6   1   3

14.   r<u>ai</u>n   l<u>oo</u>k   n<u>ou</u>n   <u>ch</u>eek   <u>shi</u>ne
               4   6   6   4   3

15.   sq<u>ui</u>nt   <u>ch</u>arm   cr<u>ow</u>   t<u>oi</u>l   <u>thi</u>ne
               1   5   4   6   3

16.   <u>wh</u>iff   tr<u>ai</u>l   imp   <u>sh</u>av<u>e</u>   <u>ch</u>ant
               1   4   1   3   1

17.   <u>ee</u>l   fam<u>e</u>   brisk   blast   strik<u>e</u>
               4   3   1   1   3

18.   <u>sh</u>eep   brin<u>e</u>   r<u>oo</u>m   p<u>oi</u>nt   c<u>oo</u>k
               4   3   6   6   6

Page 79

1. re-1-<u>s</u>ult   no-1-mad   stu-1-dent   bo-1-nus
   2   1   2   1   2   1   2   1

2. i-1-ris   re-1-<u>s</u>ist   de-1-<u>ter</u>   e-1-lect
   2   1   2   1   2   5   2   1

3. ro-1-dent   to-1-ken   se-1-<u>qu</u>el   be-1-<u>qu</u>est
   2   1   2   1   2   1   2   1

4. ze-1-ro   <u>sea</u>-1-<u>so</u>n   si-1-lent   be-1-gin
   2   2   4   1   2   1   2   1

5. a-1-dult   fo-1-cus   be-1-gan   se-1-lect
   2   1   2   1   2   1   2   1

6. re-1-<u>s</u>ent   bra-1-zen   hu-1-man   re-1-mit
   2   1   2   1   2   1   2   1

7. de-1-mand   a-1-men   jo-1-<u>ker</u>   ma-1-ki<u>ng</u>
   2   1   2   1   2   5   2   1

8. re-1-fund   mu-1-cus   de-1-fect   pre-1-<u>s</u>ent
   2   1   2   1   2   1   2   1

9. u-1-<u>sing</u>   e-1-mit   pre-1-fix   ti-1-di<u>ngs</u>
   2   1   2   1   2   1   2   1

Page 80

1. con-2-duct   ton-2-sil   can-2-non   ten-2-nis
   1   1   1   1   1   1   1   1

2. gos-2-sip   vic-2-tim   sel-2-dom   sub-2-ject
   1   1   1   1   1   1   1   1

3. <u>wh</u>ip-2-la<u>sh</u>   kid-2-nap   bla<u>n</u>-2-ket   clas-2-sic
     1   1   1   1   1   1   1   1

4. gal-2-lop   les-2-son   pub-2-li<u>sh</u>   con-2-tact
   1   1   1   1   1   1   1   1

5. af-2-f<u>or</u>d   fos-2-sil   bas-2-ket   dis-2-trict
   1   5   1   1   1   1   1   1

6. en-2-ri<u>ch</u>   in-2-<u>qu</u>est   pis-2-ton   ham-2-let
   1   1   1   1   1   1   1   1

7. cac-2-tus   nut-2-<u>sh</u>ell   co<u>n</u>-2-gress   con-2-vict
   1   1   1   1   1   1   1   1

8. frag-2-ment   con-2-<u>qu</u>est   bet-2-t<u>er</u>   in-2-sti<u>n</u>ct
   1   1   1   1   1   5   1   1

9. tin-2-sel   d<u>ow</u>n-2-t<u>ow</u>n   ran-2-sa<u>ck</u>   muf-2-fin
   1   1   6   6   1   1   1   1

10. pam-2-<u>ph</u>let   ban-2-dit   buz-2-z<u>ar</u>d   flut-2-t<u>er</u>
    1   1   1   1   1   5   1   5

11. seg-2-ment   dis-2-tant   ham-2-mo<u>ck</u>   nap-2-kin
    1   1   1   1   1   1   1   1

12. ven-2-d<u>or</u>   kin-2-dred   pub-2-lic   em-2-b<u>ar</u>k
    1   5   1   1   1   1   1   5

13. mon-2-st<u>er</u>   nos-2-tril   un-2-pa<u>ck</u>   hol-2-l<u>ow</u>
    1   5   1   1   1   1   1   4

14. skep-2-tic   at-2-tempt   snap-2-p<u>er</u>   zig-2-zag
    1   1   1   1   1   5   1   1

15. flip-2-p<u>er</u>   com-2-mon   lus-2-t<u>er</u>   stan-2-d<u>ar</u>d
    1   5   1   1   1   5   1   5

16. ob-2-ject   bel-2-l<u>ow</u>   dic-2-tat<u>e</u>   rus-2-tic
    1   1   1   4   1   3   1   1

17. con-2-fu<u>se</u>   jab-2-b<u>er</u>   drum-2-m<u>er</u>   gut-2-t<u>er</u>
    1   3   1   5   1   5   1   5

Page 81

1. <u>shr</u>u<u>n</u>-2-ken   pre-1-v<u>ai</u>l   im-2-po<u>se</u>   i-1-dol
    1   1   2   4   1   3   2   1

2. bo-1-gus   h u<u>n</u>-2-ger   mi-1-<u>ser</u>   <u>eas</u>-2-t<u>er</u>n
    2   1   1   5   2   5   4   5

3. cre-1-mat<u>e</u>   <u>wh</u>im-2-p<u>er</u>   gos-2-pel   pre-1-dict
    2   3   1   5   1   1   2   1

4. <u>ch</u>ap-2-t<u>er</u>
  1   5
	lau-1-rel
	  6 1
		gus-2-to
		  1 2
			mag-2-got
			  1 1

5. dol-2-<u>phi</u>n
  1   1
	ad-2-dict
	  1 1
		win-2-n<u>ow</u>
		  1 4
			fra-1-m<u>er</u>
			  2 5

6. <u>Au</u>-1-gust
  6   1
	spec-2-t<u>er</u>
	  1 5
		splin-2-t<u>er</u>
		  1 5
			vi-1-p<u>er</u>
			  2 5

7. i-1-con
  2   1
	hum-2-drum
	  1 1
		<u>bar</u>-1-b<u>er</u>
		  5 5
			ob-2-tr<u>u</u>d<u>e</u>
			  1 3

8. mel-2-<u>low</u>
  1   4
	pres-2-to
	  1 2
		bon-2-net
		  1 1
			re-1-tir<u>e</u>
			  2 3

9. of-2-ten
  1   1
	vo-1-t<u>er</u>
	  2 5
		<u>au</u>-1-<u>thor</u>
		  5 5
			trin-2-ket
			  1 1

10. de-1-vi<u>se</u>
  2   3
	as-2-s<u>u</u>m<u>e</u>
	  1 3
		jum-2-bo
		  1 2
			in-2-clin<u>e</u>
			  1 3

11. f<u>ur</u>-1-ni<u>sh</u>
  5   1
	t<u>ee</u>-1-p<u>ee</u>
	  4 4
		la-1-tent
		  2 1
			dis-2-put<u>e</u>
			  1 3

12. <u>sh</u>im-2-m<u>er</u>
  1   5
	l<u>aw</u>-1-y<u>er</u>
	  6 5
		f<u>oot</u>-2-print
		  6 1
			e-1-dict
			  2 1

13. pre-1-tend
  2   1
	a-1-mend
	  2 1
		<u>tor</u>-1-ment
		  5 1
			flus-2-t<u>er</u>
			  1 5

14. doc-2-t<u>or</u>
  1   5
	fe-1-mal<u>e</u>
	  2 3
		ig-2-l<u>oo</u>
		  1 6
			be-1-set
			  2 1

15. f<u>ou</u>n-2-d<u>er</u>
  6   5
	vic-2-t<u>or</u>
	  1 5
		di-1-n<u>er</u>
		  2 5
			clut-2-t<u>er</u>
			  1 5

16. <u>or</u>-1-bit
  5   1
	el-2-b<u>ow</u>
	  1 4
		e-1-mot<u>e</u>
		  2 3
			va-1-p<u>or</u>
			  2 5

17. jes-2-t<u>er</u>
  1   5
	hel-2-lo
	  1 2
		a-1-w<u>ai</u>t
		  2 4
			j<u>u</u>n-2-ket
			  1 1

18. tem-2-po
  1   2
	de-1-t<u>ai</u>l
	  2 4
		mo-1-tel
		  2 1
			a-1-cut<u>e</u>
			  2 3

19. e-1-go
  2   2
	slip-2-p<u>er</u>
	  1 5
		vul-2-g<u>ar</u>
		  1 5
			fun-2-nel
			  1 1

20. pol-2-len
  1   1
	r<u>u</u>-1-l<u>er</u>
	  2 5
		dis-2-tin̄ct
		  1 1
			me-1-t<u>er</u>
			  2 5

Page 82

1. t<u>ea</u>-1-sp<u>oo</u>n
  4 ˇˇ6
	de-1-flat<u>e</u>
	  2 ˜3
		<u>ur</u>-1-<u>ch</u>in
		  5 1
			ma-1-trix
			  2 ˜1

2. pro-1-gram
  2 ˜1
	re-1-tr<u>ea</u>t
	  2 ˜4
		spend-2-<u>th</u>rift
		  1˜˜ 1
			han̄g-2-man
			  1 1

3. be-1-st<u>ow</u>
  2 ˜ 4
	go-1-<u>ph</u>er
	  2 5
		pro-1-tr<u>u</u>d<u>e</u>
		  2 ˜3
			de-1-tract
			  2 ˜1

4. <u>or</u>-1-<u>ph</u>an
  5   1
	se-1-cret
	  2 ˜1
		bump-2-kin
		  1 ˜ 1
			re-1-spond
			  2 ˜1

151

5. <u>ou</u>t-2-<u>shi</u>ne   de-1-plete   be-1-tr<u>ay</u>   sa<u>ck</u>-2-<u>cloth</u>
     6   3   2   ⁓3   2   ⁓4   1   1

6. ran-2-<u>cher</u>   re-1-gret   re-1-print   ne-1-glect
     1   5   2   ⁓1   2   ⁓1   2   ⁓1

7. sp<u>or</u>ts-2-man   ni-1-tric   pl<u>ay</u>-1-gr<u>ou</u>nd   e-1-gret
     5 ⁓   1   2   ⁓1   4   ⁓   6   2   ⁓1

Page 83

1. bab-2-b<u>le</u>   pad-2-d<u>le</u>   bub-2-b<u>le</u>   <u>chu</u>ck-1-<u>le</u>
     1   7   1   7   1   7   1   7

2. jum-2-b<u>le</u>   puz-2-z<u>le</u>   <u>a</u>n-2-k<u>le</u>   ti<u>ck</u>-1-<u>le</u>
     1   7   1   7   1   7   1   7

3. ket-2-t<u>le</u>   <u>sh</u>a<u>ck</u>-1-<u>le</u>   g<u>ur</u>-1-g<u>le</u>   ti-1-t<u>le</u>
     1   7   1   7   5   7   2   7

4. mid-2-d<u>le</u>   he<u>ck</u>-1-<u>le</u>   ta-1-b<u>le</u>   scrib-2-b<u>le</u>
     1   7   1   7   2   7   1   7

5. fi<u>ck</u>-1-<u>le</u>   cud-2-d<u>le</u>   daz-2-z<u>le</u>   wob-2-b<u>le</u>
     1   7   1   7   1   7   1   7

6. smug-2-g<u>le</u>   j<u>i</u>n-2-g<u>le</u>   tri<u>ck</u>-1-<u>le</u>   swin-2-d<u>le</u>
     1   7   1   7   1   7   1   7

7. dim-2-p<u>le</u>   bu<u>ck</u>-1-<u>le</u>   cra<u>ck</u>-1-<u>le</u>   bat-2-t<u>le</u>
     1   7   1   7   1   7   1   7

8. fid-2-d<u>le</u>   sp<u>ar</u>-1-k<u>le</u>   m<u>a</u>n-2-g<u>le</u>   spe<u>ck</u>-1-<u>le</u>
     1   7   5 ·   7   1   7   1   7

9. dwin-2-d<u>le</u>   fum-2-b<u>le</u>   set-2-t<u>le</u>   lit-2-t<u>le</u>
     1   7   1   7   1   7   1   7

10. mud-2-d<u>le</u>   n<u>oo</u>-1-d<u>le</u>   gam-2-b<u>le</u>   stum-2-b<u>le</u>
     1   7   6   7   1   7   1   7

11. f<u>oi</u>-1-b<u>le</u>   <u>th</u>im-2-b<u>le</u>   si<u>ck</u>-1-<u>le</u>   met-2-t<u>le</u>
     6   7   1   7   1   7   1   7

12. hag-2-g<u>le</u>   rid-2-d<u>le</u>   twin-2-k<u>le</u>   ta<u>ck</u>-1-<u>le</u>
     1   7   1   7   1   7   1   7

Page 85

1. ab-2-b<u>ey</u>   con-2-str<u>ai</u>n   m<u>ai</u>-1-den   can-2-t<u>ee</u>n
     1   4   1   4   4   1   1   4

2. d<u>o</u>n-2-k<u>ey</u>   ap-2-pr<u>oa</u><u>ch</u>   h<u>ee</u>d-2-less   b<u>ea</u>-1-ten
     1   4   1   4   4   1   4   1

3. en-2-t<u>ai</u>l   vil-2-l<u>ai</u>n   med-2-l<u>ey</u>   <u>sh</u><u>ee</u>p-2-skin
     1   4   1   4   1   4   4   1

4. kid-2-n<u>ey</u>   con-2-t<u>ai</u>n   tr<u>ea</u>t-2-ment   w<u>ai</u>-1-tress
     1   4   1   4   4   1   4   ⁓1

5. <u>ch</u>im-2-n<u>ey</u>   in-2-l<u>ay</u>   al-2-l<u>ey</u>   mid-2-w<u>ay</u>
     1   4   1   4   1   4   1   4

6. trol-2-l<u>ey</u>   com-2-pl<u>ai</u>nt   in-2-cr<u>ea</u>se   mis-2-l<u>ea</u>d
     1   4   1   4   1   4   1   4

7. Yan-2-kee   m on-2-key   val-2-ley   up-2-keep
   1   4   1   4   1   4   1   4

8. squea-1-mish   ob-2-tain   im-2-peach   un-2-load
     4   1   1   4   1   4   1   4

9. rai-1-ling   mis-2-lay   in-2-deed   up-2-stream
   4   1   1   4   1   4   1   4

10. es-2-teem   con-2-straint   gal-2-ley   trea-1-son
   1   4   1   4   1   4   4   1

11. pay-1-ment   at-2-tain   jock-1-ey   black-2-mail
   4   1   1   4   1   4   1   4

12. com-2-plain   main-2-land   pea-1-cock   fif-2-teen
   1   4   4   1   4   1   1   4

13. dis-2-claim   rai-1-sin   mot-2-ley   toad-2-stool
   1   4   4   1   1   4   4   6

14. res-2-cue   fel-2-low   vol-2-ley   steam-2-ship
   1   4   1   4   1   4   4   1

15. ex-2-plain   ac-2-quaint   ap-2-peal   plain-2-tiff
   1   4   1   4   1   4   4   1

16. val-1-ue   sus-2-tain   may-1-hem   cray-1-fish
   1   4   4   4   4   1   4   1

17. ab-2-stain   dis-2-play   as-2-sail   dis-2-dain
   1   4   1   4   1   4   1   4

18. ex-2-claim   in-2-grain   mid-2-day   bow-1-ling
   1   4   1   4   1   4   4   1

19. dis-2-creet   mis-2-take   es-2-say   rain-2-drop
   1   4   1   3   1   4   4   1

20. cap-2-tain   play-1-pen   in-2-road   seam-2-stress
   1   4   4   1   1   4   4   1

Page 86

1. har-1-ness   as-2-sert   un-2-hurt   out-2-wit
   5   1   1   5   1   5   6   1

2. per-1-fect   car-1-pet   thou-1-sand   ex-2-ploit
   5   1   5   1   6   1   1   6

3. per-1-haps   a-1-noint   foo-1-lish   aug-2-ment
   5   1   2   6   6   1   6   1

4. sub-2-vert   es-2-cort   stub-2-born   bal-2-loon
   1   5   1   5   1   5   1   6

5. ver-1-dict   her-1-mit   per-1-sist   en-2-joy
   5   1   5   1   5   1   1   6

6. for-1-get   mor-1-bid   check-1-er   ap-2-point
   5   1   5   1   1   5   1   6

7. con-2-vert   im-2-port   tar-1-get   al-2-loy
   1   5   1   5   5   1   1   6

8. per-1-mit   ar-1-tist   hard-2-ship   dis-2-joint
   5   1   5   1   5   1   1   6

9. in-2-vert — 1 5   squir-1-rel — 5 1   man-2-ner — 1 5   em-2-ploy — 1 6
10. mar-1-ket — 5 1   sup-2-port — 1 5   fil-2-ter — 1 5   ac-2-count — 1 6
11. cor-1-rect — 5 1   ban-2-ner — 1 5   gar-1-den — 5 1   an-2-noy — 1 6
12. ex-2-pert — 1 5   gar-1-ment — 5 1   tran-2-sport — 1 5   sur-1-pass — 5 1
13. mon-2-soon — 1 6   var-1-nish — 5 1   mer-1-chant — 5 1   con-2-voy — 1 6
14. fer-1-ment — 5 1   plat-2-form — 1 5   rac-2-coon — 1 6   mush-2-room — 1 6
15. fas-2-ter — 1 5   con-2-tort — 1 5   tab-2-loid — 1 6   un-2-der — 1 5
16. cor-1-net — 5 1   lan-2-tern — 1 5   em-2-broil — 1 6   dew-1-drop — 6 ˜1
17. per-1-plex — 5 ˜1   sar-1-casm — 5 1   en-2-join — 1 6   aw-1-ning — 6 1
18. in-2-sert — 1 5   dis-2-tort — 1 5   maw-1-kish — 6 1   bit-2-ter — 1 5
19. hor-1-net — 5 1   pat-2-tern — 1 5   buf-2-foon — 1 6   tur-1-ban — 5 1

Page 87

1. a-1-bate — 2 3   re-1-fer — 2 5   be-1-moan — 2 4   be-1-lay — 2 4
2. ha-1-lo — 2 2   be-1-tween — 2 ˜4   hu-1-mor — 2 5   o-1-dor — 2 5
3. de-1-claim — 2 ˜4   a-1-loof — 2 6   re-1-join — 2 6   sha-1-ven — 2 1
4. be-1-tray — 2 ˜4   pro-1-claim — 2 ˜4   po-1-lite — 2 3   trig-2-ger — 1 5
5. pro-1-found — 2 6   ra-1-zor — 2 5   de-1-stroy — 2 ˜˜˜6   va-1-cate — 2 3
6. milk-2-weed — 1˜ 4   re-1-strain — 2 ˜˜4   e-1-lope — 2 3   a-1-hoy — 2 6
7. re-1-lay — 2 4   be-1-wail — 2 4   pro-1-mote — 2 3   de-1-vout — 2 6
8. o-1-bese — 2 3   re-1-mote — 2 3   ra-1-dar — 2 5   tooth-2-brush — 6 1
9. de-1-mote — 2 3   ti-1-ger — 2 5   hal-2-low — 1 4   o-1-vert — 2 5
10. a-1-tone — 2 3   re-1-late — 2 3   tu-1-mor — 2 5   de-1-feat — 2 4
11. mi-1-nor — 2 5   de-1-spoil — 2 ˜6   de-1-note — 2 3   wa-1-fer — 2 5

12. so-1-ber	de-1-mean	do-1-main	re-1-frain
2 5	2 4	2 4	2 ⌣4
13. re-1-tail	ta-1-ker	re-1-claim	di-1-lute
2 4	2 5	2 ⌣4	2 3
14. dis-2-turb	a-1-go	ru-1-mor	de-1-tain
2 5	2 2	2 5	2 4
15. ca-1-nine	re-1-proof	de-1-vour	a-1-mount
2 3	2 ⌣6	2 6	2 6
16. a-1-vail	re-1-gain	de-1-lay	pre-1-pare
2 4	2 4	2 4	2 3
17. so-1-lo	stri-1-dent	sa-1-ber	re-1-tain
2 2	2 1	2 5	2 4
18. spi-1-der	la-1-bor	vi-1-brate	de-1-cay
2 5	2 5	2 ⌣3	2 4

Page 88

1. bloo-1-mer	out-2-side	out-2-growth	poin-2-ter
6 5	6 3	6 4	6 5
2. ar-1-cade	rain-2-bow	fore-1-bode	per-1-fume
5 3	4 4	3 3	5 3
3. bee-1-line	sail-2-boat	for-1-sake	store-1-room
4 3	4 4	5 3	3 6
4. air-2-mail	per-1-spire	out-2-burst	spea-1-ker
4 4	5 ⌣3	6 5	4 5
5. car-1-toon	scoo-1-ter	name-1-sake	boy-1-hood
5 6	6 5	3 3	6 6
6. bride-1-groom	troo-1-per	out-2-lay	ver-1-bose
3 ⌣6	6 5	6 4	5 3
7. cur-1-tail	ow-1-ner	cloud-2-burst	boo-1-mer
5 4	4 5	6 5	6 5
8. coo-1-ler	side-1-board	or-1-nate	laun-2-der
6 5	3 4	5 3	6 5
9. fore-1-taste	sai-1-lor	por-1-tray	boar-2-der
3 3	4 5	5 ⌣4	4 5
10. har-1-poon	cook-2-book	floun-2-der	wea-1-ver
5 6	6 6	6 5	4 5
11. gain-2-say	side-1-ways	par-1-take	oy-1-ster
4 4	3 4	5 3	6 ⌣5
12. moon-2-shine	waist-2-line	broi-1-ler	road-2-side
6 3	4 ⌣3	6 5	4 3
13. for-1-gave	look-1-out	per-1-vade	traw-1-ler
5 3	6 6	5 3	6 5
14. mile-1-stone	grape-1-vine	clea-1-ver	toa-1-ster
3 ⌣3	3 3	4 5	4 ⌣5
15. main-2-sail	par-1-took	home-1-made	ou-1-ster
4 4	5 6	3 3	6 ⌣5

16. r<u>oo</u>m-2-mat<u>e</u>   d<u>ay</u>-1-dr<u>ea</u>m   state-1-r<u>oo</u>m   s<u>ur</u>-1-m<u>ou</u>nt
    6   3   4   ~4   3   6   5   6

17. nin<u>e</u>-1-t<u>ee</u><u>n</u><u>th</u>   s<u>ee</u>-1-k<u>er</u>   ros<u>e</u>-1-w<u>oo</u>d   s<u>au</u>n-2-t<u>er</u>
    3   4   4   5   3   6   6   6

18. r<u>ai</u>l-2-r<u>oa</u>d   cl<u>oi</u>-1-st<u>er</u>   m<u>ea</u>n-2-<u>while</u>   b<u>ar</u>-1-t<u>er</u>
    4   4   6   ~5   4   3   5   5

19. r<u>oo</u>-1-st<u>er</u>   c<u>or</u>-1-rod<u>e</u>   m<u>ois</u>-2-tur<u>e</u>   p<u>or</u>-1-t<u>er</u>
    6 ~5   5   3   6   3   5   5

Page 89

1. wa<u>tch</u>   full   so-1-da   An-2-na
   8   8   2 8   1   8

2. pro-1-ven   stall   ze-1-bra   squan-2-d<u>er</u>
   8 1   8   2 8   8   5

3. to   bald   stalk   wan-2-d<u>er</u>
   8   8   8   8   5

4. am-2-bu<u>sh</u>   waltz   bul-2-let   Cu-1-ba
   1 8   8   8 1   2 8

5. small   <u>who</u>   com-2-ma   squab-2-b<u>le</u>
   8   8   1   8   8   7

6. bull   wa<u>s</u>   al-2-so   <u>th</u>rall
   8   8   8 2   8

7. swad-2-d<u>le</u>   pu<u>sh</u>   <u>who</u>m   tu-1-na
   8   7   8   8   2 8

8. squa<u>ll</u>   squad-2-ron   fal-2-t<u>er</u>   do
   8   8 1   8 5   8

9. h<u>u</u>-1-la   bu-1-<u>sh</u>el   car<u>e</u>-1-ful   wal-2-let
   2 8   8 1   3 8   8 1

10. <u>Chi</u>-1-na   m<u>ou</u><u>th</u>-2-ful   ex-2-tra   put
   2 8   6   8   1 8   8

11. gall   balk   wa-1-t<u>er</u>   Wal-2-t<u>er</u>
   8   8   8 5   8 5

Page 91

1. bass/bass   ca-1-det   grind   tri-1-but<u>e</u>
   <u>1</u> 1   <u>2</u> 1   1   <u>2</u> <u>3</u>

2. scold   ho-1-n<u>ey</u>   <u>ch</u>am-2-b<u>er</u>   cre-1-dit
   <u>1</u>   <u>2</u> 4   <u>1</u> 5   <u>2</u> 1

3. fa-1-mi<u>sh</u>   wild   hol-2-st<u>er</u>   sa-1-lu<u>te</u>
   <u>2</u> 1   <u>1</u>   <u>1</u> 5   <u>2</u> <u>3</u>

4. mind   de-1-cad<u>e</u>   scroll   co-1-l<u>or</u>
   <u>1</u>   <u>2</u> 3   <u>1</u>   2 5

5. gross   pint   di-1-vin<u>e</u>   se-1-dat<u>e</u>
   <u>1</u>   <u>1</u>   <u>2</u> 3   <u>2</u> 3

6. po-1-li<u>sh</u>/Po-1-i<u>sh</u>   de-1-vil   mold   cli-1-mat<u>e</u>
   <u>2</u> 1   2 1   <u>2</u> 1   <u>1</u>   2 <u>3</u>

7. do-1-zen — 2 1 | bin-2-der — 1 5 | stroll — 1 | host — 1
8. poll — 1 | be-1-hold — 2 1 | kind — 1 | de-1-bit — 2 1
9. di-1-vide — 2 3 | told — 1 | di-1-sease — 2 4 | toll — 1

Page 92

1. bare — 3 | sphere — 3 | bore-1-dom — 3 1 | Ha-1-rold — 2 1
2. dire — 3 | mir-2-ror — 1 5 | com-2-pare — 1 3 | mar-2-row — 1 4
3. lure — 3 | bur-1-row — 5 4 | ad-2-here — 1 3 | e-1-rode — 2 3
4. bore — 3 | ad-2-mire — 1 3 | be-1-reft — 2 1 | spar-2-row — 1 4
5. blare — 3 | ter-2-ror — 1 5 | mire — 3 | car-2-rot — 1 1
6. fire — 3 | spi-1-rit — 2 1 | ba-1-ron — 2 1 | fan-2-fare — 1 3
7. pure — 3 | bar-2-rel — 1 1 | as-2-pire — 1 3 | pa-1-rish — 2 1
8. fore — 3 | quag-2-mire — 1 3 | sur-1-round — 5 6 | ac-2-quire — 1 3
9. care — 3 | par-2-rot — 1 1 | con-2-spire — 1 3 | fer-2-ret — 1 1
10. hire — 3 | i-1-rate — 2 3 | fare-1-well — 3 1 | pe-1-rish — 2 1
11. se-1-cure — 2 3 | en-2-snare — 1 3 | sur-1-real — 5 4 | hor-1-ror — 5 5
12. he-1-ro — 2 2 | du-1-ress — 2 1 | e-1-rupt — 2 1 | tran-2-spire — 1 3
13. Hu-1-ron — 2 1 | spire — 3 | du-1-ring — 2 1 | si-1-ren — 2 1
14. nar-2-rate — 1 3 | Ca-1-rol — 2 1 | me-1-rit — 2 1 | spa-1-ring — 2 1
15. pe-1-ril — 2 1 | I-1-ran — 2 1 | Ka-1-ren — 2 1 | er-2-ror — 1 5

Page 93

1. rab-2-bit — 1 1 | pil-2-low — 1 4 | Jo-1-seph — 2 1 | splen-2-did — 1 1
2. im-2-press — 1 1 | pud-2-ding — 8 1 | mer-1-maid — 5 4 | li-1-lac — 2 1
3. pas-2-tel — 1 1 | sir-1-loin — 5 6 | tor-1-por — 5 5 | ve-1-nom — 2 1

4. Lon-2-don 1 1	im-2-bibe 1 3	ex-2-tent 1 1	fes-2-ter 1 5
5. star-1-tle 5 7	chow-1-der 6 5	pho-1-nics 2 1	shel-2-ter 1 5
6. pat-2-ter 1 5	li-1-mit 2 1	shar-1-pen 5 1	cal-2-dron 8 1
7. re-1-deem 2 4	ex-2-pose 1 3	do-1-nate 2 3	moon-2-beam 6 4
8. clus-2-ter 1 5	ruf-2-fle 1 7	cod-2-dle 1 7	stag-2-ger 1 5
9. dit-2-to 1 2	up-2-roar 1 4	al-2-pha 1 8	ti-1-mid 2 1
10. ad-2-dress 1 1	hal-2-ter 8 5	i-1-tem 2 1	pro-1-fane 2 3
11. fla-1-grant 2 ⁓1	sec-2-tor 1 5	mu-1-sic 2 1	stam-2-pede 1 3
12. lob-2-ster 1 5	mis-2-hap 1 1	mis-2-count 1 6	mun-2-dane 1 3
13. shame-1-ful 3 8	wal-2-nut 8 1	traf-2-fic 1 1	muz-2-zle 1 7
14. re-1-flect 2 ⁓1	wax-1-en 1 1	pre-1-clude 2 ⁓3	ma-1-jor 2 5
15. pic-2-nic 1 1	lam-2-poon 1 6	fraz-2-zle 1 7	ten-2-der 1 5
16. aw-1-ful 6 8	mot-2-tle 1 7	slug-2-gish 1 1	me-1-dal 2 8
17. o-1-pen 2 1	pho-1-to 2 2	con-2-fess 1 1	sham-2-ble 1 7
18. o-1-ther 2 5	be-1-cause 2 6	ac-2-crue 1 4	snug-2-gle 1 7
19. gog-2-gle 1 7	plas-2-tic 1 1	de-1-cline 2 ⁓3	scald 8

Page 94

1. dis-2-rupt 1 1	ser-1-pent 5 1	splen-2-dor 1 5	be-1-low 2 4
2. ex-2-cuse 1 3	con-2-vent 1 1	con-2-found 1 6	main-2-tain 4 4
3. de-1-fault 2 6	re-1-call 2 8	har-1-bor 5 5	pis-2-tol 1 1
4. au-1-dit 6 1	ban-2-quet 1 1	wit-2-ness 1 1	pel-2-let 1 1
5. tat-2-too 1 6	tram-2-ple 1 7	con-2-coct 1 1	scorn-2-ful 5 8
6. ap-2-pall 1 8	poi-1-son 6 1	pol-2-ka 1 8	gob-2-lin 1 1

7. con-2-text	dar-1-ling	reck-1-on	pa-1-trol
1 1	5 1	1 1	2 1
8. out-2-law	vir-1-tue	pes-2-ter	tac-2-tics
6 6	5 4	1 5	1 1
9. wea-1-sel	os-2-trich	tem-2-per	me-1-thane
4 1	1 1	1 5	2 3
10. pain-2-less	ei-1-ther	tick-2-lish	wal-2-rus
4 1	4 5	1 1	8 1
11. far-1-ther	bick-1-er	op-2-press	Fri-1-day
5 5	1 5	1 1	2 4
12. au-1-burn	whit-2-tle	wee-1-vil	la-1-bel
6 5	1 7	4 1	2 1
13. con-2-done	whis-2-per	wel-2-come	ex-2-pel
1 3	1 5	1 3	1 1
14. tur-1-key	pitch-1-er	stag-2-nate	sea-1-board
5 4	1 5	1 3	4 4
15. be-1-fall	ex-2-hale	lo-1-ser	fi-1-nish
2 8	1 3	8 5	2 1
16. con-2-dor	mea-1-ger	ac-2-quit	mis-2-took
1 5	4 5	1 1	1 6
17. se-1-rum	in-2-form	quib-2-ble	at-2-tach
2 1	1 5	1 7	1 1
18. mag-2-net	or-1-der	e-1-ject	in-2-to
1 1	5 5	2 1	1 8

Page 96

1. ran-2-cid	wince	spice	cen-2-sor
1 1	1	3	1 5
2. farce	con-2-cern	nui-1-sance	ounce
5	1 5	4 1	6
3. com-2-merce	spruce	cei-1-ling	en-2-trance
1 5	3	4 1	1 1
4. cinch	sten-2-cil	prin-2-cess	of-2-fice
1	1 1	1 1	1 1
5. ci-1-gar	suc-2-ceed	fleece	li-1-cense
2 5	1 4	4	2 3
6. trance	force	bi-1-ceps	pro-1-cess
1	5	2 1	2 1
7. peace	con-2-cert	ac-2-cent	an-2-nounce
4	1 5	1 1	1 6
8. sen-2-tence	de-1-vice	in-2-voice	ra-1-cism
1 1	2 3	1 6	2 1
9. cease	i-1-cing	ba-1-lance	sauce
4	2 1	2 1	6
10. pounce	sub-2-stance	ad-2-vance	pin-2-cers
6	1 1	1 1	1 5

11. con-2-ceal   fur-1-nace   no-1-tice   space
    1   4   5   1   2   1   3

12. sin-2-cere   de-1-cide   ro-1-mance   chance
    1   3   2   3   2   1   1

13. di-1-vorce   a-1-cid   prac-2-tice   re-1-joice
    2   5   2   1   1   1   2   6

14. bounce   can-2-cel   em-2-brace   choice
    6   1   1   1   3   6

15. pen-2-cil   suc-2-cess   glance   truce
    1   1   1   1   1   3

Page 98

1. bridge   mer-1-ger   a-1-gent   e-1-merge
    1   5   5   2   1   2   5

2. bulge   badge   dis-2-gorge   hedge
    1   1   1   5   1

3. en-2-large   plun-2-ger   nudge   sta-1-ging
    1   5   1   5   1   2   1

4. budge   wedge   ur-1-gent   in-2-dulge
    1   1   5   1   1   1

5. strange   lounge   wa-1-ger   be-1-grudge
    3   6   2   5   2   ⌣1

6. di-1-gest   fringe   sludge   man-2-ger
    2   1   1   1   1   5

7. trudge   vi-1-gil   ex-2-change   forge
    1   2   1   1   3   5

8. ran-2-ger   huge   di-1-verge   dodge
    1   5   3   2   5   1

9. out-2-rage   ledge   gen-2-der   plunge
    6   3   1   1   5   1

10. sub-2-merge   gouge   col-2-lege   sledge
    1   5   6   1   1   1

11. smudge   barge   cringe   gin-2-ger
    1   5   1   1   5

12. en-2-gage   dis-2-charge   pledge   range
    1   3   1   5   1   3

13. in-2-gest   ridge   merge   an-2-gel
    1   1   1   5   1   1

Page 102

1. hym-2-nal   sup-2-ply   py-1-thon   py-1-lon
    1   8   1   2   2   1   2   1

2. re-1-ly   vi-1-nyl   by   here-1-by
    2   2   2   1   2   3   2

3. there-1-by   pry   hy-1-drant   thy
    3   2   2   2   ⌣1   2

4. sky	sys-2-tem	syl-2-van	al-2-ly
2	1 1	1 1	1 2
5. crys-2-tal	ty-1-phus	gy-1-rate	shy
1 8	2 1	2 3	2
6. phy-1-sics	hy-1-phen	sly	cy-1-nic
2 1	2 1	2	2 1
7. cy-1-clist	de-1-fy	thy-1-roid	mys-2-tic
2 ⁓1	2 2	2 6	1 1
8. cym-2-bal	a-1-byss	ap-2-ply	cy-1-clone
1 8	2 1	1 2	2 ⁓3
9. dry	lymph	cy-1-cle	gyp-2-sum
2	1	2 7	1 1
10. en-2-try	an-2-gry	row-1-dy	mu-1-shy
1 2	1 2	6 2	2 2
11. na-1-vy	scur-1-ry	ran-2-gy	tar-1-dy
2 2	5 2	1 2	5 2
12. hol-2-ly	diz-2-zy	pan-2-try	co-1-zy
1 2	1 2	1 2	2 2
13. dow-1-dy	on-2-ly	ru-1-by	low-1-ly
6 2	1 2	2 2	4 2
14. pu-1-ny	mar-2-ry	noi-1-sy	moo-1-dy
2 2	1 2	6 2	6 2
15. din-2-gy	mur-1-ky	whis-2-ky	gent-2-ly
1 2	5 2	1 2	1⁓ 2
16. hur-1-ry	hoo-1-ky	gloo-1-my	fris-2-ky
5 2	6 2	6 2	1 2
17. slop-2-py	hard-2-ly	bal-2-my	po-1-ny
1 2	5 2	8 2	2 2
18. dai-1-sy	ea-1-sy	du-1-ty	lof-2-ty
4 2	4 2	2 2	1 2
19. bree-1-zy	ear-1-ly	bul-2-ky	quea-1-sy
4 2	5 2	1 2	4 2

Page 103

1. cry	yams	play	bay
2	1	4	4
2. stay	fan-2-cy	fly	boun-2-ty
4	1 2	2	6 2
3. crypt	yam-2-mer	gym	type
1	1 5	1	3
4. o-1-kay	im-2-ply	tray	ci-1-ty
2 4	1 2	4	2 2
5. de-1-ny	ply	bag-2-gy	yet
2 2	2	1 2	1
6. ar-1-my	cyst	lay	de-1-cry
5 2	1	4	2 ⁓2

7. pop-2-p̲y̲ 1 2	bo-1-ny̲ 2 2	sy̲-1-rup <u>2</u> 1	sly 2
8. yen 1	man-2-ly̲ 1 2	<u>lou</u>-1-<u>sy̲</u> 6 2	pra̲y̲ 4
9. spy̲ 2	cla̲y̲ 4	lyn<u>ch</u> 1	my<u>th</u> 1
10. bo-1-dy̲ <u>2</u> 2	gra-1-vy̲ 2 2	pry̲ 2	yel-2-<u>low</u> 1 4
11. y<u>ar</u>d 5	<u>shy</u> 2	re-1-ply 2 ~2	wa-1-vy̲ 2 2
12. hy̲-1-brid 2 ~1	dum-2-my̲ 1 2	ty̲-1-<u>ph</u>oid 2 6	m<u>ay</u> 4
13. gr<u>ee</u>-1-dy̲ 4 2	<u>why</u> 2	com-2-ply 1 2	hus-2-k̲y̲ 1 2
14. ke̲y̲ 4	p<u>ay</u> 4	fus-2-sy̲ 1 2	fry̲ 2
15. my̲ 2	stod-2-g̲y̲ 1 2	en-2-vy̲ 1 2	g̲yp 1
16. fil-2-<u>thy</u> 1 2	<u>out</u>-2-cry 6 2	Yu-1-kon 2̲ 1	bel-2-ly̲ 1 2
17. de-1-fy̲ 2 2	h<u>ay</u> 4	<u>ch</u>il-2-ly̲ 1 2	Lynn 1
18. <u>oi</u>-1-ly̲ 6 2	f<u>au</u>l-2-ty̲ 6 2	lynx 1	pal-2-try̲ 8 2
19. m<u>er</u>-1-c̲y̲ 5 2	dry̲ 2	can-2-dy̲ 1 2	ve-1-ry̲ 2̲ 2
20. fr<u>ay</u> 4	ba-1-by̲ 2 2	<u>boo</u>-1-ty̲ 6̲ 2	emp-2-ty̲ 1 ~ 2

Page 105

1. cl<u>ea</u>-1-ran<u>ce</u> 4 1	symp-2-tom 1 ~ 1	gro-1-<u>c̲</u>er 2 5	m<u>ur</u>-1-d<u>er</u> 5 5
2. ca-1-b<u>le</u> 2 7	fa-1-bric 2̲ ~1	sty<u>le</u> 3	de-1-<u>c̲</u>ent 2 1
3. con-2-<u>geal</u> 1 4	fa-1-b<u>le</u> 2 7	st<u>ee</u>-1-ly̲ 4 2	sym-2-bol 1 1
4. re-1-spect 2 ~ 1	<u>cor</u>-1-n<u>er</u> 5 5	in-2-stall 1 8	ca<u>ck</u>-1-<u>le</u> 1 7
5. cro-1-ny̲ 2 2	cryp-2-tic 1 1	hu-1-man<u>e</u> 2 3	dis-2-lo<u>dge</u> 1 1
6. <u>gor</u>ge 5	<u>sur</u>-1-pri<u>se</u> 5 ~ 3	n<u>ee</u>d-2-ful 4 8	mi-1-n<u>er</u> 2 5
7. bul-2-ly̲ 8 2	con-2-gest 1 1	ly-1-ric 2̲ 1	in-2-san<u>e</u> 1 3
8. ac-2-<u>c̲</u>ess 1 1	<u>ch</u>at-2-t<u>er</u> 1 5	le-1-gend 2̲ 1	ob-2-scur<u>e</u> 1 3

9. f<u>er</u>-1-til<u>e</u>   b<u>ur</u>-1-l<u>y</u>   de-1-du<u>ce</u>   prop-2-pin<u>g</u>
   5   3   5   2   2   3̿   1   1

10. mum-2-m<u>y</u>   en-2-ra<u>ge</u>   co-1-p<u>y</u>   ta-1-b<u>le</u>
   1   2   1   3   2̲   2   2   7

11. <u>ch</u>eap-2-l<u>y</u>   re-1-<u>c</u>ess   spon<u>ge</u>   cat-2-t<u>le</u>
   4   2   2   1   1   1   7

12. syn-2-tax   <u>g</u>en-2-til<u>e</u>   re-1-<u>g</u>ent   pro-1-fil<u>e</u>
   1   1   1   3   2   1   2   3

13. strol-2-l<u>er</u>   <u>g</u>ist   ex-2-<u>c</u>ess   ty-1-rant
   <u>1</u>   5   1   1   1   2   1

14. pro-1-du<u>ce</u>   bot-2-t<u>le</u>   con-2-test   <u>cir</u>-1-c<u>le</u>
   2̿   3̿   1   7   1   1   5   7

15. pre-1-<u>c</u>i<u>n</u>ct   a-1-fr<u>ai</u>d   fol-2-l<u>y</u>   <u>for</u>-1-tress
   2̿   1   2   ˘4   1   2   5   ˘1

16. <u>ch</u>an<u>ge</u>   en-2-ti<u>ce</u>   ha<u>ck</u>-1-<u>le</u>   p<u>ur</u>-1-p<u>le</u>
   3   1   3   1   7   5   7

17. in-2-stan<u>ce</u>   r<u>oo</u>-1-st<u>er</u>   va-1-grant   ef-2-f<u>or</u>t
   1   1   6   ˘5   2   ˘1   1   5

18. tan-2-gent   <u>ch</u>am-2-b<u>er</u>   s<u>ur</u>-1-viv<u>e</u>   <u>c</u>i-1-trus
   1   1   <u>1</u>   5   5   3   2̲   ˘1

19. r<u>ea</u>l-2-l<u>y</u>   j<u>ui</u><u>ce</u>   es-2-sen<u>ce</u>   mo-1-lest
   4   2   4   1   1   2   1

20. <u>ch</u>ar-1-c<u>oa</u>l   bra<u>ce</u>-1-let   tra-1-<u>g</u>ic   di-1-vul<u>ge</u>
   5   4   3   1   2̲   1   2̲   1

Page 106

1. re-1-<u>c</u>ed<u>e</u>   con-2-trit<u>e</u>   cl<u>er</u>-1-g<u>y</u>   re-1-pel
   2   3   1   3   5   2   2   1

2. ma-1-<u>g</u>ic   sol-2-sti<u>ce</u>   es-2-cap<u>e</u>   w<u>oo</u>-1-d<u>y</u>
   2̲   1   <u>1</u>   1   1   3   6   2

3. <u>un</u>-2-c<u>le</u>   rub-2-bi<u>sh</u>   nan-2-n<u>y</u>   <u>En</u>-2-gli<u>sh</u>
   1   7   1   1   1   2   <u>1</u>   1

4. dru<u>dge</u>   no-1-b<u>le</u>   s<u>ur</u><u>ge</u>   fr<u>ee</u>-1-dom
   1   2   7   5   4   1

5. bra-1-<u>c</u>in<u>g</u>   ac-2-<u>c</u>ept   crum-2-b<u>le</u>   bal-2-lot
   2   1   1   1   1   7   1   1

6. in-2-frin<u>ge</u>   di-1-git   blis-2-t<u>er</u>   m<u>ar</u>-1-b<u>le</u>
   1   1   2̲   1   1   5   5   7

7. clam-2-m<u>y</u>   re-1-fu<u>ge</u>   pen-2-n<u>y</u>   re-1-<u>c</u>ent
   1   2   2̲   3   1   2   2   1

8. re-1-n<u>ou</u>n<u>ce</u>   <u>au</u>s-2-ter<u>e</u>   bu<u>dge</u>   im-2-pin<u>ge</u>
   2   6   6   3   1   1   1

9. e-1-vent   re-1-<u>c</u>it<u>e</u>   tr<u>ai</u>-1-t<u>or</u>   ma-1-tur<u>e</u>
   2   1   2   3   4   5   2   3

10. sli-1-m<u>y</u>   mo-1-ment   re-1-pla<u>ce</u>   j<u>er</u>-1-s<u>ey</u>
   2   2   2   1   2   ˘3   5   4

11. con-2-sole   com-2-mence   fra-1-gile   bad-2-ger
   1   3   1   1   2   3   1   5

12. Chi-1-nese   oc-2-tave   slea-1-zy   a-1-pron
   2   3   1   3   4   2   2   ~1

13. dis-2-grace   a-1-cross   ig-2-nite   gyp-2-sy
   1   3   2   ~1   1   3   1   2

14. ger-1-mane   mus-2-ket   Ro-1-man   pol-2-lute
   5   3   1   1   2   1   1   3

15. con-2-cede   tan-2-gle   re-1-duce   car-1-bon
   1   3   1   7   2   3   5   1

16. for-1-ceps   fif-2-ty   mus-2-ter   ab-2-sence
   5   1   1   2   1   5   1   1

17. cin-2-der   dis-1-own   lo-1-gic   de-1-nounce
   1   5   1   4   2   1   2   6

18. bar-1-gain   ce-1-ment   tran-2-scribe   let-2-tuce
   5   4   2   1   1   3   1   1

19. pa-1-cer   ser-1-vice   de-1-cease   pan-2-ther
   2   5   5   1   2   4   1   5

20. u-1-nit   ad-2-vice   clou-1-dy   pre-1-cise
   2   1   1   3   6   2   2   3

Page 107

1. shaped   jammed   bat-2-ted   res-2-ted
   3   1   1   1   1   1

2. wined   dimmed   rot-2-ted   tipped
   3   1   1   1   1

3. po-1-lished   mat-2-ted   scraped   baked
   2   1   1   1   3   3

4. blessed   shou-1-ted   nod-2-ded   seemed
   1   6   1   1   1   4

5. hoped   tra-1-ded   toas-2-ted   dus-2-ted
   3   2   1   4   1   1   1

6. lan-2-ded   stopped   re-1-turned   hap-2-pened
   1   1   1   2   5   1   1

7. picked   ra-1-vished   foun-2-ded   faked
   1   2   1   6   1   3

8. res-2-ted   raked   plea-1-ded   hummed
   1   1   3   4   1   1

9. wheeled   fit-2-ted   re-1-sumed   pre-1-pared
   4   1   1   2   3   2   3

10. plan-2-ted   hugged   danced   ra-1-ted
   1   1   1   1   2   1

11. flat-2-tened   ad-2-ded   poin-2-ted   marked
   1   1   1   1   6   1   5

1. <u>or</u>-1-ga-1-nic
   5   <u>2</u>   1

2. an-2-<u>c̳es</u>-2-tr<u>y</u>
   1   1   2

3. en-2-c<u>ou</u>n-2-t<u>er</u>
   1   6   5

4. con-2-stan-2-<u>c̳y</u>
   1   1   2

5. i-1-mi-1-tat<u>e</u>
   <u>2</u>   2   3

6. u-1-ten-2-sil
   2   1   1

7. rasp-2-ber-2-ry
   1   1   2

8. c<u>ou</u>n-2-se-1-l<u>or</u>
   6   <u>2</u>   5

9. dis-2-co-1-v<u>er</u>
   1   <u>2</u>   5

10. bal-2-co-1-ny
   1   2   2

11. de-1-<u>c̳i</u>-1-<u>pher</u>
   2   2   5

12. mo-1-las-2-ses
   2   1   1

13. buf-2-fa-1-lo
   1   2   2

14. den-2-si-1-ty
   1   <u>2</u>   2

15. pro-1-jec-2-t<u>or</u>
   2   1   5

16. ac-2-ro-1-bat
   1   2   1

17. in-2-sol-2-vent
   1   1   1

18. hy-1-po-1-crite
   <u>2</u>   2   3̃

19. m<u>ar</u>-1-ma-1-lad<u>e</u>
   5   2   3

20. de-1-pen-2-dent
   2   1   1

---

in-2-dus-2-tr<u>y</u>
   1   1   2

<u>gin</u>-2-g<u>er</u>-1-l<u>y</u>
   1   5   2

com-2-mu-1-nist
   1   2   1

an-2-<u>c̳es</u>-2-t<u>or</u>
   1   1   5

ad-2-ven-2-tur<u>e</u>
   1   1   3

daf-2-fo-1-dil
   1   2   1

lux-1-u-1-ry
   1   2   2

O-1-lym-2-pic
   2   1   1

oc-2-ta-1-gon
   1   2   1

re-1-m<u>ain</u>-2-d<u>er</u>
   2   4   5

of-2-fi-1-<u>c̳er</u>
   1   <u>2</u>   5

c<u>ur</u>-1-ren-2-<u>c̳y</u>
   5   1   2

em-2-bas-2-s<u>y</u>
   1   1   2

de-1-t<u>er</u>-1-gent
   2   5   1

e-1-na-1-mel
   2   <u>2</u>   1

vi-1-ne-1-g<u>ar</u>
   <u>2</u>   <u>2</u>   5

dis-1-<u>or</u>-1-d<u>er</u>
   1   5   5

o-1-v<u>er</u>-1-l<u>oo</u>k
   2   5   6

cap-2-ti-1-vat<u>e</u>
   1   <u>2</u>   3

ab-2-n<u>or</u>-1-mal
   1   5   8

---

bad-2-min-2-ton
   1   1   1

n<u>ar</u>-1-co-1-tic
   5   <u>2</u>   1

De-1-<u>c̳em</u>-2-b<u>er</u>
   2   1   5

en-2-cum-2-b<u>er</u>
   1   1   5

mag-2-ne-1-ti<u>sm</u>
   1   <u>2</u>   1

en-2-gag<u>e</u>-1-ment
   1   3   1

ad-2-v<u>er</u>-1-ti<u>se</u>
   1   5   3

re-1-tir<u>e</u>-1-ment
   2   3   1

fi-1-na-1-lize
   2   2   3

tran-2-qui-1-lize
   1   <u>2</u>   3

sanc-2-ti-1-ty
   1̃   2   2

blas-2-<u>phe</u>-1-my
   1   <u>2</u>   2

ex-2-pe-1-dit<u>e</u>
   1   <u>2</u>   3

t<u>or</u>-1-men-2-t<u>or</u>
   5   1   5

sy-1-nop-2-sis
   <u>2</u>   1   1

sum-2-ma-1-r<u>y</u>
   1   2   2

a-1-de-1-quate
   <u>2</u>   <u>2</u>   3

in-2-no-1-<u>c̳ent</u>
   1   2   1

di-1-sen-2-gag<u>e</u>
   <u>2</u>   1   3

ec-2-<u>c̳en</u>-2-tric
   1   1   1

---

com-2-pen-2-sat<u>e</u>
   1   1   3

con-2-so-1-nant
   1   2   1

t<u>er</u>-1-mi-1-nus
   5   <u>2</u>   1

pro-1-se-1-cute
   <u>2</u>   <u>2</u>   3

p<u>or</u>-1-cu-1-pin<u>e</u>
   5   2   3

im-2-p<u>or</u>-1-tant
   1   5   1

in-2-<u>c̳i</u>-1-dent
   1   <u>2</u>   1

un-2-com-2-mon
   1   1   1

de-1-<u>lin</u>-2-<u>quent</u>
   2   1   1

po-1-ta-1-to
   2   2   2

m<u>er</u>-1-<u>chan</u>-2-dis<u>e</u>
   5   1   3

di-1-sin-2-fect
   <u>2</u>   1   1

syl-2-la-1-b<u>le</u>
   1   2   7

fur-1-ni-1-tur<u>e</u>
   5   <u>2</u>   3

sta-1-bi-1-liz<u>e</u>
   2   <u>2</u>   3

al-2-<u>pha</u>-1-bet
   1   2   1

in-2-<u>for</u>-1-mant
   1   5   1

en-2-t<u>er</u>-1-pri<u>se</u>
   1   5   3̃

b<u>ur</u>-1-si-1-tis
   5   2   1

ra-1-ti-1-fy
   <u>2</u>   <u>2</u>   2

Answer Key for Sections One Through Three

Page 109

1. im-2-pe-1-tus
    1   2   1
   ba-1-che-1-lor
    2   2   5
   sub-2-sti-1-tute
    1   2   3
   im-2-po-1-lite
    1   2   3

2. a-1-gree-1-ment
    2 ˘ 4   1
   fas-2-ci-1-nate
    1   2   3
   de-1-ploy-1-ment
    2 ˘ 6   1
   for-1-mu-1-late
    5   2   3

3. ap-2-pe-1-tite
    1   2   3
   pas-2-sen-2-ger
    1   1   5
   com-2-pu-1-ter
    1   2   5
   u-1-ni-1-verse
    2   2   5

4. ex-2-cel-2-lent
    1   1   1
   un-2-der-1-mine
    1   5   3
   tur-1-bu-1-lent
    5   2   1
   ab-2-do-1-men
    1   2   1

5. e-1-di-1-ble
    2   2   7
   mag-2-ne-1-tize
    1   2   3
   won-2-der-1-land
    1   5   1
   em-2-pha-1-size
    1   2   3

6. to-1-ma-1-to
    2   2   2
   in-2-ter-1-cept
    1   5   1
   pa-1-ra-1-dise
    2   2   3
   in-2-di-1-rect
    1   2   1

7. po-1-pu-1-lar
    2   2   5
   in-2-tel-2-lect
    1   1   1
   do-1-cu-1-ment
    2   2   1
   ma-1-jes-2-tic
    2   1   1

8. re-1-mem-2-ber
    2   1   5
   as-2-sess-2-ment
    1   1   1
   re-1-ple-1-nish
    2 ˘2 1
   Oc-2-to-1-ber
    1   2   5

9. al-2-co-1-hol
    1   2   1
   ex-2-cite-1-ment
    1   3   1
   chal-2-len-2-ger
    1   1   5
   vol-2-ca-1-no
    1   2   2

10. per-1-pe-1-trate
    5   2 ˘3
   e-1-quip-2-ment
    2   1   1
   ap-2-pre-1-hend
    1   2   1
   pro-1-to-1-type
    2   2   3

11. a-1-no-1-ther
    2   2   5
   tor-1-na-1-do
    5   2   2
   di-1-mi-1-nish
    2   2   1
   e-1-di-1-tor
    2   2   5

12. hy-1-dro-1-gen
    2 ˘2 1
   tux-1-e-1-do
    1   2   2
   sa-1-tel-2-lite
    2   1   3
   em-2-broi-1-der
    1   6   5

13. mar-1-ke-1-ting
    5   2   1
   com-2-pre-1-hend
    1   2   1
   per-1-ma-1-nent
    5   2   1
   de-1-com-2-pose
    2   1   3

14. as-2-sis-2-tant
    1   1   1
   di-1-rec-2-tor
    2   1   5
   fre-1-quent-2-ly
    2   1˘ 2
   ten-2-den-2-cy
    1   1   2

15. tor-1-pe-1-do
    5   2   2
   ac-2-com-2-plish
    1   1   1
   ob-2-so-1-lete
    1   2   3
   in-2-fan-2-cy
    1   1   2

16. ap-2-pen-2-dix
    1   1   1
   lu-1-na-1-tic
    2   2   1
   a-1-muse-1-ment
    2   3   1
   es-2-ti-1-mate
    1   2   3

17. con-2-fi-1-dent
    1   2   1
   am-2-ber-1-jack
    1   5   1
   at-2-ti-1-tude
    1   2   3
   e-1-ner-1-gy
    2   5   2

18. as-2-to-1-nish
    1   2   1
   bul-2-le-1-tin
    1   2   1
   pub-2-li-1-sher
    1   2   5
   con-2-sul-2-tant
    1   1   1

19. or-1-ga-1-nize
    5   2   3
   con-2-su-1-mer
    1   2   5
   type-1-set-2-ter
    3   1   5
   re-1-por-1-ter
    2   5   5

20. cen-2-ti-1-pede
    1   2   3
   en-2-ter-1-tain
    1   5   4
   po-1-li-1-cy
    2   2   2
   fi-1-nan-2-cing
    2   1   1

Page 110

1. o-3-a-1-sis
    2   2   1
   mow-3-er
    4   5
   vi-3-o-1-lin
    2   2   1
   fi-3-er-3-y
    2   5   2

2. for-3-est   ro-1-de-3-o   pe-3-o-1-ny   or-3-ange
    5   1   2   2   2   2   2   2   5   1

3. bay-3-o-1-net   ma-1-nu-3-al   po-3-et   hy-3-e-1-na
    4   2   1   2   2   8   2   1   2   2   8

4. vi-3-o-1-lent   vow-3-el   nau-1-se-3-ate   cre-3-ate
    2   2   1   6   1   6   2   3   2   3

5. vi-1-de-3-o   gra-1-du-3-ate   tow-3-el   flam-2-boy-3-ant
    2   2   2   2   2   3   6   1   1   6   1

6. voy-3-age   me-1-te-3-or   cow-3-ard   fu-1-ner-3-al
    6   3   2   2   5   6   5   2   5   8

7. de-1-fi-3-ant   glor-3-y   re-3-ac-2-tor   ar-1-ter-3-y
    2   2   1   5   2   2   1   5   5   5   2

8. brew-3-er-3-y   mo-1-sa-3-ic   ly-3-ing   co-3-erce
    6   5   2   2   2   1   2   1   2   5

9. roy-3-al   hy-3-a-1-cinth   pli-3-a-1-ble   he-1-ro-3-ism
    6   8   2   2   1   2   2   7   2   2   1

10. de-1-ni-3-al   prow-3-ess   sto-3-ic   po-1-di-3-um
    2   2   8   6   1   2   1   2   2   1

11. Cre-3-ole   ge-1-nu-3-ine   me-1-di-3-ate   mi-1-ser-3-y
    2   3   2   2   3   2   2   3   2   5   2

12. ca-1-me-3-o   gi-3-ant   vi-3-o-1-let   may-3-or
    2   2   2   2   1   2   2   1   4   5

13. punc-2-tu-3-ate   vi-3-al   au-1-di-3-o   o-1-per-3-ate
    1˘   2   3   2   8   6   2   2   2   5   3

14. pray-3-er   po-3-e-1-try   sew-3-er   how-3-it-2-zer
    4   5   2   2   ˜2   6   5   6   1   5

15. i-3-o-1-dine   mack-1-er-3-el   ce-1-ler-3-y   gor-3-y
    2   2   3   1   5   1   2   5   2   5   2

16. ce-1-re-3-al   fli-3-er   ne-3-on   i-1-di-3-ot
    2   2   8   2   5   2   1   2   2   1

17. di-3-ag-2-nose   foy-3-er   glor-3-i-1-fy   re-3-u-1-nite
    2   1   3   6   5   5   2   2   2   2   3

18. vi-3-o-1-lence   his-2-tor-3-y   fu-3-el   plow-3-ing
    2   2   1   1   5   2   2   1   6   1

19. ru-3-in   di-3-a-1-lect   re-3-act   pi-3-e-1-ty
    2   1   2   2   1   2   1   2   2   2

Page 112

1. sanc-2-tion   cru-1-cial   con-2-fes-2-sion   par-1-tial
    1˜   1   2   8   1   1   1   5   8

2. wrack   con-2-clu-1-sion   ma-1-gi-1-cian   ex-2-ten-2-sion
    1   1   2   1   2   2   1   1   1   1

3. pen-2-sion   af-2-fec-2-tion   wrap   in-2-volve
    1   1   1   1   1   1   1   1

4. re-1-serve   wreck   po-1-si-1-tion   in-2-va-1-sion
    2   5   1   2   2   1   1   2   1

5. e-1-mis-2-sion   fa-1-cial   wretch   vin-2-dic-2-tive
   2   1   1   2   8   1   1   1   1

6. frac-2-tion   men-2-tion   col-2-lec-2-tion   mar-1-quee
   1   1   1   1   1   1   1   5   4

7. pas-2-sion   wrench   de-1-serve   trans-2-fu-1-sion
   1   1   1   2   5   1 ˘   2   1

8. so-1-cial   ex-2-plo-1-sion   wrap-2-per   mos-2-qui-1-to
   2   8   1   2   1   1   5   1   2   2

9. per-1-cus-2-sion   suc-2-ces-2-sive   de-1-ser-1-tion   re-1-gres-2-sion
   5   1   1   1   1   1   2   5   1   2   ˜1   1

10. wreath   clique   of-2-fi-1-cial   col-2-li-1-sion
   4   3   1   2   8   1   2   1

11. trac-2-tion   con-2-di-1-tion   se-1-clu-1-sion   ex-2-ten-2-sive
   1   1   1   2   1   2   ˜2   1   1   1   1

12. phy-1-si-1-cian   ad-2-he-1-sive   delve   man-2-sion
   2   2   1   1   2   1   1   1   1

13. wren   li-1-quor   cor-1-rup-2-tion   re-1-volve
   1   2   5   5   1   1   2   1

13. gro-1-tesque   cur-1-sive   tax-1-a-1-tion   a-1-bra-1-sion
   2   3   5   1   1   2   1   2   ˜2   1

Page 113

1. com-2-pas-2-sion   du-1-ra-1-tion   ma-1-gi-1-cian   plaque
   1   1   1   2   2   1   2   2   1   3

2. wring-1-er   ad-2-di-1-tive   quo-1-ta-1-tion   in-2-ci-1-sion
   1   5   1   2   1   2   2   1   1   2   1

3. ob-2-ses-2-sion   con-2-quer   cor-1-rec-2-tion   ex-2-tinc-2-tion
   1   1   1   1   5   5   1   1   1   1˜   1

4. di-1-vi-1-sion   ex-2-pres-2-sion   heave   so-1-lu-1-tion
   2   2   1   1   1   1   4   2   2   1

5. tur-1-quoise   ig-2-ni-1-tion   wrin-2-kle   wri-1-ter
   5   6   1   2   1   1   7   2   5

6. ex-2-clu-1-sive   i-1-ni-1-tial   ex-2-cur-1-sion   ten-2-sion
   1   2   1   2   2   8   1   5   1   1   1

7. per-1-fec-2-tion   mor-1-ti-1-cian   re-1-pul-2-sive   com-2-mo-1-tion
   5   1   1   5   2   1   2   1   1   1   2   1

8. wrig-2-gle   e-1-ro-1-sion   sta-1-tu-3-esque   pro-1-tec-2-tive
   1   7   2   2   1   2   2   3   2   1   1

9. ab-2-sorp-2-tion   cre-3-a-1-tion   gla-1-cial   re-1-cep-2-tive
   1   5   1   2   2   1   2   8   2   1   1

10. per-1-spec-2-tive   nerve   il-2-lu-1-sion   torque
   5   ˘1   1   5   1   2   1   5

11. mu-1-si-1-cian   pro-1-ba-1-tion   re-1-vul-2-sion   wrest
   2   2   1   2   2   1   2   1   1   1

12. pre-1-ci-1-sion   wrath   lu-1-cra-1-tive   pro-1-fes-2-sion
   2   2   1   1   2   ˜2   1   2   1   1

13. fes-2-ti<u>ve</u>   ex-2-clu-1-<u>sio</u>n   pro-1-duc-2-ti<u>ve</u>   e-1-rup-2-<u>tio</u>n
   1 1   1 2 1   2 1 1   2 1 1

14. de-1-<u>c</u>ep-2-ti<u>ve</u>   na-1-ti<u>ve</u>   pro-1-mo-1-<u>tio</u>n   in-2-clu-1-<u>sio</u>n
   2 1 1   2 1   2 2 1   1 2 1

15. fan-2-ta-1-<u>sia</u>   con-2-<u>c</u>es-2-<u>sio</u>n   ra-1-<u>c</u>ial   ap-2-pro<u>ve</u>
   1   2   8   1 1 1   2   8   1 8

16. mos<u>que</u>   <u>c</u>i-1-ta-1-<u>tio</u>n   <u>wrong</u>   pre-1-ven-2-<u>tio</u>n
   <u>3</u>   2 2 1   1   2 1 1

17. sus-2-pi-1-<u>ci</u>on   man-2-ne-1-<u>qui</u>n   vi-1-<u>si</u>on   in-2-<u>c</u>en-2-ti<u>ve</u>
   1   <u>2</u> 1   1   <u>2</u> 1   <u>2</u> 1   1 1 1

18. im-2-pul-2-si<u>ve</u>   im-2-pres-2-<u>sio</u>n   re-1-mo<u>ve</u>   n<u>u</u>-1-tri-1-<u>tio</u>n
   1   1   1   1   1   1   2   8   <u>2</u> ˜<u>2</u> 1

19. con-2-fu-1-<u>sio</u>n   gr<u>oo</u><u>ve</u>   de-1-scrip-2-ti<u>ve</u>   spe-1-<u>c</u>ial
   1   2   1   6   2 ˜˜˜1 1   <u>2</u>   8

Page 117

1. col-2-<u>lie</u>   un-2-v<u>ei</u>l   gri<u>eve</u>   blue-1-b<u>i</u>rd
   1   6   1   6   6   <u>4</u>   5

2. <u>c</u>ei-1-ling   w<u>ie</u>ld   gr<u>e</u>y-1-h<u>ou</u>nd   t<u>ie</u>
   4   1   6   6   6   4

3. pr<u>ai</u>-1-r<u>ie</u>   de-1-<u>c</u>ei<u>ve</u>   bl<u>ar</u>-1-n<u>e</u>y   y<u>ie</u>ld
   4   6   2   4   5   4   6

4. pr<u>e</u>y   re-1-<u>c</u>ei<u>ve</u>   be-1-l<u>ie</u>f   rein-2-d<u>ee</u>r
   6   2   4   2   6   6   4

5. pul-2-l<u>e</u>y   <u>shie</u>ld   ca-1-<u>shie</u>r   vir-1-t<u>ue</u>
   8   4   6   <u>2</u>   6   5   4

6. <u>g</u>e-1-n<u>ie</u>   cl<u>ue</u>   re-1-<u>c</u>eipt   fon-2-d<u>ue</u>
   2   6   <u>4</u>   2   4~   1   <u>4</u>

7. v<u>ei</u>n   s<u>ur</u>-1-v<u>e</u>y   cad-2-d<u>ie</u>   be-1-s<u>iege</u>
   6   5   6   1   6   2   6

8. <u>ar</u>-1-g<u>ue</u>   <u>thieve</u>s   turn-2-k<u>e</u>y   don-2-k<u>e</u>y
   5   4   6   5   4   1   4

9. ca-1-l<u>or</u>-3-<u>ie</u>   <u>ei</u>-1-<u>ther</u>   be-1-l<u>ieve</u>   d<u>ue</u>
   <u>2</u>   5   6   4   5   2   6   <u>4</u>

10. tr<u>ue</u>   br<u>ie</u>f   <u>shrie</u>k   th<u>ei</u>r
    <u>4</u>   6   6   6

11. os-2-pr<u>e</u>y   <u>c</u>hief   con-2-<u>c</u>eit   re-1-l<u>ie</u>f
   1   4   6   1   4   2   6

12. be-1-l<u>ie</u>   re-1-v<u>er</u>-3-<u>ie</u>   <u>thie</u>f   o-1-b<u>e</u>y
   2   4   <u>2</u>   5   6   6   2   6

13. lad-2-d<u>ie</u>   b<u>ei</u><u>ge</u>   pr<u>ie</u>st   sta-1-t<u>ue</u>
   1   6   6   6   <u>2</u>   4

14. de-1-<u>c</u>eit   a-1-<u>chieve</u>   con-2-v<u>e</u>y-3-an<u>c</u>e   gr<u>ie</u>f
   2   4   2   6   1   6   1   6

Page 118

1. br<u>ow</u>-1-n<u>ie</u> cr<u>ui</u><u>se</u> trol-2-l<u>ey</u> h<u>ei</u>r
   6   6   4   1   4   ~ 6

2. <u>qu</u>a-1-li-1-f<u>ie</u>d bar-1-be-1-c<u>ue</u> dis-2-be-1-l<u>ie</u>f mo-1-n<u>ey</u>
   8   <u>2</u>   4   5   <u>2</u>   4   1   2   6   <u>2</u>   4

3. con-2-v<u>ey</u> ab-2-b<u>ey</u> r<u>ei</u>n dig-2-ni-1-f<u>ie</u>d
   1   6   1   4   6   1   <u>2</u>   4

4. hy-1-g<u>ie</u>ne w<u>ei</u>rd sub-2-d<u>ue</u> val-<u>1</u>-<u>ue</u>
   2   6   4   1   4   1   4

5. <u>c</u>er-1-ti-1-f<u>ie</u>d h<u>ock</u>-1-<u>ey</u> dis-<u>1</u>-o-1-bey b<u>ar</u>-1-l<u>ey</u>
   5   <u>2</u>   4   1   4   1   2   6   5   4

6. h<u>ei</u>-1-ress im-2-b<u>ue</u> bl<u>ue</u> n<u>ie</u>ce
   ~ 6   1   1   4   4   6

7. ho-1-n<u>ey</u> f<u>ie</u>nd gr<u>ue</u>-1-some l<u>ei</u>-1-s<u>u</u>re
   <u>2</u>   4   6   4   <u>3</u>   4   3

8. kid-2-n<u>ey</u> a-1-ve-1-n<u>ue</u> las-2-s<u>ie</u> wh<u>ey</u>
   1   4   <u>2</u>   <u>2</u>   4   1   6   6

9. j<u>ui</u>ce con-2-ti-1-n<u>ue</u> ap-2-pl<u>ie</u>d s<u>ue</u>
   4   1   <u>2</u>   4   1   4   4

10. s<u>ei</u>-1-zure re-1-tr<u>ie</u>v<u>e</u> vol-2-l<u>ey</u> p<u>ie</u>
   4   3   2   ~6   1   6   4

11. m<u>on</u>-2-key th<u>ey</u> p<u>ur</u>-1-v<u>ey</u> gl<u>ue</u>
   1   4   6   5   6   4

12. dr<u>ie</u>d <u>ch</u>im-2-n<u>ey</u> re-1-l<u>ie</u>v<u>e</u> ac-2-cr<u>ue</u>
   4   1   4   2   6   1   4

13. jer-1-<u>sey</u> res-2-c<u>ue</u> per-1-<u>c</u>e<u>i</u>v<u>e</u> tur-1-k<u>ey</u>
   5   5   1   4   5   4   5   4

14. gr<u>ie</u>-1-van<u>ce</u> f<u>ei</u>nt h<u>ey</u> no-1-ti-1-f<u>ie</u>d
   6   1   6   6   2   <u>2</u>   4

15. br<u>ui</u><u>se</u> p<u>ie</u>ce la<u>ck</u>-<u>1</u>-<u>ey</u> par-1-l<u>ey</u>
   4   6   1   4   5   4

16. al-2-l<u>ie</u>d n<u>ei</u>-1-<u>th</u>er pars-2-ley p<u>ur</u>-1-s<u>ue</u>
   1   4   4   5   5   4   5   <u>4</u>

17. s<u>ur</u>-1-v<u>ei</u>-2-lan<u>ce</u> re-1-ve-1-n<u>ue</u> cr<u>ie</u>d jo<u>ck</u>-1-<u>ey</u>
   5   6   1   <u>2</u>   <u>2</u>   4   4   1   4

18. med-2-l<u>ey</u> c<u>ue</u> ag-2-gr<u>ie</u>v<u>e</u> fal-2-si-1-f<u>ie</u>d
   1   4   4   1   6   8   <u>2</u>   4

19. s<u>ie</u>ge gal-2-l<u>ey</u> s<u>ei</u>ze fr<u>ie</u>d
   6   1   4   4   4

Page 121

1. n<u>eigh</u>-1-b<u>or</u> pug-2-na-1-<u>ci</u>ous j<u>ea</u>-1-l<u>ou</u>s ner-1-v<u>ou</u>s
   6   5   1   2   6   6   6   5   6

2. t<u>augh</u>t fa-1-m<u>ou</u>s h<u>ea</u>-1-<u>th</u>er st<u>ea</u>-1-d<u>y</u>
   6   2   6   6   5   6   2

3. dealt — 6
lea-1-ther — 6 5
worm — 5
young-2-ster — 6 5

4. plea-1-sant — 6 1
trou-1-ble — 6 7
high — 4
wea-1-pon — 6 1

5. re-1-ward — 2 5
dread — 6
ha-1-zar-1-dous — 2 5 6
bear — 6

6. se-1-ri-3-ous — 2 2 6
heal-2-thy — 6 2
fraught — 6
mea-1-dow — 6 4

7. plight — 4
coun-2-try — 6 2
world — 5
stealth — 6

8. cou-1-ple — 6 7
realm — 6
eight — 6
pi-3-ous — 2 6

9. dou-1-ble — 6 7
wart — 5
fri-1-vo-1-lous — 2 2 6
sweat — 6

10. slaugh-1-ter — 6 5
read — 4/6
flight — 4
wealth — 6

11. lead — 4/6
quart — 5
vi-1-cious — 2 6
threat — 6

12. bread — 6
night — 4
cu-1-ri-3-ous — 2 2 6
dead — 6

Page 122

1. cleanse — 6
thigh — 4
eigh-1-teen — 6 4
warp — 5

2. dis-2-traught — 1 6
wor-1-thy — 5 2
phea-1-sant — 6 1
de-1-li-1-cious — 2 2 6

3. ligh-1-ter — 4 5
thwart — 5
ma-1-li-1-cious — 2 2 6
break-2-fast — 6 1

4. pre-1-cious — 2 6
caught — 6
weigh-1-ty — 6 2
war-1-ble — 5 7

5. trea-1-cher-3-y — 6 5 2
en-2-vi-3-ous — 1 2 6
air-2-tight — 4 5
word — 5

6. swar-1-thy — 5 2
quartz — 5
zea-1-lot — 6 1
te-1-na-1-cious — 2 2 6

7. freight — 6
dan-2-ger-3-ous — 1 5 6
daugh-1-ter — 6 5
spright-2-ly — 4 2

8. worth — 5
in-2-stead — 1 6
spa-1-cious — 2 6
pre-1-vi-3-ous — 2 2 6

9. gla-1-mor-3-ous — 2 5 6
al-2-migh-1-ty — 8 4 2
wea-1-ther — 6 5
in-2-fec-2-tious — 1 1 6

10. on-2-slaught — 1 6
wharf — 5
joy-3-ous — 6 6
mo-1-men-2-tous — 2 1 6

11. fea-1-ther — 6 5
weight — 6
work — 5
rea-1-di-1-ly — 6 2 2

12. e-1-nor-1-mous — 2 5 6
gra-1-cious — 2 6
swarm — 5
cou-1-sin — 6 1

13. w<u>or</u>-1-<u>shi</u>p   sw<u>ea</u>-1-t<u>er</u>   de-1-l<u>igh</u>t   h<u>augh</u>-1-t<u>y</u>
    5   1   6   5   2   4   6   2

14. pros-2-p<u>er</u>-3-<u>ou</u>s   w<u>ar</u>-1-den   sl<u>eigh</u>   <u>au</u>s-2-pi-1-<u>cio</u>us
   1   5   6   5   1   6   6   2   6

15. <u>thr</u>ead   <u>augh</u>t   h<u>or</u>-1-ren-2-d<u>ou</u>s   y<u>ou</u>ng
    6   6   5   1   6   6

16. fa-1-bu-1-l<u>o</u>us   sl<u>igh</u>t   w<u>or</u>st   a-1-h<u>ea</u>d
   2   2   6   4   5   2   6

17. am-2-bi-1-t<u>iou</u>s   <u>eigh</u>-1-t<u>y</u>   dw<u>ar</u>f   te-1-di-3-<u>ou</u>s
   1   2   6   6   2   5   2   2   6

18. n<u>augh</u>-1-t<u>y</u>   w<u>or</u>se   m<u>igh</u>-1-t<u>y</u>   br<u>ea</u><u>th</u>
   6   2   5   4   2   6

19. va-1-ri-3-<u>ou</u>s   h<u>ea</u>-1-v<u>y</u>   w<u>or</u>-1-r<u>y</u>   w<u>eigh</u>
   2   2   6   6   2   5   2   6

Page 125

1. <u>cha</u>-1-p<u>er</u>-3-one   g<u>ui</u>de   a-1-<u>sc</u>end   <u>tech</u>
   2   5   3   3   2   1   1

2. <u>or</u>-1-<u>ch</u>id   <u>kn</u>ack   <u>gh</u>ost   <u>chr</u>ome
   5   1   1   1   3

3. <u>sc</u>i-3-en<u>ce</u>   <u>Rh</u>ode<u>s</u>   <u>s</u>chwa   a<u>ch</u><u>e</u>
   2   1   3   8   3

4. <u>ch</u>e-1-mist   re-1-<u>s</u>ign   rog<u>ue</u>   <u>ch</u>or-3-al
   2   1   2   1   3   5   8

5. <u>rh</u>i-1-no   <u>chr</u>o-1-nic   re-1-<u>sc</u>ind   ma-1-<u>ch</u>i<u>ne</u>
   2   2   2   1   2   1   2   x

6. de-1-<u>s</u>ign   an-2-<u>ch</u>or   lep-2-re-1-<u>ch</u>a<u>u</u>n   <u>kn</u>ead
   2   1   1   5   1   2   6   4

7. bro-1-<u>ch</u>ure   <u>sc</u>ent   <u>Chr</u>ist   mo-1-n<u>ar</u>-1-<u>ch</u><u>y</u>
   2   3   1   1   2   5   2

8. <u>kn</u>eel   h<u>ar</u>p-2-si-1-<u>ch</u>ord   as-2-sign   g<u>ui</u>-1-tar
   4   5   2   5   1   1   2   5

9. ob-2-<u>sc</u>ene   <u>gh</u>et-2-to   <u>ch</u>ar-1-la-1-tan   <u>Rh</u>i<u>ne</u>
   1   3   1   2   5   2   1   3

10. l<u>ea</u>g<u>ue</u>   be-1-ni<u>gn</u>   <u>kn</u>it   <u>or</u>-1-<u>ch</u>es-2-tra
   4   2   1   1   5   1   8

11. <u>ch</u>ev-2-ron   <u>kn</u>ife   tran-2-<u>sc</u>end   <u>Ch</u>er
   1   1   3   1   1   1

12. as-2-sig<u>n</u>-2-ment   ri-1-co-1-<u>ch</u>et   <u>rh</u>u-1-b<u>ar</u>b   <u>Chr</u>ist-2-mas
   1   1   1   2   2   xx   2   5   1~~   1

13. <u>s</u><u>ch</u>e-1-dule   ca-1-ta-1-log<u>u</u> e   <u>ch</u>ute   <u>kn</u>ob
   2   3   2   2   3   3   1

14. <u>ch</u>ef   <u>ch</u>a<u>s</u>m   <u>sc</u>is-2-<u>s</u>ors   ar-2-r<u>ai</u><u>gn</u>
   1   1   1   5   1   4

15. s<u>or</u>-1- <u>gh</u>u m   <u>ch</u>e-1-mis-2-tr<u>y</u>   <u>kn</u>ot   cro-1-<u>ch</u>et
   5   1   2   1   2   1   2   xx

16. knuck-1- le   rhe-1-tor-3-ic   sign   chlor-3-ide
     1   7   2   5   1   1   5   3

17. ar-1-chi-1-tect   cre-1-scent   chi-1-val-2-ry   sto-1-mach
     5   2   1   2   1   2   8   2   2   1

18. cam-2-pai gn   cha-1-rac-2-ter   guise   li-1-chen
     1   4   2   1   5   3   2   1

Page 126

1. con-2-de-1-scend   An-2-chor-3-age   rhythm   van-2-guard
    1   2   1   1   5   3   1   1   5

2. spa-1-ghet-2-ti   mus-2-tache   plague   knoll
    2   1   x   1   3   3   1

3. scho-1-lar   schoo-1-ner   cham-2-pagne   mus-2-cle
    2   5   6   5   1   3   1   7

4. pa-1-ra-1-chute   gui-1-dance   knock   fa-1-tigue
    2   2   3   2   1   1   2   x

5. tech-2-nique   a-1-lign   co-1-logne   guile
    1   x   2   1   2   3   3

6. tra-1-ve-1-logue   sce-1-ner-3-y   e-1-cho   rhap-2-so-1-dy
    2   2   3   2   5   2   2   2   1   2   2

7. chro-1-ni-1-cle   for-3-eign   e-1-che-1-lon   chris-2-ten
    2   2   7   5   6   2   2   1   1   ~1

8. che-1-mi-1-cal   chlor-3-o-1-phyll   sy-1-na-1-gogue   known
    2   2   8   5   2   1   2   2   3   4

9. sci-3-en-2-tist   ghast-2-ly   ar-1-chan-2-gel   in-2-trigue
    2   1   1   1   2   5   1   1   1   x

10. e-1-pi-1-logue   kni ves   ma-1-chi-1-nist   scheme
    2   2   3   3   2   x   1   3

11. chlor-3-o-1-form   dis-2-guise   ab-2-scess   reign
    5   2   5   1   3   1   1   6

12. a-1-scent   rhine-1-stone   school   tra-1-che-3-a
    2   1   3   3   6   2   2   8

13. cha-3-os   cha-1-grin   guar-1-di-3-an   bron-2-chi-1-tis
    2   1   8   ~1   5   2   1   1   2   1

14. en-2-sign   ar-1-chi ve   knight   de-1-scent
    1   1   5   3   4   2   1

15. chif-2-fon   strych-2-nine   a-1-ghast   morgue
    1   1   1   3   2   1   5

16. di-1-sci-1-ple   di-3-a-1-logue   non-2-cha-1-lance   con-2-sign
    2   2   7   2   2   3   1   2   8   1   1

17. rhyme   knee   tech-2-ni-1-cal   chro-1-mi-3-um
    3   4   1   2   8   2   2   1

18. gua-1-ran-2-tee   gnash   cho-1-ler-3-a   chi-1-val-2-rous
    2   1   4   1   2   5   8   2   8   6

19. chlo-1-rine   sce-1-nic   gnaw   chor-3-us
    2   x   2   1   6   5   1

Page 128

1. ex-2-pla-1-na-1-<u>tio</u>n
    1   2   2   1

2. ap-2-pro-1-pri-3-at<u>e</u>
    1   2   ~2 3

3. pe-1-nin-2-s<u>u</u>-1-la
    <u>2</u> 1 <u>2</u> 8

4. com-2-pa-1-ri-1-son
    1 <u>2</u> <u>2</u> 1

5. il-2-lus-2-tra-1-<u>tio</u>n
    1 1   2   1

6. re-1-m<u>ar</u>-1-ka-1-b<u>le</u>
    2   5   2   7

7. e-1-v<u>er</u>-3-<u>y</u>-1-d<u>ay</u>
    <u>2</u>   5 <u>2</u> 4

8. con-2-tri-1-bu-1-t<u>ed</u>
    1   <u>2</u> 2 1

9. va-1-ri-3-a-1-<u>tio</u>ns
    <u>2</u> <u>2</u> 2 1

10. ex-2-pe-1-di-1-<u>tio</u>n
     1   <u>2</u> <u>2</u> 1

11. h<u>or</u>-3-i-1-zon-2-tal
      5 <u>2</u> 1 8

12. ra-1-di-3-a-1-<u>tio</u>n
     2 <u>2</u> 2 1

13. u-1-ra-1-ni-3-um
     2 2 <u>2</u> 1

14. Co-1-l<u>or</u>-3-a-1-do
     <u>2</u> 5 8 2

15. un-<u>1</u>-ex-2-pec-2-t<u>ed</u>
     1 1   1   1

16. u-1-s<u>u</u>-3-al-2-l<u>y</u>
     2 2 8 2

17. b<u>ea</u>-3-u-1-ti-1-ful
     4   2 <u>2</u> 8

18. tem-2-p<u>er</u>-3-a-1-tur<u>e</u>
      1   5   2 3

19. lo-1-co-1-mo-1-tiv<u>e</u>
     2 2 2 1

20. in-2-vi-1-si-1-b<u>le</u>
     1   <u>2</u> <u>2</u> 7

a-1-l<u>u</u>-1-mi-1-num
2 <u>2</u> 2 1

in-2-t<u>er</u>-1-sec-2-<u>tio</u>n
1   5   1   1

se-1-cre-1-ta-1-r<u>y</u>
<u>2</u> ~2 2 2

f<u>or</u>-1-tu-1-nat<u>e</u>-1-l<u>y</u>
5   2   3   2

co-1-lo-1-ni-3-al
2 2 <u>2</u> 8

di-1-vi-1-s<u>i</u>-1-b<u>le</u>
<u>2</u> 2 <u>2</u> 7

ma-1-j<u>or</u>-3-i-1-t<u>y</u>
<u>2</u> 5 2 2

he-1-li-1-cop-2-t<u>er</u>
2 2 1   5

Fe-1-br<u>u</u>-3-a-1-r<u>y</u>
<u>2</u> ~~<u>2</u> 2 2

e-1-co-1-no-1-m<u>y</u>
2 <u>2</u> 2 2

al-2-to-1-ge-1-<u>ther</u>
8 8 <u>2</u>   5

e-1-mo-1-<u>tio</u>n-1-al
2 2   1 8

in-2-t<u>er</u>-1-rup-2-t<u>ed</u>
1   5   1   1

de-1-ve-1-lop-2-ment
2 <u>2</u> 1   1

o-1-p<u>er</u>-3-a-1-<u>tio</u>n
<u>2</u> 5 2 1

po-1-li-1-ti-1-cal
2 <u>2</u> <u>2</u> 8

e-1-q<u>ui</u>-1-va-1-lent
2 <u>2</u> 2 1

com-2-bi-1-na-1-<u>tio</u>n
1   <u>2</u> 2 1

<u>or</u>-3-i-3-en-2-tal
5 <u>2</u> 1 8

in-2-dus-2-tri-3-al
1   1   <u>2</u> 8

e-1-co-1-no-1-mic
2 <u>2</u> 2 1

as-2-tro-1-no-1-m<u>ers</u>
1   <u>2</u> 2 5

ad-2-di-1-<u>tio</u>n-<u>1</u>-al
1   <u>2</u> 1 8

<u>au</u>-1-<u>thor</u>-3-i-1-t<u>y</u>
6   5   <u>2</u> 2

punc-2-tu-3-a-1-<u>tio</u>n
<u>1</u> ~ 2 2 1

Ja-1-nu-3-a-1-r<u>y</u>
<u>2</u> 2 2 2

<u>au</u>-1-to-1-ma-1-tic
6 2 <u>2</u> 1

pa-1-ren-2-<u>the</u>-1-sis
<u>2</u> 1   <u>2</u> 1

me-1-<u>cha</u>-1-ni-1-cal
<u>2</u>   2   <u>2</u> 8

pe-1-ri-1-me-1-t<u>er</u>
<u>2</u> 2 <u>2</u> 5

com-2-pli-1-ca-1-t<u>ed</u>
1   <u>2</u> 2 1

pro-1-fes-2-<u>sio</u>n-<u>1</u>-al
2 1   1 8

un-2-d<u>er</u>-1-wa-1-t<u>er</u>
1   5   8 5

con-2-ti-1-nen-2-tal
1   <u>2</u> 1   8

A-1-me-1-ri-1-can
2 <u>2</u> <u>2</u> 1

ma-1-te-1-ri-3-al
<u>2</u> 2 <u>2</u> 8

e-1-v<u>er</u>-3-<u>y</u>-1-<u>thing</u>
<u>2</u>   5 <u>2</u> 1

in-2-t<u>er</u>-3-es-2-ting
1   5   1   1

sin-2-<u>ce</u>-1-ri-1-t<u>y</u>
1   <u>2</u> 2 2

dif-2-f<u>er</u>-3-en-2-<u>tia</u>l
1   5   1   8

Page 129

1. es-2-ti-1-ma-1-<u>tio</u>n
    1   <u>2</u> 2 1

so-1-<u>ci</u>-3-e-1-t<u>y</u>
2 <u>2</u> 2 2

com-2-pre-1-hen-2-<u>sio</u>n
1   2   1   1

2. gra-1-du-3-al-2-ly
   <u>2</u>   2   8   2

3. ac-2-tu-3-al-2-ly
   1   2   8   2

4. com-2-mu-1-ni-1-ty
   1   2   <u>2</u>   2

5. ve-1-ge-1-ta-1-bles
   <u>2</u>   <u>2</u>   2   7

6. ob-2-ser-1-va-1-tion
   1   5   2   1

7. re-1-ver-1-ber-3-ate
   2   5   5   3

8. tem-2-per-3-a-1-ture
   1   5   2   3

9. de-3-o-1-dor-3-ant
   2   2   5   1

10. in-2-ter-1-rup-2-tion
   1   5   1   1

11. vi-3-o-1-li-1-nist
   2   2   <u>2</u>   1

12. cir-1-cu-1-la-1-tion
   5   2   2   1

13. ge-1-ner-3-a-1-tion
   <u>2</u>   5   2   1

14. im-2-pos-2-si-1-ble
   1   1   <u>2</u>   7

15. re-1-ser-1-va-1-tion
   <u>2</u>   5   2   1

16. pre-1-his-2-tor-3-ic
   2   1   5   1

17. in-2-car-1-na-1-tion
   1   5   2   1

18. cor-1-por-3-a-1-tion
   5   5   2   1

19. cal-2-cu-1-la-1-ting
   1   2   2   1

20. dif-2-fi-1-cul-2-ty
   4   <u>2</u>   1   2

di-3-a-1-me-1-ter
   2   <u>2</u>   2   5

in-2-dus-2-tri-3-al
   1   1   <u>2</u>   8

val-1-u-3-a-1-ble
   1   2   2   7

ter-2-ri-1-tor-3-y
   1   <u>2</u>   5   2

se-1-con-2-da-1-ry
   <u>2</u>   1   <u>2</u>   2

dis-2-con-2-ti-1-nue
   1   1   <u>2</u>   4

dis-2-ho-1-nes-2-ty
   1   ~<u>2</u>   1   2

con-2-si-1-der-3-ate
   1   <u>2</u>   5   3

par-1-ti-1-cu-1-lar
   5   <u>2</u>   2   5

sa-1-tis-2-fac-2-tion
   <u>2</u>   1   1   1

re-3-ad-2-just-2-ment
   2   1   1   1

in-1-at-2-ten-2-tion
   1   1   1   1

u-1-ni-1-ver-1-sal
   2   <u>2</u>   5   8

ir-2-re-1-gu-1-lar
   1   <u>2</u>   2   5

pe-1-ri-3-o-1-dic
   2   <u>2</u>   2   1

ex-2-pe-1-ri-1-ment
   1   <u>2</u>   <u>2</u>   1

tri-1-bu-1-ta-1-ry
   <u>2</u>   2   2   <u>2</u>

in-2-spir-3-a-1-tion
   1   5   2   1

mys-2-te-1-ri-3-ous
   1   2   <u>2</u>   6

con-2-so-1-li-1-date
   1   <u>2</u>   <u>2</u>   3

re-1-tri-1-bu-1-tion
   2   ~<u>2</u>   2   1

po-1-pu-1-la-1-tion
   <u>2</u>   2   2   1

va-1-ri-3-e-1-ty
   <u>2</u>   2   <u>2</u>   2

o-1-per-3-a-1-tion
   <u>2</u>   5   2   1

su-1-per-1-so-1-nic
   <u>2</u>   5   <u>2</u>   1

com-2-for-1-ta-1-ble
   1   5   2   7

fa-1-vor-3-a-1-ble
   2   5   2   7

in-1-ac-2-cu-1-rate
   1   1   2   3

ex-2-pe-1-ri-3-ence
   1   2   <u>2</u>   1

in-2-ti-1-mi-1-date
   1   <u>2</u>   <u>2</u>   3

dis-1-ad-2-van-2-tage
   1   1   1   3

or-3-i-1-gi-1-nal
   5   <u>2</u>   <u>2</u>   8

in-2-ter-1-mis-2-sion
   1   5   1   1

jur-3-is-2-dic-2-tion
   5   1   1   1

ne-1-ces-2-sa-1-ry
   <u>2</u>   1   <u>2</u>   2

pho-1-to-1-gra-1-phy
   2   2   ~2   2

vi-1-gor-3-ous-2-ly
   <u>2</u>   5   6   2

de-1-mo-1-cra-1-cy
   2   2   ~<u>2</u>   2

Page 131

1. bou-1-le-1-vard   soul   cough   cour-3-age
   6 <u>2</u> 5   4   6   5   3

2. can-2-ta-1-loupe   mourn   so-1-journ   dis-2-course
   1   2   4   4   2   5   1   4

3. en-2-cour-3-age   group   troupe   un-2-couth
   1   5   3   6   6   1   6

4. rough — 6 | soup — 6 | gla-1-mour — 2 5 | a-1-cous-2-tics — 2 6 1

5. jour-1-ney — 5 4 | wound/wound — 6 6 | through-3-out — 6 6 | con-2-course — 1 4

6. four — 4 | youth — 6 | rou-1-lette — 6 3 | dis-2-cour-1-te-3-ous — 1 5 2 6

7. ca-1-ri-1-bou — 2 2 6 | course — 4 | tough — 6 | flou-1-rish — 4 1

8. shoul-2-der — 4 5 | jour-1-nal — 5 8 | dough-1-nut — 4 1 | fought — 6

9. nour-3-ish — 5 1 | cou-1-pon — 6 1 | wrought — 6 | youth-2-ful — 6 8

10. thor-3-ough — 5 4 | scourge — 5 | nour-3-ish-2-ment — 5 1 1 | though — 4

11. rough-3-en — 6 1 | ad-2-journ — 1 5 | cour-1-te-1-sy — 5 2 2 | you — 6

12. sou-1-ve-1-nir — 6 2 1 | cour-1-te-3-ous — 5 2 6 | fur-1-lough — 5 4 | court-2-yard — 4 ˘ 5

13. re-1-source — 2 4 | cou-1-gar — 6 5 | thought — 6 | gourd — 4

14. drought — 6 | e-1-nough — 2 6 | boul-2-der — 4 5 | al-2-though — 8 4

15. rou-1-tine — 6 x | thor-3-ough-1-bred — 5 4 ˘ 1 | brought — 6 | through — 6

16. route/route — 6 6 | dis-2-cour-3-age — 1 5 3 | source — 4 | bay-3-ou — x 6

Page 133

1. re-1-ver-1-ber-3-a-1-tion — 2 5 5 2 1 | quar-1-ter-1-mas-2-ter — 5 5 1 5 | re-3-in-2-car-1-na-1-tion — 2 1 5 2 1

2. con-2-gra-1-tu-1-la-1-tions — 1 2 2 1 | com-2-mu-1-ni-1-ca-1-tion — 1 2 2 2 1 | in-2-di-1-vi-1-du-3-al — 1 2 2 2 8

3. ad-2-mi-1-nis-2-tra-1-tion — 1 2 1 2 1 | as-2-so-1-ci-3-a-1-tion — 1 2 2 2 1 | ci-1-vi-1-li-1-za-1-tion — 2 2 2 2 1

4. in-2-tox-1-i-1-ca-1-tion — 1 1 2 2 1 | ge-1-ner-3-a-1-li-1-za-1-tion — 2 5 2 2 2 1 | qua-1-li-1-fi-1-ca-1-tion — 8 2 2 2 1

5. in-2-stan-2-ta-1-ne-3-ous — 1 1 2 2 6 | pre-1-pos-2-ter-3-ous — 2 1 5 6 | su-1-per-1-sti-1-tious — 2 5 ˘2 6

6. in-1-ex-2-pe-1-ri-3-ence — 1 1 2 2 1 | com-2-mis-2-sion-1-er — 1 1 1 5 | un-2-ne-1-ces-2-sa-1-ri-1-ly — 1 2 1 2 2 2

7. pro-1-fes-2-sor-1-ship — 2 1 5 1 | ir-2-re-1-spon-2-si-1-ble — 1 2 ˘1 2 7 | su-1-pe-1-ri-3-or-3-i-1-ty — 2 2 2 5 2 2

8. re-1-tar-1-da-1-tion — 2 5 2 1 | per-1-so-1-na-1-li-1-ty — 5 2 2 2 2 | ex-2-pe-1-ri-1-men-2-ta-1-tion — 1 2 2 1 2 1

176

9. un-2-for-1-tu-1-nate
   1   5   2   3

10. con-2-ta-1-mi-1-na-1-tion
    1   2   2   2   1

11. dis-1-in-2-te-1-gra-1-tion
    1   1   2   2   1

12. hal-2-lu-1- ci-1-na-1-tion
    1   2   2   2   1

13. dis-1-ap-2-pea-1-rance
    1   1   4   1

14. as-2-sas-2-si-1-na-1-tion
    1   1   2   2   1

15. ma-1-the-1-ma-1-ti-1-cal
    2   2   2   2   8

16. in-2-tel-2-lec-2-tu-3-al
    1   1   1   2   8

17. il-2-le-1-gi-1-ti-1-mate
    1   2   2   2   3

18. me-1-tro-1-po-1-li-1-tan
    2   2   2   2   1

19. sta-1-bi-1-li-1-za-1-tion
    2   2   2   2   1

20. ar-1-bi-1-tra-1-ri-1-ly
    5   2   2   2   2

de-1-si-1-ra-1-ble
  2   2   2   7

dis-2-pro-1-por-1-tio n
  1   2   5   1

un-1-ac-2-coun-2-ta-1-ble
  1   6   2   7

re-3-in-2-force-1-ment
  2   1   5   1

cor-1-re-1-spon-2-dent
  5   2   1   1

de-1-no-1-mi-1-na-1-tion
  2   2   2   2   1

ma-1-tri-1-mo-1-ni-3-al
  2   2   2   2   8

con-2-gre-1-ga-1-tio n
  1   2   2   1

re-1-ha-1-bi-1-li-1-ta-1-tion
  2   2   2   2   2   1

mul-2-ti-1-pli-1-ca-1-tion
  1   2   2   2   1

mi-1-ra-1-cu-1-lous
  2   2   2   6

bib-2-li-3-o-1-gra-1-phy
  1   2   2   2   2

pro-1-por-1-tion-1-ate-1-ly
  2   5   1   3   2

dis-2-sa-1-tis-2-fac-2-tio n
  1   2   1   1   1

mas-2-cu-1-li-1-ni-1-ty
  1   2   2   2   2

pro-1-fes-2-sion-1-al
  2   1   1   8

in-2-ter-1-de-1-pen-2-dence
  1   5   2   1   1

ex-2-com-2-mu-1-ni-1-ca-1-tion
  1   1   2   2   2   1

ton-2-sil-2-lec-2-to-1-my
  1   1   1   2   2

coun-2-ter-1-re-1-vo-1-lu-1-tion
  6   5   2   2   2   1

con-2-si-1-der-3-a-1-tio n
  1   2   5   2   1

flex-1-i-1-bi-1-li-1-ty
  1   2   2   2   2

per-1-pen-2-di-1-cu-1-lar
  5   1   2   2   5

tu-1-ber-1-cu-1-lo-1-sis
  2   5   2   2   1

Page 134

1. hy-1-po-1-the-1-ti-1-cal
    2   2   2   2   8

2. chi-1-ro-1-prac-2-tic
    2   2   1   1

3. bi-3-o-1-gra-1-phi-1-cal
    2   2   2   2   8

4. so-1-li-1-ci-1-tous
    2   2   2   6

5. de-1-ro-1-ga-1-tive
    2   2   2   1

6. tri-1-bu-1-la-1-tio n
    2   2   2   1

7. glor-3-i-1-fi-1-ca-1-tio n
    5   2   2   2   1

8. ques-2-tion-1-a-1-ble
    1   1   2   7

9. ob-2-se-1-qui-3-ous
    1   2   2   6

10. li-1-qui-1-da-1-tion
    2   2   2   1

pre-3-oc-2-cu-1-py
  2   1   2   2

ab-2-so-1-lu-1-tion
  1   2   2   1

vir-1-tu-3-o-1-si-1-ty
  5   2   2   2   2

chor-3-e-1-o-1-gra-1-pher
  5   2   2   2   5

un-2-pre-1-ce-1-den-2-ted
  1   2   2   1   1

flab-2-ber-1-gas-2-ted
  1   5   1   1

re-1-ver-1-ber-3-a-1-ting
  2   5   5   2   1

la-1-bor-3-a-1-tor-3-y
  2   5   2   5   2

Ne-3-o-1-li-1-thic
  2   2   2   1

pan-2-de-1-mo-1-ni-3-um
  1   2   2   2   1

de-1-per-1-so-1-na-1-lize
  2   5   2   8   3

u-1-ti-1-li-1-ta-1-ri-3-an
  2   2   2   2   2   1

me-1-ta-1-mor-1- pho-1-sis
  2   2   5   2   1

u-1-bi-1-qui-1-tous
  2   2   2   6

ef-2-fer-1-ve-1-scent
  1   5   2   1

un-1-im-2-pea-1-cha-1-ble
  1   1   4   2   7

in-2-flam-2-ma-1-ble
  1   1   2   7

pre-1-pon-2-der-3-ance
  2   1   5   1

mis-2-cel-2-la-1-ne-3-ous
  1   1   2   2   6

me-1-mor-3-a-1-bi-1-li-3-a
  2   5   2   2   2   8

11. ni-1-tro-1-gly-1-c͟er-3-in   in-2-cre-1-du-1-l͟o͟us   re-3-ac-2-t͟i͟on-1-a-1-ry
    2 ͝2 ͝<u>2</u> 5 1   1 <u>2</u> 2 6   2 1 1 <u>2</u> 2

12. ho-1-mo-1-g͟e-1-ne-3-o͟u͟s   se-1-mi-3-an-2-nu-3-al   f͟er-1-ti-1-li-1-za-1-t͟i͟on
    2 2 2 2 6   <u>2</u> 2 1 2 8   5 <u>2</u> <u>2</u> 2 1

13. sa-1-ga-1-c͟i-1-ty   mo-1-no-1-syl-2-la-1-b͟l͟e   pre-1-d͟e-1-c͟es-2-s͟or
    <u>2</u> <u>2</u> <u>2</u> 2   <u>2</u> 2 1 2 7   <u>2</u> <u>2</u> 1 5

14. de-1-fi-1-c͟ien-2-cy   ir-2-re-1-spon-2-si-1-b͟l͟e   p͟ho-1-to-1-syn-2-t͟he-1-siz͟e
    2 <u>2</u> 1 2   1 2 ͝1 <u>2</u> 7   2 2 1 <u>2</u> 3

15. tri-3-a͟n-2-gu-1-l͟ar   Je-1-r͟u-1-sa-1-lem   pa-1-ra-1-p͟her-1-na-1-li-3-a
    2 1 2 5   <u>2</u> <u>2</u> 2 1   <u>2</u> 2 5 2 <u>2</u> 8

16. in-2-dus-2-tri-3-a-1-liz͟e   in-2-com-2-pre-1-hen-2-s͟i͟on   e-1-lec-2-tri-1-c͟i-1-ty
    1 1 <u>2</u> 2 3   1 1 2 1 1   2 1 <u>2</u> <u>2</u> 2

17. in-2-tro-1-v͟er-1-s͟i͟o n   ac-2-q͟ui-3-e-1-sc͟en͟ce   mo-1-no-1-li-1-t͟hic
    1 2 5 1   1 <u>2</u> 2 1   <u>2</u> 2 <u>2</u> 1

18. un-2-s͟e͟a-1-s͟o-1-na-1-b͟l͟e   sa-1-ni-1-ta-1-ri-3-um   ex-2-pe-1-di-3-en-2-c͟y
    1 4 <u>2</u> 2 7   <u>2</u> 2 2 <u>2</u> 1   1 2 <u>2</u> 1 <u>2</u>

19. dan-2-d͟e-1-li-3-on   pas-2-s͟i͟on-1-at͟e-1-l͟y   ex-2-tra-3-o͟r-1-di-1-na-1-r͟y
    1 2 2 1   1 1 3 2   1 8 5 <u>2</u> <u>2</u> 2

20. ste-1-re-3-o-1-typ͟e   un-2-s͟er-1-vic͟e-1-a-1-b͟l͟e   hy-1-po-1-gly-1-c͟e-1-mi-3-a
    <u>2</u> 2 2 3   1 5 1 2 7   2 2 ͝2 2 <u>2</u> 8

Section Four

Section Four is the intensive spelling portion of this program. Three word lists, each consisting of 800 words and composing some of the most frequently-used words in the English language, are used for spelling dictation. Word List A contains the most common words in our language. Word List B consists of the next group of frequently-used words in our language, and Word List C continues with other often-used words. An Answer Key is also provided for each separate word list and consists of those same lists of words with each word divided into syllables when appropriate and with each syllable or word marked, using the same system that has been used throughout the preceding portions of this workbook. These word lists were compiled from the study *Phoneme-Grapheme Correspondences as Cues to Spelling Improvement* under the direction of Paul R. Hanna.

This spelling section is an intrinsic part of the overall phonics program. However much your students may have improved up to this point, they can fully expect to see a similar or increased rate of improvement as they proceed through Section Four. In fact by the time students have gone through all three word lists– A, B, and C– using the procedure about to be outlined, they will continue to see profound improvement in their decoding, comprehension, spelling, and pronunciation skills.

Up to this point in the program we have focused primarily upon decoding skills while spending relatively little time on developing spelling skills. Of course any separation between these two skill areas is to a large extent artificial. Decoding and spelling are actually opposite ends of the same process. Decoding is the process of looking at and accurately identifying a written word. Spelling, on the other hand, is the process of starting with identity of the word known and then accurately translating the known word to the letters which spell it.

The skill of reading of which spelling is a vital subpart is a hierarchical activity. An important step in becoming a good speller is to become a fluent reader. At first the person attempting to master the decoding process must look at and sound out virtually every word he encounters. But gradually as he perseveres in this process, he will begin to recognize an ever-increasing number of words instantly until at some point he is able to read almost anything he encounters instantaneously without the need to sound out large numbers of words within the selection first. This ability to recognize words instantly is referred to as decoding fluency and is the goal of everyone who desires to master the skill of reading.

Several factors work in the favor of the student to enable his degree of decoding fluency to improve rapidly as he proceeds further through this book. First is the fact that the more familiar your student becomes in working with the sounds of the language and the letter combinations that represent those sounds, then the faster that student will be able to sound out unknown words when encountered. Second is the fact that by virtue of having worked carefully through the first three sections of the book, the student has gained a thorough understanding of the phonetic basis of our language. With this knowledge as a foundation he then has the capability to look at any word and determine what that word is, never needing to guess again. Finally in normal conversation people tend to use a very limited number of vocabulary words. Thus by learning the most commonly-used words in our language, an individual learns those words which have the highest frequency of appearance in written form. Working from this list of commonly-used words then, one has an excellent foundation upon which to build decoding proficiency over a period of time.

The appropriate time to begin to concentrate on spelling skills is the point at which the student begins to develop decoding proficiency. At this juncture in the program the teacher focuses his instructional time exclusively on spelling. Becoming a good speller takes longer than developing decoding proficiency. Do not, however, either as an instructor or student let that fact dissuade you.

The key to mastering the skill of spelling is to understand that spelling is not primarily a process of memorizing words. Spelling, instead, is a process of listening to sounds words make and then applying phonic principles in attempting to spell those words properly. Never allow or encourage your students to rely on memory alone in spelling a word. Memory is useful, but learning to associate letters with sounds in relationship to the way a word is spelled is the key to developing spelling mastery.

In some of the words found in Word Lists A, B, and C, teams are marked that have not been listed in Section One through Section Three; teams in this category have not been previously mentioned because of their infrequent use in the English language.

Occasionally while marking words, you will find that there is more than one way that a particular word may be marked. In those instances when your marking varies from the marking found in the book and you feel that your marking is the more accurate, feel free to disagree. Do not get overly involved in disputing minor points. The whole purpose of this marking system is to enable a person to analyze systematically a word for purposes of decoding and spelling. To the extent that it accomplishes that task, it is a useful tool. Beyond the successful analysis of a word for decoding and spelling purposes, this marking system was never intended to be a precise linguistic tool for the categorization of the English language. Use this marking system in that spirit.

This practice of marking the word is very important for spelling because it serves to reinforce the phonic principles already learned and also serves as a mnemonic aid in enabling the student to learn the spelling system. Marking words forces students to pay attention to every aspect of the word; first the student must mentally note the phonic elements within the word and then demonstrate his understanding of how the word is constructed phonetically by accurately marking those elements. Thus even students who possess relatively strong reading and spelling skills will find themselves challenged when attempting to spell and mark words correctly within this program.

This marking system demonstrates the consistency of English phonics, the fact that a a direct relationship exists between letters and sounds in our language. To most poor spellers the spelling system appears completely arbitrary and thus largely unlearnable and grossly unfair. One of the benefits of the marking system used in this book is that through using it, the student develops an awareness that spelling and decoding in our language are activities based upon a logical and coherent system of rules; thus the student can see that once he has mastered an understanding of the logic and rules, he has the capability to learn both reading and spelling skills. He realizes that he is not being asked to memorize by sight thousands of individual words, a task which for many would be impossible. This realization is of very great importance. A student needs to know that while the learning process he is embarked upon entails a significant personal commitment and a great deal of time, it is not a process where no end will ever be within sight. Instead with certainty and conviction he comes to the understanding that his goal of learning to read and spell is an eminently realistic and achievable one.

Spelling Dictation for Word Lists A, B, and C

Follow this procedure when dictating words from the word lists.

When dictating vowel sounds, the teacher should stress the vowel sound so that it is in agreement with the actual spelling of the word as much as is possible. As an example in the second syllable of the word *thousand* the normal pronunciation for *sand* is *zund*. Vowels in unaccented syllables lose their stress and thus tend to be pronounced with the schwa sound, which is in effect the short *u* sound. For dictating words, be careful to dictate the unaccented syllables with full stress, thus causing the vowel sounds in unaccented syllables to retain their original clear sound. Thus the correct way to pronounce the second syllable in *thousand* is *zand*.

Students use practice paper when they first spell the word pronounced; once the word has been discussed and checked in class, the word is transferred to the student's notebook from which the student will review and practice words away from class.

First the teacher pronounces without any special emphasis the spelling word as it is spoken in conversation. The teacher then reads the sentence containing that word from the word list. Students do not see the word. The teacher must be sure that everyone understands what the word is and knows the meaning of the word.

Here is the procedure for dictating the one-syllable word *peace*. The teacher pronounces *peace* and then reads from Word List A the sentence, "*Peace* on earth." The teacher asks, "How many sounds are in the word *peace*?" The students respond, "Three." The teacher now shows three fingers, then closes his fingers and shows only one finger. This gesture is a signal for the students to make the first sound of the word. They do not call out the name of the letter *p* but instead in unison they make the sound *p* and write the letter *p* on their practice paper as they make the sound.

The instructor then shows two fingers. This hand movement is a signal for the students to make the second sound in the word *peace*. Students again answer in unison, not by saying the names of the letters *ea* but instead by making the sound *ee*. When a sound may be represented by more than one letter or letter team such as the *ee* sound, which can be spelled in at least six different ways, the instructor asks his students the following question: "Which *ee*?" The teacher never calls out the names of letters but refers to them only by making their sounds. Students again answer, not by naming the letter team *ea* but instead by pronouncing the two sounds which the vowel team *ea* makes: *ee, eh*. The team *ea* is then written on the paper next to the letter *p*.

The teacher holds up three fingers which signal to the students to make the third sound in the word *peace*. Students again answer in unison, not by saying the names of the letters *ce* but instead by making the sound *s*. Because there is more than one way the sound *s* can be spelled, the instructor asks the students, "Which *s*?" The students answer with the following phrase: "A two-letter team whose only sound is *s*." Students write the *ce* team down, and the spelling is complete.

The teacher now faces the board with his back to the students and raises one finger with his left hand as he holds the chalk stick in his right hand. Students make the sound *p* while the teacher writes the letter *p* on the board. The teacher then raises two fingers, and the students make the sound *ee*. The teacher asks, "Which *ee*?" The students answer by making the sounds *ee, eh* as the teacher writes *ea* on board. The teacher raises three fingers, and the students make the sound *s*. The teacher asks, "Which *s*?" The students reply, "A two-letter team with only one sound," as the teacher writes *ce* on the board. Students check to make sure that they have spelled the word correctly. If there are no questions at this point, students are asked to mark fully the word, using the marking system they have learned in Section One through Section Three.

The marking procedure for words is as follows:

Step One - Underline all vowel and consonant teams.

Step Two - Double underline any *c* or *g* letters which make their second sounds.

Step Three - If a word ends with a silent letter *e*, underline the letter *e* once to indicate it is silent.

Step Four - Place dots under all vowels which make sounds. Place one centered dot under each vowel team.

Step Five - The word is already divided into syllables. Determine the syllable rule number which applies, and write that number either above the letters or between the syllables. Identify any consonant blends which must be protected.

Step Six - Determine the vowel group number for each vowel sound in the word, and write that number directly under the vowel or vowel team.

Step Seven - After each student has marked the word individually, the teacher marks the word on the board and answers any questions. Finally the student transfers the marked word to his notebook.

When dictating words of two or more syllables in length, the teacher should use the same procedure as the one indicated for one-syllable words. Using the word *visit* as an example, the teacher pronounces the word and reads from Word List A the sentence, "I want to *visit* her soon." Students do not see the word. The teacher must be sure that everyone understands what the word is and knows the meaning of the word.

The teacher asks, "How many syllables are in the word *visit?*" Students answer, "Two." The teacher says, "Say the first syllable." The students make the sound *vi*. The teacher asks, "How many sounds are in the first syllable?" The students reply, "Two." The teacher shows two fingers.

The teacher then shows a closed fist and then shows one finger. This hand movement is a signal for the students to make the first sound of the syllable *vi*. The students do not call out the name of the letter *v* but instead in unison they make the sound *v* and write the letter *v* on their practice paper as they make the sound.

The instructor shows two fingers. This hand movement is a signal for the students to make the second sound in the syllable *vi*. Students again answer in unison, not by saying the name of the letter *i* but instead by making the sound *ih*. When a sound may be represented by more than one letter or letter team such as the *i h* sound which can be spelled in one of two ways, the instructor asks his students the following question: "Which *ih*?" The teacher never calls out the names of letters but refers to them only by making their sounds. Students again answer, not by naming the letter *i* but instead by pronouncing the two sounds which the vowel *i* makes: *ih and i* (the long *i* sound.) The letter *i* is then written on the paper next to the letter *v*.

The teacher asks, "What is the sound of the second syllable?" The students reply, "Zit." The teacher asks, "How many sounds are in the second syllable?" The students reply, "Three." The teacher holds up three fingers, then closes his fist and shows only one finger. This hand movement is a signal for the students to make the first sound of the second syllable *sit*. Students do not call out the name of the letter *s* but instead in unison make the sound *z*. When a sound may be represented by more than one letter or letter team such as the *z* sound, which can be spelled in one of three ways, the teacher asks his students the following question: "Which *z*?" Students again answer, not by naming the letter *s* but instead by pronouncing the two sounds which the letter *s* makes: *s* and *z*. The letter *s* is then written on the paper.

The instructor then shows two fingers. This hand gesture is a signal for the students to make the second sound in the syllable *sit*. Students again answer in unison, not by saying the name of the letter *i* but instead by making the sound *ih*. The teacher asks his students, "Which *ih*?" Students again answer, not by naming the letter *i* but instead by pronouncing the two sounds which the vowel *i* makes: *ih and i* (the long *i* sound.) The letter *i* is then written on the paper next to the letter *s*.

The instructor then shows three fingers. This hand movement is the signal for the students to make the third sound in the syllable *sit*. Students again answer in unison, not by saying the name of the letter *t* but instead by making the sound *t*. The sound *t* is represented only by the letter *t*. Students write the letter *t* down, and the spelling is complete.

The teacher now faces the board with his back to the students and raises one finger with his left hand as he holds the chalk stick in his right hand and says, "First syllable." The students respond by making the sound *vi*. The teacher closes his fist and then shows one finger. Students make the sound *v* while the teacher writes the letter *v* on the board. The teacher then raises two fingers, and the students make the sound *ih*. The teacher asks, "Which *ih*," and the students reply by making the sounds *ih* and *i* (the long *i* sound) while the teacher writes *i* on the board.

Now the teacher, still facing the board, shows two fingers and says, "Second syllable." The students respond by making the sound *zit*. The teacher closes his fist

184

and then shows one finger. Students make the sound *z*. The teacher asks, "Which *z*?" The students respond by making the sounds *s* and *z* while the teacher writes the letter *s* on the board. The teacher then raises two fingers, and the students make the sound *ih*. The teacher asks, "Which *ih*?" The students respond by making the sounds *ih* and *i* (the long *i* sound) as the teacher writes the letter *i* on board. The teacher raises three fingers, and the students make the sound *t*. The teacher writes *t* on the board. Students check to make sure that they have spelled the word correctly. If there are no questions at this point, students are asked to mark each word, using the marking system they have learned in Section One through Section Three of the book.

This process constitutes the spelling procedure to be used with each word. Once a word is covered in class, students are responsible for spelling that word correctly in daily spelling tests. Each day prior to dictating new spelling words, the instructor should give a brief spelling quiz on the words covered thus far in the program. The instructor may concentrate on the most recent words covered or choose words from any portion of the spelling list which has already been dictated. Keep a daily record of each student's score. Students need to understand that there is a great deal to cover and that it is in their best interest to study as much as possible away from class. These test scores will serve as an incentive for students to study outside of class. Those students who put in the most study time will see the most dramatic results. Remind your students of the fact that it takes a lot of practice to become a good speller.

Prior to beginning any spelling lesson, it is highly desirable to provide to students a brief yet concise review of all phonic elements of our language. Please read carefully the following page titled "Phonics Review" before dictating words for spelling.

Phonics Review

Now that your student has finished the basic phonics' portion of this workbook, he should be capable of correctly associating sounds with both individual letters and letter teams. Two charts immediately follow in this book: *The Major English Letters and Letter Teams* and *The Forty-two Sounds of the English Language*. These charts together constitute a complete and thorough review of the sounds in our language and the letters and letter teams which we use to represent those sounds. These charts were developed to provide a concise review mechanism for the teacher and student. Begin each spelling session with a review of one of these charts.

Start with *The Major English Letters and Letter Teams'* chart. Have your student give the proper sound or combination of sounds which each letter or letter team represents in each of the individual boxes. Some letters may represent one sound; others may represent as many as four different sounds. In the course of this review procedure, ask questions of your student to be certain that he understands the phonic principles behind the marking system. For instance ask your student in what circumstances are the teams *ck*, *tch*, and *dge* used? Your student needs to memorize all of the sounds represented by all eighty letters and letter teams on the chart. It is not necessary to review every single letter or letter team every day. Once you have determined that your students know the single consonants which will likely be the case at this point in the program, concentrate on those letter teams about which they are less sure. The important point to stress here is that a student must learn the information presented on this chart until he can repeat the sounds for each letter and letter team without pause for thought; in other words this activity needs to become an automatic process.

Only after you have determined that your student has mastered the information on *The Major English Letters and Letter Teams'* chart should you proceed to the chart entitled *The Forty-Two Sounds of the English Language*. This chart reverses the process taught in the previous chart. The entire English language is composed of only the forty-two sounds represented on this chart. All of our words are simply a result of choosing from and then combining from these forty-two discrete sounds into endless combinations. The teacher makes any one of the forty-two sounds found on the chart and asks the student to write down all of the various letters and letter combinations which represent that particular sound. Some sounds are represented by only one letter. Other sounds can be represented by many different combinations of letters. An answer key is provided following both charts.

As your student becomes increasingly familiar with the sound-symbol relationship of the letters of our alphabet, he will be capable of completing this review process in increasingly shorter periods of time. Eventually he will review both charts with such accuracy and rapidity that it will become obvious that the review process is no longer necessary.

186

The Major English Letters and Letter Teams

1 b	2 c	3 d	4 f	5 g	6 h
7 j	8 k	9 l	10 m	11 n	12 p
13 qu	14 r	15 s	16 t	17 v	18 w
19 x	20 y	21 z	22 a	23 e	24 i
25 o	26 u	27 ng	28 ch	29 tch	30 ck
31 ph	32 sh	33 th	34 wh	35 ai	36 ay
37 ea	38 ee	39 ey	40 oa	41 oe	42 ou
43 ow	44 ue	45 ui	46 ar	47 er	48 ir
49 or	50 ur	51 oo	52 oi	53 oy	54 au
55 aw	56 ew	57 le	58 ce	59 ge	60 dge
61 ci	62 si	63 ti	64 ve	65 ed	66 augh
67 ei	68 eigh	69 ie	70 igh	71 ear	72 our
73 gh	74 gn	75 gu	76 kn	77 rh	78 sc
79 wr	80 ough				

Answer Key for The Major English Letters and Letter Teams

1. b- bus
2. c-cat/cent
The letter *c* has no sound of its own. When *c* is followed by the letter *e, i,* or *y*, it always makes its second sound.
3. d-dog
4. f-fan
5. g-gum/gem
When *g* is followed by the letter *e, i,* or *y*, it sometimes makes its second sound.
6. h-hat
7. j-jet
The letter *j* is never used as the last letter in a word. The teams *ge* or *dge* are used instead.
8. k-kite
The letter *k* is used before *e,i,* or *y* to represent the *k* sound.
9. l-lamp
10. m-map
11. n-nut/n-rink
12. p-pot
13. qu-queen/con quer
The letter *q* has no sound of its own and is always followed by the letter *u*.
14. r-rat
15. s-sun/hose
The letter *s* can never follow the letter *x*.
16. t- tan
17. v-van
18. w-watch
19. x-box(x=ks)/Xerox
The letter *x* has no sound of its own.
20. y-yard/gym/my
21. z-zebra
22. a- apple/make/call
8
23. e-egg/be
24. i-igloo/ice
25. o-ostrich/note/do
8

26. u- umbrella/ mule/dude/put
8
27. ng-ring
28. ch-church/school/chef
29. tch-match
30. ck-rock
The letter team *ck* may be used only when it directly follows after a short vowel.
31. ph-phone
32. sh-shut
The letter team *sh* may be used only at the beginning of a word or at the end of any syllable. The letter teams *si, ti,* and *ci* are used to represent the *sh* sound at the beginning of any syllable following the first syllable in the word.
33. th-thumb/this
34. wh-whale/who
35. ai-rain
This team cannot be used at the end of a word.
36. ay-pray
The letter team *ay* usually represents the sound *ai* at the end of words.
37. ea-tea/bread
38. ee-feel
39. ey- key/they
40. oa- boat
41. oe-toe
42. ou- out/ fa mous/ soup/ soul
This team cannot be used at the end of a word.
43. ow-blow/cow
44. ue-hue/sue
45. ui- fruit
This team cannot be used at the end of a word.
46. ar-arm/warm
47. er-her
48. ir-girl

188

Answer Key for The Major English Letters and Letter Teams

49. or- c_or_n/w_or_k
50. ur-b_ur_n
51. oo-b_oo_t/f_oo_t
52. oi-_oi_l
This team cannot be used at the end of a word.
53. oy-b_oy_
54. au-_Au_gust
This team cannot be used at the end of a word.
55. aw- s_aw_
56. ew-f_ew_
57. le-can d_le_
58. ce-dan_ce_
59. ge-bar_ge_
60. dge-do_dge_
The letter team *dge* may only be used when it
directly follows after a short vowel.
61. ci-spe _ci_al
The letter teams *si*, *ti*, and *ci* are used only at the beginning of a syllable following the first syllable to represent the *sh* sound.
62. si-mis _si_on/vi _si_on
The letter teams *si*, *ti*, and *ci* are used only at the beginning of a syllable following the first syllable to represent the *sh* sound.
63. ti- na _ti_on
The letter teams *si*, *ti*, and *ci* are used only at the beginning of a syllable following the first syllable to represent the *sh* sound.
64. ve-ha_ve_
Words never end in the letter *v*; the team *ve* is used instead.

65. ed- lan d_ed_ / dimm_ed_
This team represents past tense.
66. augh-c_augh_t
67. ei-re c_ei_ve/th_ei_r
68. eigh-_eigh_t
69. ie-p_ie_/f_ie_ld
70. igh-s_igh_
71. ear-h_ear_d
The letter team *ear* usually forms a team when followed by a consonant.
72. our-j_our_ney
The letter team *our* usually forms a team when followed by a consonant.
73. gh-_gh_ost
The letter team *gh* is a team only at the beginning of a syllable.
74. gn-_gn_at
75. gu-_gu_itar
This team is primarily used to prevent the letter *g* from being followed by *e*, *i*, or *y* which could cause the *g* to make its second sound.
76. kn-_kn_ot
The letter team *kn* may be used only at the beginning of a syllable.
77. rh-_rh_yme
78. sc-_sc_ience
The letter team *sc* must be followed by *e*, *i*, or *y* in order to form a team.
79. wr-_wr_ite
The letter team *wr* may be used only at the beginning of a word.
80. ough-(The letter team *ough* makes many different sounds. Its most common sound is the long *o* sound.)

189

The Forty-Two Sounds of the English Language

1 b	2 d	3 f	4 g	5 h	6 j
7 k	8 l	9 m	10 n	11 p	12 r
13 s	14 t	15 v	16 w	17 y	18 z
19 ch	20 ng	21 sh	22 <u>si</u>	23 th	24 <u>th</u>
25 a Short sound of letter *a*.	26 e Short sound of letter *e*.	27 i Short sound of letter *i*.	28 o Short sound of letter *o*.	29 u Short sound of letter *u*.	30 a Long sound of letter *a*.
31 e Long sound of letter *e*.	32 i Long sound of letter *i*.	33 o Long sound of letter *o*.	34 u Long sound of letter *u*.	35 ar	36 er
37 or	38 au	39 oi	40 oo	41 <u>oo</u>	42 ou

Answer Key for Forty-one Sounds of the English Language Chart

1. b-boy
2. d- dog
3. f- fan
   ph- phone
4. g- gun
   gh- ghost
   gu-guitar
5. h-house
   wh-who
6. j- jet
   g- gent
   ge-barge
   dge-dodge
7. c-cat
   k-kite
   ck-rock
   ch-school
   qu-conquer
8. l-lamb
9. m-man
10. n-nut
    kn-knot
    gn-gnat
11. p-pot
12. r-rabbit
    wr-wrap
    rh-rhythm
13. s- sun
    c-cent
    ce-dance
    sc-scene
14. t- tent
15. v- van
    ve-have
16. w-wagon
    wh-whale
17. y-yard
18. z-zebra
    s-hose
    x-xylophone

19. ch-church
    tch-match
    ti- question
20. ng- ring
    n- bank
21. sh- ship
    ti-nation
    si-mission
    ch-chef
    ci-commercial
22. si-television
23. th- thank
24. th-that
25. a(1st sound)-
    band
26. e(1st sound)-egg
    ea-bread
27. i(1st sound)-trim
    y-gym
28. o(1st sound)-fog
29. u(1st sound)-bus
    ou-country
30. a(2nd sound)-
    make
    ai-rain
    ay-pray
    ei-their
    ey-they
    eigh-eight
31. e(2nd sound)-he
    y-baby
    ea-tea
    ee-feel
    ey-key
    ei-receive
32. i(2nd sound)-hi
    y-my
    igh-high

33. o(2nd sound)-
    home
    oa-boat
    ow-blow
    ou-soul
    oe-toe
34. u(2nd sound)-
    mule
    ue-argue
    ew-few
35. ar-car
36. er-her
    ur-turn
    ir-bird
    or-work
    our-journey
    ear-heard
37. or-corn
    ar-warm
38. au-August
    a-all
    8 8
    aw-saw
    augh-caught
39. oi-oil
    oy-boy
40. oo-boot
    u-rude
    ou-soup
    ui-fruit
    ue-sue
    ew-new
    o-to
    8 8
41. oo-foot
    u-put
    8 8
42. ou-out
    ow-how

191

Word List A

1. Give the man **a** quarter.
2. I want to **visit** her soon.
3. **Peace** on earth.
4. The plane is flying **low**.
5. Watch the **end** of this game.
6. The **lady** has blonde hair.
7. The moon is a **silver** color.
8. Take it **from** the start.
9. Make an **example** of them.
10. Go to **bed**.
11. Climb the **hill**.
12. The doctor is **in**.
13. The **art** gallery is open.
14. **I** like ice cream.
15. She **sat** on the bench.
16. The frog became a **prince**.
17. Put soap in your **mouth**.
18. **Practice** makes perfect.
19. Give **him** the keys.
20. To win you must finish **first**.
21. The **ship** was sunk.
22. I **was** about to graduate.
23. Can you **add**?
24. The **horse** is beautiful.
25. That magazine **article** is true.

26. **Enter** at your own risk.
27. **His** bike is stolen.
28. Please sit in the **chair**.
29. Your speed **boat** is fast.
30. He can **spike** the basketball.
31. My **stock** is dropping fast.
32. I **put** it in the closet.
33. I **dare** you.
34. **Several** people visited us.
35. **History** is my best subject.
36. Go easy on the **butter**.
37. What **size** do you wear?
38. Give me a **thousand** dollars.
39. I **also** am Irish.
40. **More** is not always better.
41. What is the **difference**?
42. Put a **period** after the word.
43. My **roof** leaks.
44. Get in the **car**.
45. I **did** not do it.
46. That **felt** great.
47. The **company** is friendly.
48. The **department** store is big.
49. I **accept** your offer.
50. Let's spend some **money**.

51. **Count** your blessings.

52. **Live** from New York.

53. Walk **straight** down the line.

54. Can you **catch** the ball?

55. I hope to find a **job**.

56. He **kept** his promise.

57. **This** is it.

58. My favorite **color** is blue.

59. The **baby** is sick.

60. She **and** I will go.

61. **According** to him I am shy.

62. Please go **along** with the joke.

63. The car is **very** old.

64. What do you **fear**?

65. **Who** is it?

66. I **tried** to convince him.

67. The **news** is so depressing.

68. I **left** the party early.

69. Will you **come** with us?

70. Walk the **line**.

71. It is wrong to **kill**.

72. The **three** soldiers were hit.

73. We have little in **common**.

74. The line began to **advance**.

75. **Ten** minutes to show time.

76. **Either** you go, or I do.

77. **Destroy** the enemy.

78. The fire **station** is always open.

79. I live in the **city**.

80. The **producer** is in charge.

81. Don't go **between** the lines.

82. We know that **person**.

83. **Share** the wealth with all.

84. What **sort** of tool is that?

85. The **rule** is clear.

86. That is a **lie**.

87. She is one **pretty** woman.

88. The **battle** lasted all night.

89. Let's give him a **lift**.

90. **Food** is an essential item.

91. I **came** to talk business.

92. Watch out for the **hole**.

93. My you **grew** fast.

94. We **honor** all credit cards.

95. The **gentleman** was elderly.

96. **We** went to the ball game.

97. The food is too **sweet**.

98. That is a **fact**.

99. All may go **except** you.

100. We must **continue** to win.

Word List A

101. She did it **herself**.

102. **Leave** us alone.

103. What **if** we fail?

104. Whose **side** are you on?

105. The movie **starred** Cher.

106. Please pay **attention**.

107. One **mile** left to walk.

108. I gave **her** my promise.

109. I would **rather** sit on the aisle.

110. Take it to the lost and **found**.

111. My shirt is made of **cotton**.

112. Will you accept my **check**?

113. I **knew** the answer to that.

114. What a beautiful **cloud**.

115. You are too **late** for dinner.

116. **Take** whatever you want.

117. The **cast** was itching me.

118. What does it meant to be **free**?

119. The **general** is in command.

120. We **supply** the city with water.

121. You must **listen** carefully.

122. We **understand** your belief.

123. The **best** is still ahead.

124. We all are **human**.

125. **Let** it go.

126. Everyone has **gone** to the store.

127. One **hundred** dollars was lost.

128. We may **rest** now.

129. The **tree** was hit by lightning.

130. **Morning** has broken.

131. **Express** yourself.

132. To **whom** are you speaking?

133. The honor **society** chose me.

134. Please tell us a good **story**.

135. Today is **warm**.

136. The **subject** is taxes.

137. This problem is too **hard**.

138. How many **men** will come?

139. My **class** reunion was last year.

140. Who will **find** the prize?

141. Look **behind** the building.

142. Who can draw a perfect **circle**?

143. **Sleep** is what we all need.

144. The stove is **hot**.

145. **Pass** the football.

146. I **want** a pizza.

147. What a **strange** comment.

148. You are **being** childish.

149. What do they **suggest** we do?

150. I try and exercise **daily**.

151. The weather is **pleasant**.

152. We will go **forward**.

153. What is your **interest** in this?

154. **Run** for your life.

155. Use persuasion not **force**.

156. The legal **system** is a mess.

157. I love to **read**.

158. What shall I **wear**?

159. Please **include** a signed check.

160. The **notice** was posted today.

161. I **cannot** afford another car.

162. **Give** to the needy.

163. I want your **picture**.

164. That was one **long** class.

165. The **knight** went into battle.

166. What **other** thing can we do?

167. I have a better **idea**.

168. **Together** we stand united.

169. Where is your **coloring** book?

170. She is **tall**.

171. Where is the town **square**?

172. You are too **much** for me.

173. **Shop** till you drop.

174. **Smile** and the world is yours.

175. Did I **mention** I saw him?

176. We found him **under** the car.

177. I want an **oil** well in my name.

178. It **began** as a joke.

179. Did you forget **it** again?

180. Catch the **wave**, dude.

181. The judge will **decide** today.

182. We must find the **enemy**.

183. Let's go to the **lake**.

184. I **held** a strong hand.

185. Don't **tear** your pants on that.

186. We walked a great **distance**.

187. **Six** minutes remained.

188. We could **tell** you knew.

189. Your **face** is pale.

190. They have **taken** over.

191. Our **trip** was very expensive.

192. The **railroad** is slow.

193. **Set** the table for five.

194. Walk **toward** the light.

195. **Now** is the time to act.

196. Have you been **hurt**?

197. Do you know the **way**?

198. The **army** is not just a job.

199. Each must walk **alone**.

200. All things are **possible**.

Word List A

201. **Close** the door.

202. I want to be a **teacher**.

203. Is all this fuss really **necessary**?

204. My wedding **ring** is gold.

205. **Hang** your shirt up, please.

206. I broke the old **record**.

207. **Blue** is my favorite color.

208. **Each** of us has a gift to offer.

209. **Every** person must do his duty.

210. **How** do you do?

211. **Early** morning we will rise.

212. Children love to **play**.

213. I will **be** there.

214. Someone is **coming**.

215. **Fishing** takes patience.

216. Don't **dream** your life away.

217. I **often** think of you.

218. **Lay** the carpet in this room.

219. **Even** I wanted to go.

220. **Ride** the horse with care.

221. What **number** did you pick?

222. **Whatever** you say goes.

223. The **Lord** is my shepherd.

224. I **made** an A in algebra.

225. **Clothes** are very expensive.

226. I **became** confused.

227. Remember what is **important**.

228. The lawyer won the **case**.

229. He wrote her a love **letter**.

230. Make your **move**.

231. What a beautiful **day**.

232. My **house** is on that street.

233. She **fell** off the swing.

234. We won **because** of you.

235. My **mother** was born here.

236. I want to join this **club**.

237. Look **around** the building.

238. The **grass** needs cutting.

239. I am **twenty** today.

240. Lets meet **after** school.

241. I can barely **hear** you.

242. Neither you **nor** I may go.

243. **Though** I tried, I failed.

244. The **account** is closed.

245. Your **voice** is beautiful.

246. It has been **good** to know you.

247. Yes, **sir**.

248. I did not make that **claim**.

249. The tree's bark is **brown**.

250. We must **sell** at a better price.

251. That **amount** is incorrect.

252. What **hour** do we leave?

253. We went **rolling** down the hill.

254. My **dear** friend just phoned.

255. The **air** is so warm.

256. The wet cloth is **cool**.

257. Our **neighbor** is never home.

258. They had **themselves** to blame.

259. Don't go looking for **trouble**.

260. Your rent is **due**.

261. The river is **narrow** here.

262. Turn **right** at the corner.

263. The weather is **bad** tonight.

264. Turn your **paper** in now.

265. The police **chief** resigned.

266. The **command** was given.

267. I sometimes **miss** you.

268. You **seem** to be tired.

269. The **wind** blows outside.

270. I will be **there** tomorrow.

271. Take your **pick**.

272. I **too** want to go.

273. My first **date** was a disaster.

274. We **thank** you for your help.

275. **May** I be of some help?

276. The **forest** is dark and deep.

277. **No** announcement was made.

278. The sky is **gray**.

279. **Nothing** is as it seems.

280. I do not **draw** very well.

281. I hate to **march**.

282. We made the **crossing**.

283. Give me one good **reason**.

284. Sign your name **here**.

285. She is very **short**.

286. The boys are **thirsty**.

287. Don't **subject** me to your lies.

288. **Tomorrow** is another day.

289. My **dog** is my best friend.

290. The old man is **sick**.

291. The **new** model is improved.

292. One must take care of his **body**.

293. **England** is a large island.

294. The painting is very **old**.

295. What **else** is there to eat?

296. You must be **strong** to play.

297. I **declare** I am innocent.

298. Please be **on** time.

299. He did me a **favor** once.

300. Make a wish upon a **star**.

301. I am **going** now.
302. Will you make a **reply**?
303. I **use** only the best.
304. **Fair** skin easily burns.
305. Turn left at the next **corner**.
306. We drove **by** the river.
307. She **threw** him out.
308. The answer is **simple**.
309. I **have** not yet done my chores.
310. What is your favorite **game**?
311. They **sent** us many gifts.
312. We **went** to Texas last year.
313. **Mark** your name on the box.
314. I **still** don't understand.
315. I **trust** that you are comfortable.
316. The shoe **industry** is in decline.
317. You will **receive** your reward.
318. **Round** up the usual suspects.
319. You better learn your **lesson**.
320. What is the **proper** response?
321. What is the largest **animal**?
322. The **fight** continued all night.
323. That dog is **wild**.
324. Cut the **board** in half.
325. I will **direct** traffic.

326. We **own** our home.
327. The potato salad is **great**.
328. The **red** flag was displayed.
329. We **read** that story yesterday.
330. Let's **discuss** the situation.
331. The **train** is running late.
332. Stay off the **center** line.
333. Still water runs **deep**.
334. The **president** issued the order.
335. Our **nation** is a democracy.
336. Things will **happen** soon.
337. The **next** person will win.
338. Walk the **length** of the room.
339. The **shore** is highly developed.
340. Can you **divide** this prize?
341. We must **remain** loyal to him.
342. **Up** and away we go.
343. The **moment** is everything.
344. That **suit** looks good on you.
345. Our produce is **fresh**.
346. Reach **below** the counter.
347. The freezer door was **open**.
348. The Falcons finished **third**.
349. The **colored** glasses were sold.
350. She is a **famous** ballerina.

351. **Waste** not, want not.

352. We **care** about you.

353. Your **conduct** is inexcusable.

354. We live on Walnut **street**.

355. How much **further** is it?

356. I'll **race** you to the stairs.

357. **Joy** to the world.

358. We drove in **front** of you.

359. I **offer** you my congratulations.

360. The **children** were excited.

361. **Lead** the way.

362. Allow me to **explain**.

363. **Till** you came, we were lost.

364. Let's **shout** the team song.

365. You must **study** to succeed.

366. We will **provide** for you.

367. The **captain** gave the order.

368. We cannot **fail** our mission.

369. We bought him a **watch**.

370. Plant the seed in good **soil**.

371. She walked a narrow **path**.

372. We gave **them** a ride.

373. The **future** looks good.

374. Had we **but** known.

375. The **paint** is very colorful.

376. **When** do you expect to arrive?

377. He seemed **normal** enough.

378. The **fence** is too high to climb.

379. We **were** there today.

380. **Hold** your horses, mister.

381. My **brother** is older than I.

382. **Gather** all the team together.

383. We lose **unless** you play.

384. **Allow** me to introduce myself.

385. **Follow** the leader.

386. The **sign** said closed.

387. My **hair** needs cutting.

388. I was **born** in July.

389. We must **instruct** the class.

390. Very **few** from the group came.

391. **Everything** is turning up roses.

392. The desert is a **dry** place.

393. What **name** did you use?

394. Our **government** is elected.

395. The **man** owns a nice home.

396. I **feel** great.

397. We **need** a score right now.

398. Wait **outside** while I change.

399. She **stood** under the light.

400. Please **spread** the jam evenly.

401. I was **afraid** that might happen.

402. The **child** was lost.

403. The prom **queen** cried.

404. **Silence** is golden.

405. I will **never** leave this country.

406. We do **not** plan to attend.

407. My **nose** is cold.

408. It is difficult to **master** this.

409. At **least** you tried.

410. **Knock** on the door.

411. My **office** is upstairs.

412. **All** is well.

413. Watch your **step**.

414. I **do** believe you.

415. Fill out the **form**.

416. That **stick** is very dangerous.

417. I agree on one **condition**.

418. The team has good **spirit**.

419. We went on a long **drive**.

420. Will you **dance** with me?

421. She is in great **shape**.

422. My **sense** is not to go.

423. You must **pay** the band.

424. My **uncle** is coming to visit.

425. That **rock** is too big to move.

426. Both of **us** want to go.

427. **Life** is precious.

428. Give **me** your attention.

429. I am **filling** up the gas tank.

430. He **sprang** at us with a knife.

431. We will leave this **afternoon**.

432. I will **blow** up the balloon.

433. **Many** people came to the party.

434. The **plan** is very simple.

435. He ran **across** the open field.

436. What is your favorite **bird**?

437. I grew up on rock and **roll**.

438. He **beat** the drum hard.

439. I **cut** my finger on that blade.

440. Can you sing this high **note**?

441. I **think** you are a genius.

442. We are **near** the airport.

443. The **ground** is muddy.

444. She **sold** her violin.

445. I am stating a **plain** fact.

446. Go **west**, young man.

447. I am **tired** of your comments.

448. We are **riding** in a boat.

449. He had **an** egg in his hand.

450. **Cross** the street carefully.

Word List A

451. We have had **such** fun.

452. Our **table** is overloaded.

453. What **college** will you attend?

454. I **teach** English.

455. The river is **wide** here.

456. Let's go for a **walk**.

457. I **keep** to myself at times.

458. The dog began to **growl**.

459. The **cost** was high in the end.

460. The **dollar** is weak in Europe.

461. I **told** you not to do that.

462. What an ugly **tie**.

463. I **met** my friends at the mall.

464. We spoke, **then** shook hands.

465. I finally **see** your point.

466. Are you quite **finished**, sir?

467. I will **require** more money.

468. **Summer** is a time for fun.

469. My heart is too **full** to speak.

470. Will you **become** famous?

471. The **storm** lasted all night.

472. Either you **or** I must do it.

473. **Exercise** is a good thing to do.

474. You need to **speak** when called.

475. We must **hurry** for the bus.

476. The **former** athlete is poor.

477. My **dad** smokes a pipe.

478. Lets take a **break**.

479. Your **point** is well taken.

480. My **son** lives in Boston.

481. A free **press** is important to us.

482. **Eat** more green vegetables.

483. I am **tying** his shoes.

484. The **show** was sold-out.

485. I brought you a **present**.

486. That **drug** store is open.

487. Can you **reach** that shelf?

488. Place the book **beside** my table.

489. The **poor** woman lost her pet.

490. His **father** goes to work early.

491. We went **to** the market.

492. My **boy** plays ball at school.

493. We must **win** tonight.

494. He is **favored** to finish first.

495. Bring me **another** hamburger.

496. We will **discover** the truth.

497. The **road** is long and winding.

498. Our **family** is together today.

499. I **might** just change my mind.

500. A **leader** must lead.

501. The **moth** flew into the flame.

502. The pencil has **lead** in it.

503. I will **carry** my own pack.

504. Try and **finish** what you start.

505. I **desire** to make good grades.

506. He **took** the girl fishing.

507. **Land** is very expensive.

508. This **crayon** is broken.

509. The **bear** looked hungry to me.

510. The **snow** is so beautiful.

511. The **whole** world is watching.

512. **He** is my best friend.

513. Boss, may I have a **raise**?

514. I am **certain** of the directions.

515. The trees tower **above** us.

516. I have **fifty** dollars on me.

517. The sun is **bright** and warm.

518. All of a **sudden,** he left.

519. The **moon** is full tonight.

520. Fried **fish** is fattening.

521. Your statement was **clear**.

522. I **like** you.

523. Let's walk **among** the flowers.

524. He must **suffer** a great deal.

525. May I **present** my wife to you?

526. **Water** is essential for life.

527. I **sometimes** miss the company.

528. **Where** could they have gone?

529. I **suppose** you may be right.

530. We **control** our own destiny.

531. The **church** is very old.

532. I seem to **spend** more each day.

533. We must **seek** protection.

534. Don't fall over the **edge**.

535. **Rush** this order to them.

536. Her **beauty** was known to all.

537. The **well** finally gave out.

538. She **gave** him a motorcycle.

539. We **really** wish you all the best.

540. He was **led** away.

541. **Soon** night will come.

542. I **just** stopped by to say hi.

543. I have had my **fill** of food.

544. What does the will **contain**?

545. My **button** is missing.

546. Her **skin** is dry.

547. I am not the greatest **cook**.

548. The **light** slowly faded.

549. We go to bed late each **night**.

550. That **girl** is singing for joy.

551. That police **officer** is young.

552. He was pronounced **dead**.

553. **Start** your engines.

554. I like the **taste** of your soup.

555. That **experience** changed me.

556. **The** mayor lost the election.

557. We **are** all going together.

558. I **believe** you just made a guess.

559. Roll the boulder **over**.

560. My **arm** is sore from lifting.

561. Turn to the next **page**.

562. **Lower** taxes would help.

563. My **foot** is sore.

564. We plan to **arrive** early.

565. You look as if you are **ill**.

566. The **white** cat has thick fur.

567. I am too **large** for that coat.

568. She was **paid** for the job.

569. I think **their** lawn is nice.

570. His **hat** looked ridiculous.

571. We **will** deliver the package.

572. The **string** needs to be tied.

573. Let's make some kind of **deal**.

574. The workers will **strike** today.

575. He said **that** to all present.

576. I **am** leaving soon.

577. They **saw** the crime happen.

578. The **guard** fell asleep.

579. The **glass** is fragile.

580. I must make a **report**.

581. What she said is the **truth**.

582. **These** are difficult days.

583. Let's **party**.

584. Leave **space** at the end.

585. I had an **egg** for breakfast.

586. The furniture is very **modern**.

587. I like to **sit** and watch people.

588. The grass is **green**.

589. In **God** we trust.

590. I like to **camp** outdoors.

591. He is afraid of the **dark**.

592. The paper costs one **quarter**.

593. I need to **clean** my car.

594. I don't **quite** know what to say.

595. What is the **cause** of the crash?

596. He **has** a great sense of humor.

597. Her **loss** was a blow to us all.

598. My **turn** came at last.

599. I want to learn to **fly**.

600. My **ear** is ringing.

601.	The **south** freeway is closed.	626.	He is too **thin**.
602.	We must take **action**.	627.	I will **prepare** a feast.
603.	The sun will **rise** at six o'clock.	628.	He talks like a **robot**.
604.	For **myself** I ask for nothing.	629.	She **ran** like a swift horse.
605.	The **doctor** was not friendly.	630.	It happened once **upon** a time.
606.	One more **minute** and we go.	631.	I want to **ask** you something.
607.	I **guess** we should turn here.	632.	Name the **state** capitol.
608.	You need to go **into** the office.	633.	We will **lose** if we don't score.
609.	What is your **purpose**?	634.	I want to **surprise** her.
610.	Don't **drop** the television.	635.	The **judge** was very harsh.
611.	**Mount** Everest is in Nepal.	636.	We have been sad **since** then.
612.	He received his **degree** today.	637.	I will **bring** you all you need.
613.	The **deer** can be seen at dusk.	638.	May I **stay** here with you.
614.	I eat **meat** and potatoes.	639.	The **shoulder** pads were tight.
615.	He **traveled** everywhere.	640.	**Today** we march.
616.	Keep the **cover** clean.	641.	I **already** let the cat out.
617.	I am **about** finished.	642.	May I **help** you with directions.
618.	That **fellow** is a real fan.	643.	The **stop** sign was removed.
619.	My **coat** needs mending.	644.	What a **happy** day it is.
620.	He is **different** from the others.	645.	The choir will **sing** Sunday.
621.	We like the **same** things.	646.	His **return** will be welcomed.
622.	Here comes the **sun**.	647.	The **special** show was a success.
623.	I live on the **top** floor.	648.	I am older **than** you.
624.	We must **save** the earth.	649.	He is a **nice** guy.
625.	The **bridge** was washed out.	650.	Bury the treasure **beneath** here.

651. Her **husband** is away.

652. We buy coffee by the **ounce**.

653. My **pair** of shoes is worn.

654. **School** closed early.

655. We **indeed** had a good time.

656. My **feet** are frozen.

657. The **passage** was difficult.

658. The dance **hall** is packed.

659. The umpire called him **out**.

660. The **valley** is remote.

661. I want to learn to **sail**.

662. **She** has great intelligence.

663. **What** is the weather like?

664. **Dinner** was fantastic.

665. The **danger** has passed for now.

666. My **head** is killing me.

667. I neither want **nor** seek the prize.

668. We live in the **middle** of town.

669. She will **appear** next week.

670. Throw the **ball**.

671. I **love** cookies.

672. Why won't you **admit** it?

673. What did he **say**?

674. I **refuse** to be intimidated.

675. All was **ready** at home.

676. This is the **most** we've seen.

677. My **leg** is cramping.

678. Be careful with **fire**.

679. I wish you great **success**.

680. He took every **cent** I had.

681. The **wait** seems forever.

682. She **is** coming with us.

683. Just **enjoy** yourselves.

684. I am **through** with this paper.

685. The **elephant** is a big animal.

686. Only a **member** may apply.

687. We left **during** intermission.

688. We must make a great **effort**.

689. I can't get the **spot** out.

690. We need everyone's **support**.

691. The **affair** ended rather badly.

692. We must **agree** to one goal.

693. We are **down** but not out.

694. The **ice** is melting.

695. What you say is all **true**.

696. I **still** like to drink milk.

697. We went **before** the rest.

698. **Meet** me in St. Louis.

699. I will **try** one more time.

700. We **realize** now our mistake.

701. Have you **lost** your way?

702. She is an expert **guide**.

703. We need to **produce** more.

704. The **sky** is overcast.

705. The **store** will stay open late.

706. Turn the **heat** down.

707. The **price** of gas has increased.

708. I **regard** him as my friend.

709. **Those** days are gone forever.

710. The **field** was harvested.

711. That **tire** needs air.

712. **Whose** sock is this?

713. Don't **burn** in the sun.

714. The **plant** announced layoffs.

715. I want to join a music **group**.

716. **Eight** flights were added.

717. I **object** to that statement.

718. Go **for** it!

719. We went **away** for a trip.

720. I finally **begin** to understand.

721. He is **ever** the optimist.

722. This is the **last** game.

723. The **pain** seems to be less.

724. I like **country** music.

725. Place the **object** in the bag.

726. Where is the **Gulf** of Mexico?

727. The **gate** was left open.

728. Some must **learn** the hard way.

729. Don't catch my **cold**.

730. Wait **until** your father arrives.

731. The **bank** is no longer open.

732. Do not **attempt** to escape.

733. How may I **obtain** a copy?

734. **Nine** days are left in this year.

735. Don't **spring** a surprise on me.

736. Try and **fit** into our plans.

737. I don't remember a **thing**.

738. The test **result** is not in.

739. Do **as** you wish.

740. He is very **kind** to all.

741. **Off** we went on adventure.

742. **While** we slept, she left.

743. The machine is **broken**.

744. The **branch** fell to the ground.

745. Open up a **can** of tuna.

746. **Which** way did they go?

747. The **village** was so peaceful.

748. I **hope** all is well.

749. Your **dress** needs ironing.

750. Try and **act** your age.

Word List A

751. Please **remove** your shoes.

752. We scored **seven** runs.

753. What do you **gain** from it.

754. We need to paint the **wall**.

755. He was last **seen** at the theater.

756. We must **complete** the project.

757. Climb the **mountain**.

758. The cat's fur is so **soft**.

759. We had **better** build it right.

760. We **shall** overcome.

761. Let's be **real**.

762. I have **various** ways to do it.

763. My **neck** is an average size.

764. Do you have a **problem**?

765. That man is **huge**.

766. The girl grew by an entire **inch**.

767. May I fix you a **drink**.

768. Mom's **health** is excellent.

769. We will **increase** our reserves.

770. I shed a **tear** over you.

771. You can't **always** be sleeping.

772. You have been **given** a lot.

773. Head **north** for the mountains.

774. The team made a good **trade**.

775. The **window** is open.

776. He **must** be joking.

777. That ring is a good **value**.

778. That was a **close** call.

779. The **flower** needed water.

780. To whom does this **belong**?

781. The **crowd** screamed for more.

782. Thanks a **lot**.

783. That store offers good **service**.

784. Let's **go** and win the big one.

785. Will you be **able** to do the job?

786. I can't tell **whether** it will rain.

787. The **rate** of change increases.

788. What time **zone** are we in?

789. **Look** for the positive in life.

790. What is the **matter** with you.

791. My **sister** plays piano.

792. I want to **join** a chess club.

793. Don't act like a **fool**.

794. The **king** was not popular.

795. You must take a **chance**.

796. **Labor** is part of life.

797. This dessert is too **rich**.

798. He had **less** than most.

799. He is a very **fine** man.

800. I will come **at** noon.

Word List B

1. My car was in an **accident**.
2. I will follow **directly** after you.
3. **Victory** was achieved at great cost.
4. You have an **honest** face.
5. The **professor** taught biology.
6. Your **influence** over her is strong.
7. He gave one final, **mighty** effort.
8. We have only just **begun**.
9. The **meal** was very satisfying.
10. The **actual** mileage was higher.
11. **Tax** time comes in April.
12. What in **particular** don't you like?
13. I **imagine** you are extremely tired.
14. There is no **virtue** in blind struggle.
15. The house's **foundation** is solid.
16. I can't quite **recall** what was said.
17. On whose **authority** do you come?
18. That was a **smart** move.
19. Don't point that **gun** at me.
20. My parents made a great **sacrifice**.
21. I looked through the **seed** catalog.
22. The baseball **league** is profitable.
23. We will **cease** all hostilities.
24. Place the **stamp** on the envelope.
25. My **expense** account is generous.
26. The **crop** looks good for the year.
27. **Accompany** me to the airport.
28. The **nurse** was near retirement age.
29. The **electric** motor was noisy.
30. Our **household** is always busy.
31. His only **possession** was his bag.
32. I **forgot** to set the alarm.
33. His **anger** overflowed.
34. I **represent** the people of my ward.
35. He was a **slave** to his bank account.
36. We cross the **border** tomorrow.
37. The **route** was long and dangerous.
38. That **individual** left the game.
39. The **colony** of artists was small.
40. Please be **careful**.
41. The **regular** clerk was off.
42. I think I will **bake** some bread.
43. What were you **taught** today?
44. I can't **possibly** attend.
45. That man is very **religious**.
46. He **wound** up to throw.
47. I have great **confidence** in him.
48. The baby **cried** all night.
49. I will walk to the **farther** shore.
50. He is my favorite **author**.

Word List B

51. Next **year** will be better.
52. You are an honored **guest**.
53. I **simply** can't eat another bite.
54. I hope you feel **secure** with us.
55. She is the **leading** authority.
56. Your answer is **correct**.
57. Climb the **stairs** with caution.
58. The sea was **calm**.
59. Their **crime** was a serious one.
60. The **community** came together.
61. **Numerous** reports were filed.
62. We **elect** our leaders.
63. The **load** was too heavy for me.
64. He will **possess** the prize soon.
65. We might **hire** him.
66. **Ancient** history is not my favorite.
67. Let me **repeat** myself.
68. He has a **sufficient** supply of food.
69. The **journey** began in a rainstorm.
70. Please **shut** the door.
71. She did not **indicate** her choice.
72. That **calendar** is twenty years old.
73. Sign the **contract** on the dotted line.
74. He was no **match** for his opponent.
75. The **burst** of sunlight was unexpected.

76. Our **task** is difficult.
77. Fill the **pan** with water.
78. That boy runs very **slow**.
79. The **vessel** slipped into the water.
80. Our country stands for **liberty**.
81. The **fare** will go up again next week.
82. My **aunt** is very sweet.
83. **Trick** or treat.
84. The doctor removed a **growth**.
85. Get your **stuff** together.
86. Our tickets are in the next **section**.
87. The **latter** part of the book got better.
88. I **wonder** if we will see him again.
89. The **sailor** reported to his new ship.
90. The speed limit will sometimes **vary**.
91. **Boil** the soup for about ten minutes.
92. He had **title** to the car.
93. I am buying a **ticket** to the circus.
94. My **pocket** needs mending.
95. Everyone treated him like a **kid**.
96. I put a **nail** in the board.
97. I will apply for that **position**.
98. He looks **lean** and mean.
99. It is great to be **alive**.
100. Sugar was the missing **element**.

101. I need a **treat** after all that.

102. The **bond** between us is strong.

103. We must **strip** the paint off the wall.

104. The **police** could not find him.

105. Call **collect** any time.

106. The **devil** made me do it.

107. There was a **mass** of people forming.

108. I always try and **compare** prices.

109. She told a grim **tale**.

110. The **pale** blue sky revealed itself.

111. I like to smoke a **pipe**.

112. I eat one **vegetable** every day.

113. The **profit** from this business is small.

114. He tried to get **fancy** with his plans.

115. **Attitude** is very important.

116. Don't go the **wrong** way.

117. You certainly have **grown**.

118. No **trace** of him was ever found.

119. We have a **secret** to tell.

120. Our **language** is very rich.

121. I work in a large **factory**.

122. **Dawn** is still hours away.

123. The **desk** is made of solid oak.

124. My **credit** is good here.

125. **Thy** will be done.

126. **Quality** is job number one.

127. Stay in school and get an **education**.

128. Please don't get **personal**.

129. She was given a tiny **portion**.

130. My job is to **fold** the laundry.

131. I have **pity** for him.

132. The view was **splendid**.

133. Her cheeks were pale and **hollow**.

134. Their **product** is sold everywhere.

135. The **famed** actor was spotted.

136. I want to **improve** my golf game.

137. Put a **coin** in the turnstile.

138. We **exist** in a mysterious world.

139. They have been **married** forty years.

140. I want to be sure you are on the **level**.

141. The bird's **tail** was a bright red.

142. The **palace** guard was about to march.

143. She is such a **proud** parent.

144. The ocean is **vast**.

145. The **adventure** is just beginning.

146. He **fancied** himself to be a scholar.

147. He will **defend** his honor.

148. I can **afford** to buy all I want.

149. We **greet** the sun with thankfulness.

150. Things could always be **worse**.

Word List B

151. We continue to **search** our files.
152. The **lamp** wouldn't work.
153. The **funny** man kept us laughing.
154. My **sport** is football.
155. The lawyer will **examine** the facts.
156. The movie left a **glow** in us.
157. **Throw** out the trash.
158. The **sand** burned my feet.
159. The **editor** was hard to like.
160. Private **property**; no trespassing.
161. The ocean **port** was always busy.
162. Baking **flour** is necessary for cooking.
163. Look **beneath** the shelf.
164. That **religion** started in India.
165. The election **campaign** was over.
166. The raft would **bob** up and down.
167. She **shook** her head no.
168. I find your request is **impossible**.
169. Please heat my **coffee**.
170. We all love our **freedom**.
171. **Marriage** is a serious commitment.
172. He competed in just one **event**.
173. He drew his **sword** to attack.
174. The accident was **terrible**.
175. I can only **conclude** you are right.

176. **Bless** this house.
177. I take **cream** with my coffee.
178. Her **throat** is still sore.
179. The **attack** came without warning.
180. The **bee** sting was quite painful.
181. I visit the **grave** often.
182. He was **active** in his organization.
183. She slapped his **cheek**.
184. There was no **lack** of opportunity.
185. People are **hungry**.
186. Don't **spoil** this beautiful day.
187. He soon would turn **forty**.
188. We will **create** our own luck.
189. It rained **throughout** the event.
190. I will **slip** on the jacket.
191. **Economic** sanctions were taken.
192. Believe that you are **worthy**.
193. I kept the **porch** light on for her.
194. The **flood** caused great damage.
195. My **cat** is spoiled.
196. No **relief** was anywhere in sight.
197. Her **bare** shoulders were burned.
198. I live on the next **block**.
199. My **work** is different all the time.
200. You look **lovely** in that dress.

201. We drove down the **coast**.

202. The **hospital** was full of patients.

203. My **map** is inaccurate.

204. **Folk** music is very popular.

205. The children love to **swing**.

206. The **pace** at work is very hectic.

207. The **situation** is very confusing.

208. The **citizen** was upset with the law.

209. The **rope** was strong enough to hold.

210. **Fame** can be very fleeting.

211. I **ate** the whole pizza.

212. We are trying to raise **capital**.

213. The **grand** piano was very heavy.

214. Try and stay **awake**.

215. **Science** is of great importance.

216. **Knock** and the door will be opened.

217. You know it was **worth** it.

218. I am in **utter** awe of what you did.

219. The **prison** was depressing.

220. The homeless **shelter** was crowded.

221. My **plate** is full.

222. **Supper** was delicious.

223. I live in the **eastern** part of the city.

224. That **silk** dress looks good on you.

225. The **population** continued to grow.

226. The **revolution** went on for years.

227. Don't **copy** my paper.

228. What **relation** are you to him?

229. Put the nails in the empty **bin**.

230. The man was **blind**.

231. Please **shine** my shoes.

232. The **noise** level kept rising.

233. Use this **cloth** to wash your face.

234. The **lion** gave his loud roar.

235. The **temperature** kept climbing.

236. We **deliver** all our orders.

237. We **understood** what he said.

238. The **owner** sold his business.

239. You must work to **succeed**.

240. The **valuable** painting is in a vault.

241. I like to **shoot** pool.

242. He gave a **false** statement.

243. I want to **assure** you of my intentions.

244. We **hung** around all day.

245. Please say **grace**.

246. He had a **brush** with the law.

247. We will **scatter** the seeds.

248. The **kingdom** was under attack.

249. The fisherman's **net** was torn.

250. I will win in **spite** of you.

251. We had our **lesson** today.

252. The **cow** stood in the pasture.

253. Don't **threaten** me.

254. The **trial** went on for days.

255. Our team won **easily**.

256. You must **struggle** to be free.

257. She was **popular** with the students.

258. The **flight** left right on time.

259. The test was most **difficult**.

260. We did not have a **spare** in the trunk.

261. The **prize** was a frozen turkey.

262. The **brook** silently flowed.

263. My **furniture** looks shabby.

264. The **association** was very powerful.

265. He was watched **closely**.

266. The **murder** suspect was the butler.

267. I can **manage** this situation.

268. What a **delight** to be here today.

269. They held a **benefit** concert.

270. How much do you **owe**?

271. The **traveler** was alone.

272. Try not to be so **vain**.

273. He was a **private** in the army.

274. The **fallen** comrade was missed.

275. I **assume** you want to enroll.

276. We can **develop** this property.

277. The **governor** was popular.

278. **Everybody** celebrated the victory.

279. I **scarcely** knew him.

280. Will you **kindly** explain yourself.

281. The **pine** tree has a fragrant smell.

282. We **spent** the whole day at the fair.

283. **Mix** all the ingredients together.

284. My **cousin** is in Iowa.

285. Cut the **thread**.

286. She is my favorite **writer**.

287. Mix the **powder** in the water.

288. What is the **total** amount due?

289. The **political** candidate spoke.

290. He **flew** in from the coast.

291. Her **expression** was one of shock.

292. In what **region** do you live?

293. The **desert** is a harsh environment.

294. I don't **blame** you.

295. I found a **shell** to keep at the beach.

296. I answered him **twice**.

297. The **clock** was ten seconds fast.

298. Who can **perform** this task?

299. The **majority** rules.

300. The pilot announced a slight **delay**.

Word List B

301. The first **aid** course was excellent.

302. We have only **ourselves** to blame.

303. She **hit** the ball out of the park.

304. No one made a **bid** for the property.

305. The **oak** tree has stood for years.

306. The scientist was testing his **theory**.

307. Life is a **beach**.

308. Please **excuse** my son's absence.

309. Life **goes** on.

310. The **democratic** party is in decline.

311. That **scale** is off by five pounds.

312. Life is the most **precious** gift.

313. We need to **protect** the environment.

314. His **speed** is blinding.

315. There was a **pause** in the action.

316. The allies acted with **courage**.

317. The walls were one foot **thick**.

318. May I offer you some **advice**?

319. I want to **earn** as much as possible.

320. The path was **worn** through use.

321. **Somewhere** I took a wrong turn.

322. He made the **standard** reply.

323. I am **fully** prepared to respond.

324. I want to **reduce** my debt.

325. There is not much **evidence**.

326. The tea was **bitter** without sugar.

327. Fill out this **sheet**.

328. My **salary** has been increased.

329. We will **climb** the mountain.

330. We have **similar** backgrounds.

331. This is a **major** opportunity for us.

332. The **defense** held them scoreless.

333. **Behold**, I bring you good tidings.

334. It better start; **otherwise** we walk.

335. We built an **addition** to the house.

336. It was business as **usual**.

337. We will **print** what you write.

338. I have no **immediate** plans.

339. We **had** no gas in the car.

340. They punted on **fourth** down.

341. Don't let him get your **goat**.

342. The **broad** river was one mile across.

343. I **smell** something burning.

344. Where did I put my **key**?

345. Don't be **sad** today.

346. The **upper** floors were occupied.

347. They tried to **prevent** the loss.

348. We must **combine** our resources.

349. What is the **sum** of those numbers?

350. **Civil** war broke out in the republic.

351. The **dust** has not settled yet.

352. We still have much to **accomplish**.

353. The north **pole** is a cold place.

354. The **fleet** of fishing boats went out.

355. Our profits were **huge**.

356. We will **recover** from the loss.

357. You are **perfect** to me.

358. The **birth** of the child was a blessing.

359. The **sheep** were herded together.

360. I **slept** like a dead man.

361. The **clerk** was working on commission.

362. **Row** your boat.

363. The **main** event was later.

364. Please do not **harm** them.

365. The **cast** was outstanding in the play.

366. The **original** copy is valuable.

367. **Balance** is important in all sports.

368. You may still be **useful** to us.

369. I agree in **principle**.

370. Hang **loose**.

371. There is a **pattern** emerging.

372. Bees make **honey**.

373. The **official** was booed.

374. I will make a **brief** statement.

375. You look **swell**.

376. How can you **justify** your behavior?

377. The preacher told us not to **sin**.

378. The **southern** route is longer.

379. The old **mill** is abandoned.

380. The city **council** met last week.

381. The **theater** is showing old movies.

382. The **development** project is off.

383. The **duke** received his visitors.

384. His batting **average** was low.

385. The **poet** was not well known.

386. The **flat** tire was a surprise.

387. The **local** folks were friendly.

388. I did not **recognize** you at first.

389. We left just after **midnight**.

390. I will not buy **fur** products.

391. The **sale** ends today.

392. We will **arrange** for your arrival.

393. The play was set in **motion**.

394. A **sigh** of relief was heard.

395. That **magazine** article is false.

396. They will **defeat** the home team.

397. The **convention** will meet here.

398. The **organization** is influential.

399. They will **bury** him today.

400. These colors are in **fashion** this year.

401. Take **pride** in your heritage.

402. **Nobody** is going to go.

403. She is a true **artist**.

404. It is not **likely** that you will win.

405. There is no **glory** in war.

406. **Breathe** deeply and relax.

407. I am a member of **troop** 416.

408. **Justice** will be done.

409. I made the **basket** to end the game.

410. What is the **source** of the problem?

411. That **military** base might be closed.

412. Watch me **disappear** on you.

413. The **test** was difficult.

414. The **operator** will connect you.

415. I **drove** at top speed all day.

416. She **broke** the school record.

417. The **poem** is found on the next page.

418. The **flash** bulb failed to work.

419. I took the job out of **necessity**.

420. My **recent** appearance was recorded.

421. He took a **leap** of faith.

422. What else **besides** that do you need?

423. It is a **shame** you can't come.

424. The **treaty** was signed.

425. The **fencing** coach retired.

426. That was a **stroke** of good fortune.

427. He seems to be **mad** about you.

428. I will sign the **deed** over.

429. You must **devote** yourself to the goal.

430. I'll have an **orange**.

431. He will **compel** us to leave.

432. The **cattle** truck was loaded.

433. The **settlement** was isolated.

434. He was **bound** to make a mistake.

435. The **exchange** was a heated one.

436. Don't be a **drag** on us.

437. Take a **glance** behind you.

438. You can see my **breath** in this cold.

439. He **wrote** a masterpiece.

440. Everyone **jump** up and shout.

441. The **track** was muddy.

442. The trainer **sought** advice.

443. That is one **tiny** dog.

444. I heard a **faint** cry.

445. We set out for the **territory**.

446. Every **detail** was perfect.

447. She **drew** an incredible picture.

448. I **wore** my best suit.

449. I buy in large **quantity**.

450. The **flame** was bright.

Word List B

451. I like apple **pie**.

452. The **bone** appeared broken.

453. My **minister** is not from here.

454. He **bent** the tent pole.

455. **Shake** hands.

456. His **wound** was not serious.

457. This is a difficult **circumstance**.

458. I don't like your **tone** of voice.

459. The **machinery** was oiled.

460. The **decline** in this industry is sad.

461. What a **noble** person she is.

462. I am **opposite** the grocery store.

463. We **depend** on your energy.

464. I **propose** we close the meeting.

465. You must **preserve** your dignity.

466. Will you **publish** my book?

467. He **arose** early this morning.

468. Work to **perfect** your swing.

469. I have a **gift** to give you.

470. The chicken **breast** was fried.

471. The winner will receive her **crown**.

472. The **judgment** went against him.

473. We will **worship** together.

474. I am **sorry** for your misfortune.

475. We said a **prayer** for them.

476. The play was **successful**.

477. The tree's **bark** was rough.

478. The **choice** is entirely yours.

479. **Stretch** your dollars.

480. He gave me his **word**.

481. They **satisfy** their customers.

482. The **flag** flew at half mast.

483. You need a sense of **proportion**.

484. The **rear** of the line was disorderly.

485. He was locked in his **cell**.

486. There was no cure for the **disease**.

487. He stood in his **shadow**.

488. We will **adopt** a child.

489. I **chose** the winner.

490. The **worker** was always on time.

491. I am **lying** down and resting.

492. I will deal from the **deck** of cards.

493. They are a **friendly** family.

494. We will **oppose** you.

495. The **holiday** season is for good times.

496. We are afraid of the **unknown**.

497. I **prefer** not to go.

498. He is considered to be a **saint**.

499. You must live in my **area**.

500. The **production** was elaborate.

501.	The player was a **giant**.	526.	We have an **opportunity** to win.
502.	**Breakfast** is my favorite meal.	527.	I will be **forever** thankful.
503.	People **beg** when they are hungry.	528.	The **university** is too big.
504.	This sets the **stage** for next week.	529.	I want to make a **statement**.
505.	This **activity** is illegal.	530.	Her **skirt** is torn.
506.	I have great **sorrow** about him.	531.	The **approach** to town is blocked.
507.	The **metal** was cold to the touch.	532.	The sand paper is **rough** to touch.
508.	They went to **hunt** deer.	533.	She **generally** is on time.
509.	My **term** of office is over.	534.	**Bread** is a basic food.
510.	We **fought** the good fight.	535.	The deck was short one **card**.
511.	I want one **dozen** cookies.	536.	We **invite** you to reply.
512.	Wear your **wool** socks.	537.	I look **awful** this morning.
513.	The **alarm** went off.	538.	He will go **anyway.**
514.	I will **fix** your car.	539.	Who will deliver the **message**?
515.	The city was in **ruin** after the war.	540.	Put a **log** in the fire.
516.	The **reader** made an informed choice.	541.	Pitch the **tent** on level ground.
517.	I stepped on his **heel**.	542.	This land is considered **holy**.
518.	The **pink** sunset lasted a short while.	543.	The first **division** moved out.
519.	I **tend** to be conservative in politics.	544.	We need more **wood** on the fire.
520.	The chief wanted to **appoint** her.	545.	On the **surface**, things were quiet.
521.	He was **shown** the door.	546.	The **firm** was having a slow year.
522.	We **depart** for Hawaii tomorrow.	547.	The **trail** was well maintained.
523.	I am a **lover** not a fighter.	548.	A **ray** of sun came in the window.
524.	You must pay off your **debt**.	549.	I **hate** beets.
525.	The **hotel** was booked solid.	550.	**Corn** on the cob is best with butter.

551. The **servant** was fired.

552. Bake a **cake** for my birthday.

553. The **chicken** factory was closed.

554. The **stranger** seemed mysterious.

555. **Northern** countries get very cold.

556. **Pack** the bags.

557. I forgot my grocery **list**.

558. The **operation** lasted five hours.

559. Let's play **hide** and seek.

560. Workers of the world **unite**.

561. We had to **separate** them.

562. This person is **evil**.

563. He is a **model** prisoner.

564. We saw a **distant** light.

565. I have a **score** to settle with you.

566. One must be **brave**.

567. What is the **content** of your speech?

568. Please **introduce** me to her.

569. I don't want to **burden** you.

570. I was **somewhat** surprised.

571. **Merry** Christmas.

572. She **nevertheless** feels she must go.

573. My arm is still **tender**.

574. The **royal** family left the castle.

575. This **district** needs more support.

576. This has been a **wonderful** day.

577. The **tribe** had a feast.

578. This is my **final** offer.

579. The **student** applied for aid.

580. What **rank** does he hold?

581. The **passenger** lost his bag.

582. Are you having some **difficulty**?

583. This accusation is **serious**.

584. Your **conduct** is outrageous.

585. The crowd let out a loud **cheer**.

586. His demand put a **strain** on us all.

587. There is **plenty** of opportunity.

588. Make a **dash** for the border.

589. Not even a **murmur** was heard.

590. **Seize** the day.

591. The **entrance** was blocked.

592. The **yellow** dress was noticed by all.

593. Please **pray** for the children.

594. Let's find some buried **treasure**.

595. Did you **apply** for the job?

596. The **string** became tangled.

597. I need some **gas**.

598. Her **brain** is bursting with ideas.

599. What a **fright** you gave me.

600. That is an **interesting** plan.

Word List B

601. Her **companion** was tall and dark.

602. **Someone** show me the door.

603. I **merely** said I thought he would.

604. The **band** played all night.

605. The lawyer filed an **appeal**.

606. Don't be **cheap**.

607. The **steel** town was in decline.

608. The **float** was readied for the parade.

609. The book was **written** in six months.

610. At **fifteen** I was living on my own.

611. The **tower** was on fire.

612. The firing **range** is crowded.

613. I **hardly** knew him.

614. May I **extend** my congratulations.

615. The **series** went to seven games.

616. The **design** won an award.

617. I want to **manufacture** parts.

618. **Stir** the soup periodically.

619. You must **push** against the door.

620. **Darkness** came to the land.

621. Did you obtain a **permit**?

622. When did all this **occur**?

623. The **entire** band contributed.

624. My **aim** is true.

625. He received a lot of **praise**.

626. There was **considerable** doubt.

627. An **apple** a day is good for you.

628. The **roar** of the lion scared us all.

629. Get in the **habit** of studying.

630. I shot the **bow**.

631. Please **excuse** us.

632. I **intend** to help out.

633. Do you **deny** your involvement?

634. The **social** worker was naive.

635. The **mere** fact is you were there.

636. The **protest** was very shrill.

637. The **temple** is full of worshipers.

638. My **pen** is out of ink.

639. The **display** was outstanding.

640. We **won** the playoff game.

641. The **automobile** was new.

642. **Maybe** next year we will go.

643. We **worry** about your safety.

644. The **railway** station was busy.

645. The **harbor** was full of ships.

646. Let's have some **fun**.

647. My **teeth** need cleaning.

648. The **patient** was cooperative.

649. What will the trial **reveal**?

650. The music was a bit **loud**.

651. We will **surround** the enemy.

652. She is **dangerous**.

653. We hopefully are making **progress**.

654. We hope to **occupy** our home soon.

655. The fire **engine** was a shining red.

656. The **bell** rang all night.

657. One must be **practical** at times.

658. Fill out the **address** form.

659. The couple made a rare **appearance**.

660. We will walk down the **avenue**.

661. This matter is of great **importance**.

662. Take a **bow** on stage.

663. The picture **frame** was attractive.

664. I am making **instant** coffee.

665. All people are created **equal**.

666. This razor gives a **smooth** shave.

667. The **merchant** had a record year.

668. **Safety** is our top concern.

669. **Ease** into this slowly.

670. **Proceed** with caution.

671. I will fix a **dish** of pasta.

672. We will **wander** all over the park.

673. He acts like a **beast**.

674. Let's put a **fence** around the yard.

675. The house comes on one **acre** of land.

676. The hand **rail** was broken.

677. **Happiness** can prove elusive.

678. I want to make a **purchase**.

679. The **senate** was in session.

680. He made a **fortune** in lumber.

681. His **charm** began to wear thin.

682. The **steam** was coming out the vent.

683. He suffered a **slight** wound.

684. That **custom** seems very outdated.

685. They had a terrible **row**.

686. This is a happy **occasion**.

687. We will **engage** in further discussion.

688. The **castle** was in shambles.

689. This engine is very **powerful**.

690. I don't want to make a **mistake**.

691. The **central** division is the weakest.

692. I have made a great **discovery**.

693. The station **wagon** is new.

694. The **effect** on us all has been hard.

695. The **horn** section was outstanding.

696. She will **insist** that you come.

697. The **commission** issued its report.

698. I can **swim**.

699. My **memory** is weak.

700. The ship will **sink** in this storm.

701. The **telephone** kept ringing.

702. I **rode** the elevator.

703. I want to be **independent**.

704. **Wake** me up when it's over.

705. I lost my **cap**.

706. I will **feed** you soon.

707. **Avoid** mistakes when you can.

708. Please be **quiet**.

709. He is a **handsome** man.

710. I will **locate** him soon.

711. He had a poor sense of **self**.

712. What is the **moral** of your story?

713. This **chapter** is the last one.

714. The rain made a **steady** sound.

715. Don't act so **superior**.

716. The **curtain** was torn.

717. The **silent** fog filled the street.

718. **Observe** how I handle this.

719. The store's shelves were **empty**.

720. The **conversation** became dull.

721. The children were **asleep**.

722. The **bush** needs trimming.

723. We must keep them **apart**.

724. Show some **respect**.

725. He gave us a **nod**.

726. I **bought** a new television.

727. You must set some kind of **limit**.

728. Clean out the **inside** of the car.

729. **Commerce** is a basic part of life.

730. The **county** is losing people.

731. The snow is about to **melt**.

732. There is no **substance** to this story.

733. You look so **angry**.

734. He is **representative** of his club.

735. It is impolite to **stare**.

736. I want to **write** a good novel.

737. My parents gave their **consent**.

738. The **feature** is about to start.

739. You have not been **forgotten**.

740. I will make a **quick** change.

741. I can **handle** this situation.

742. The **nest** is high up the tree.

743. Won't you **select** a tie for me?

744. The **leather** coat is expensive.

745. The **chamber** was empty.

746. I plan to **attend** the party.

747. The child would **tremble** in a storm.

748. The river's **current** was strong.

749. He **struck** the man a blow.

750. The dog did not **obey** his master.

751. The plant will **employ** ten people.

752. I gave her a **diamond**.

753. I will **pour** the milk.

754. I have a lot of **concern** about that.

755. I am a **creature** of habit.

756. The **reserve** force was held back.

757. The **plane** was one hour late.

758. I reached the **bottom** of the barrel.

759. The **motor** was running smoothly.

760. The **information** is new to me.

761. The chair is **comfortable**.

762. I need to rake the **yard**.

763. I **meant** what I said.

764. They **admire** his honesty.

765. The **team** was ready to play.

766. Her **passion** for her job was real.

767. Sometimes you have to go on **faith**.

768. He made minimum **wage**.

769. How did you **determine** that?

770. She is my **favorite**.

771. The **committee** agreed.

772. We had another **quarrel**.

773. The blade is **sharp**.

774. **Pile** your dirty clothes at the washer.

775. I **seldom** go out anymore.

776. One **parent** stayed home.

777. The pilot determined his **longitude**.

778. We will win for the **sake** of our coach.

779. That person can be a **bore**.

780. Aren't you a little **curious**?

781. **Tonight** is a big night.

782. I **urge** you to reconsider.

783. He created an **empire**.

784. The **experiment** was a failure.

785. **Potato** chips are fattening.

786. Let me **describe** the situation.

787. I want to **announce** my retirement.

788. You may make one **request**.

789. The **pupil** was tardy.

790. He opened another **bottle**.

791. I like her **style**.

792. We will **inform** you of the results.

793. **Comfort** is important.

794. The team stayed **ahead**.

795. What is the **meaning** of that word.

796. The **worst** is finally over.

797. Would you like **tea** or coffee?

798. We were in a state of **shock**.

799. We will **furnish** you everything.

800. The **volume** of traffic is heavy.

Word List C

1. We will **abandon** the ship.
2. **Dip** the brush in the paint.
3. I took a **shower** after the game.
4. **Upward** mobility is good.
5. I am not **guilty.**
6. The **pillow** was soft.
7. He is an **honorable** man.
8. The **liquid** spilled on the floor.
9. The ceiling **beam** is not smooth.
10. **Laughter** could be heard.
11. She **absolutely** refuses to attend.
12. My **stomach** is growling.
13. He has great **musical** talent.
14. I bet **heavily** on the game.
15. My **vacation** was incredible.
16. We will start a **file** on you.
17. The **priest** said mass.
18. I will **attach** tape to that.
19. Did I **scare** you?
20. The **ghost** appeared each Friday.
21. I like to eat **raw** oysters.
22. We must **resolve** the situation.
23. You **inspire** me.
24. The **chase** began in two cars.
25. I feel **silly** in this outfit.

26. The crowd had tremendous **energy.**
27. The **crow** made a shrill cry.
28. The musician has great **ability.**
29. Our **mayor** has lost many votes.
30. I do not go **duck** hunting.
31. The **harvest** was better than before.
32. She wore an eye **patch.**
33. The **federal** army won the war.
34. **Ambition** is necessary to succeed.
35. I live in a large **province.**
36. We **sadly** said our goodbyes.
37. The **blaze** was out of control.
38. The **rabbit** ate from my garden.
39. The **highway** is about to open.
40. They will **condemn** the building.
41. The **Catholic** church is growing.
42. The **prohibition** was lifted.
43. He had an **ax** to grind.
44. He **stole** the show.
45. They stormed the **fort.**
46. We can fix it **properly.**
47. I leave next **week.**
48. I was unable to **contact** him.
49. The **crew** was close to mutiny.
50. I cannot make an **exception.**

51. The **atmosphere** is polluted.
52. He **wheeled** in during the storm.
53. He **gently** held the child.
54. I need to buy a **ruler.**
55. He has a good **reputation.**
56. He stepped on the **insect.**
57. The **corporation** went bankrupt.
58. He sent a **signal** to his players.
59. Superman always wears a **cape.**
60. The **criminal** was put in jail.
61. She is the **conscience** of her people.
62. The sailor's **mate** went on leave.
63. That **drum** is very loud.
64. The **international** student graduated.
65. Give yourself a **pat** on the back.
66. He would not let his **grief** show.
67. **Altogether** now.
68. This weapon is for my **protection.**
69. The **spoon** fell onto the floor.
70. The **idle** men were unemployed.
71. He forgot his fishing **rod.**
72. The **hidden** camera worked.
73. I can only draw one **conclusion.**
74. How may I **contribute**?
75. The fast **lane** was crowded.

76. He lit a **candle** in her memory.
77. The **stocking** needed mending.
78. His **muscle** was aching.
79. He took a **savage** beating.
80. That was an **unusual** call.
81. His **instrument** was stolen.
82. You must have **exact** change.
83. My **associate** will assist you.
84. **Toss** the ball to me.
85. That child is a **genius.**
86. I am **sure** that I saw you.
87. The **republic** was in danger.
88. The woman was **innocent.**
89. His only **vice** is overeating.
90. Please **refer** to your manual.
91. I am **unable** to help you.
92. The **blade** cuts both ways.
93. It is a **thrill** to see you.
94. His violence caused **terror.**
95. We already gave **ours** away.
96. He made an **imprint** of the drawing.
97. May I help you, **madam**?
98. The horse was in the **pasture.**
99. I **instantly** liked her.
100. You must show more **patience.**

Word List C

101. The **prospect** was not pleasing.

102. My **toe** is killing me.

103. The **blank** paper was torn.

104. He heard a **sob** from the child.

105. The **oxen** pulled the sled.

106. She was unable to **conceal** it.

107. The morning **dew** was everywhere.

108. He is gentle as a **lamb.**

109. This is a grave **consequence.**

110. You seem **stiff** today.

111. The **mud** made the walk nasty.

112. She took me to the **opera.**

113. He has **universal** appeal.

114. **Pin** the tale on the donkey.

115. The **eternal** flame burned.

116. How may I **assist** you?

117. My shirt is dripping **wet.**

118. Please be **generous** this year.

119. The **tiger** roamed the jungle.

120. I took my car to the **repair** shop.

121. The **inhabitant** of the house left.

122. We were treated **equally.**

123. The **customer** was satisfied.

124. I **deserve** to succeed.

125. He **crept** up on us.

126. She lost her **temper.**

127. The **pond** had lots of fish.

128. The **driver** was pulled over.

129. He made a good **observation.**

130. My **partner** went to the bank.

131. He wore a **feather** in his hat.

132. We must **operate** immediately.

133. The **sheriff** took out his gun.

134. We heard a **groan.**

135. The **pig** was their pet.

136. The **estate** sale was Saturday.

137. The **herd** began to stampede.

138. I will **compose** a response.

139. We must **endure** difficulty.

140. She wore a **lace** dress.

141. His **instruction** was clear.

142. The teacher had a **stern** gaze.

143. The **mouse** ran into the hole.

144. We will **plow** the field.

145. You look **unhappy.**

146. She had lots of **nerve.**

147. The **estimate** was a bit high.

148. Throw the **dart** to the board.

149. **Afterward** we decided to leave.

150. This **generation** is full of hope.

151.	He offered a **wealth** of experience.	176.	The **constitution** was approved.
152.	I must **renew** my license.	177.	I am in a **bind** over this situation.
153.	The **industrial** giant kept growing.	178.	The baby started to **crawl.**
154.	I am very **fond** of her.	179.	The animal was very **swift.**
155.	Can you drive a **shift** ?	180.	The **assembly** line was moving.
156.	The **emperor** was all powerful.	181.	I like to **bathe** everyday.
157.	Don't **frighten** the children.	182.	The **garment** was torn.
158.	I heard a **tap** at the window.	183.	I will be **absent** tomorrow.
159.	The **reign** of terror finally ended.	184.	Our **civilization** is at risk.
160.	The snow **drift** was shoulder high.	185.	**Independence** is important to him.
161.	We live on **planet** Earth.	186.	The horse ate **hay.**
162.	Let's sit in the front **parlor.**	187.	The soldier raised his **shield.**
163.	The **feast** went on for days.	188.	The **fever** kept rising.
164.	The **bedroom** needed cleaning.	189.	Sometimes he acts **crazy.**
165.	You must show **proof** of age.	190.	I have a lot of **sympathy** for her.
166.	They made a dramatic **capture.**	191.	There is no **satisfaction** in losing.
167.	The dog may **bite.**	192.	I **dread** the first day of school.
168.	She gave him a **robe.**	193.	The **weed** grew everywhere.
169.	The **hen** made a loud cry.	194.	Please **pardon** my ignorance.
170.	Don't **complain** about the food.	195.	The **fastening** on the belt snapped.
171.	The **financial** district was hectic.	196.	She is a great **champion.**
172.	I like to **knit** my own clothes.	197.	The **project** was canceled.
173.	The **elder** sister was excited.	198.	The **barn** caught fire.
174.	He cut the **stem** of the flower.	199.	The **bishop** retired.
175.	The **sunlight** poured into the room.	200.	I **vow** not to quit.

201. Put the **jar** on the counter.

202. He will not **commit**.

203. Hit the **hammer**.

204. The **kitten** was tiny.

205. The **feathered** bird flew away.

206. I will **steer** away from the boulder.

207. He received a **mortal** wound.

208. The **sacred** painting was restored.

209. He grabbed her by the **collar**.

210. The man decided to **quit**.

211. Your cooperation is **essential**.

212. We will **assemble** the toy.

213. The **carriage** left the garage.

214. The **funeral** procession was long.

215. I eagerly **await** your reply.

216. The **remedy** is sleep and rest.

217. Her **income** jumped in size.

218. Our **wedding** was very small.

219. She took a **tumble**.

220. The **photograph** was cherished.

221. He is a **rival** of mine.

222. We must **organize** our neighborhood.

223. The **stable** hand quit his job.

224. The lines are now **drawn**.

225. He was **rude** to her.

226. My **papa** was very kind.

227. She left her **purse** in the car.

228. The **copper** wire was taken.

229. Our figures **project** a large profit.

230. They have a **capable** group.

231. Happy **birthday**.

232. The **roast** was served for dinner.

233. The **marble** statue was moved.

234. They made a **commercial**.

235. What is your **intention**?

236. That was a **striking** example.

237. The **deer** continued to graze.

238. They have a great **tradition**.

239. **Moreover** I will sue if you don't.

240. I want to learn to **spell**.

241. I would like a **twist** of lemon.

242. The **robin** chirped.

243. We found the **error**.

244. He is **ashamed** of his behavior.

245. We must **hasten** our efforts.

246. The Christmas **fund** was empty.

247. The animal left his **cage**.

248. We had a **remarkable** performance.

249. We rolled down the **incline**.

250. The **maiden** in distress called out.

251. The **shepherd** tended his flock.

252. I will **instruct** the new students.

253. The plane **crash** shocked the city.

254. We were **swept** up in the party.

255. The hammer is a common **tool.**

256. My **drain** is clogged.

257. **Somehow** we will find a way.

258. He tried to read my **palm.**

259. **Farewell** my good and true friends.

260. He led us with **dignity.**

261. She has a **severe** cold.

262. I need to go in for a **physical.**

263. I have lost my **button.**

264. We must learn to **forgive** others.

265. The **arrow** went through the flesh.

266. I have no **comment.**

267. Let's go out for **lunch.**

268. He learned to **kick** in karate class.

269. The **decision** was not an easy one.

270. The **beginning** was the best part.

271. We built a **monument** to her.

272. The **tin** can was kicked.

273. I kept whistling the **tune.**

274. He mumbled the **phrase.**

275. The soldier stood **erect.**

276. The **ash** got on the rug.

277. The **destruction** was extensive.

278. Our **function** is to help others.

279. **Eleven** players took the field.

280. We hope to **relieve** them.

281. We got a home **improvement** loan.

282. The **olive** tree grows in Greece.

283. The tools were kept in the **shed.**

284. The **loan** officer was nasty.

285. **Crack** is a dangerous drug.

286. **Sweep** the floor before leaving.

287. We **welcome** you home.

288. The **pearl** divers took great risks.

289. The **thunder** shook the house.

290. Guess what's in my **package.**

291. The **fan** felt great on the skin.

292. This watermelon is **enormous.**

293. The **program** started late.

294. We will **descend** into the gorge.

295. Never **betray** your friends.

296. She took a **risk** to see him.

297. The **toy** was not made well.

298. The **commander** issued the order.

299. I finished my **novel.**

300. I am very **keen** to meet him.

301. The story was planned to **deceive.**

302. The **agriculture** department closed.

303. Don't **mock** me.

304. We **grieve** this loss.

305. He won a black **belt.**

306. In the **meantime** we must wait.

307. **Swallow** the chips carefully.

308. On what **basis** did you decide?

309. I **encourage** you to apply.

310. I like **frozen** drinks.

311. He was **definite** about his choice.

312. The prisoner obtained his **release.**

313. I **perceive** you to be hostile.

314. The lawyer will **plead** the case.

315. The man can **sew** like a master.

316. The children suffered **neglect.**

317. You offer me wise **counsel.**

318. The balcony sometimes would **sway.**

319. I **advise** you to forget all about it.

320. Look for the **dot.**

321. I am too **warm.**

322. He will **scream** when he wins.

323. The **faithful** kept coming.

324. They developed a far **flung** empire.

325. She is a **professional.**

326. They **embrace** when they meet.

327. I can **bend** this rod.

328. I love **ripe** tomatoes.

329. The **register** malfunctioned.

330. The **combination** was hard to beat.

331. My **rug** needs cleaning.

332. The **jury** took a long time.

333. The **decoy** wore sun glasses.

334. The **bean** salad was spicy.

335. The **mixture** is a company secret.

336. You must **accustom** yourself to this.

337. The **tube** was almost empty.

338. My **philosophy** is to do your best.

339. I will trim the **hedge.**

340. He got a quick **glimpse** of her.

341. The **film** lasted two hours.

342. The **frost** nipped at our toes.

343. The **bureau** was moved.

344. The **scheme** was discovered.

345. She makes a bad **impression**

346. **Reading** is my favorite subject.

347. They arrived in **triumph.**

348. The changes were **permanent.**

349. The **conference** lasted two days.

350. The cat **sprang** at the squirrel.

351. The art **collection** is priceless.

352. He bought a **domestic** car.

353. I will travel **abroad** next year.

354. He put a yoke on the **ox.**

355. His **introduction** was short.

356. We must make **haste.**

357. I **proclaim** today to be a holiday.

358. The **notion** was a strange one.

359. The **bench** was made of wood.

360. She aimed her **rifle** at the target.

361. He **sang** a sweet song.

362. The **column** of soldiers moved out.

363. The man was in a **rage.**

364. The **junior** officer was popular.

365. We must **govern** with compassion.

366. The **cave** was dark and dank.

367. The **mistress** of the house was gone.

368. She **bade** him farewell.

369. Her **trunk** weighed a ton.

370. I will **persuade** her to change.

371. The **invitation** was for tomorrow.

372. The **arrest** was unexpected.

373. The alpine **meadow** was beautiful.

374. There is **merit** in your argument.

375. We had a **bunch** of people over.

376. The **statue** was made in Toledo.

377. The **import** market is growing.

378. I am **running** in the marathon.

379. **Seventy** people came.

380. The **literary** magazine sold out.

381. The **correspondent** reported.

382. I **suspect** that they already know.

383. The **device** was an original.

384. She wanted a **doll** house.

385. The **audience** went wild.

386. The **owl** hooted all night.

387. The power **failure** was massive.

388. I don't want to **interrupt** you.

389. It is a **privilege** to know you.

390. I love clean **linen.**

391. He is sometimes **foolish.**

392. We **regret** we cannot attend.

393. His **armor** did not protect him.

394. We all need **luck** at times.

395. Would you **rub** my back?

396. Orange **juice** is a healthy drink.

397. He is a **darling** child.

398. The location is **convenient** to me.

399. The **missing** children were found.

400. He gave her **candy** as a gift.

401. I didn't mean to **excite** you.

402. She has a great **personality.**

403. The **manager** was friendly.

404. The **arrangement** worked for all.

405. The **insurance** company lost money.

406. I am a **frequent** flyer.

407. The **bad** dog was punished.

408. We will go **towards** the center.

409. You have a great **imagination.**

410. All the **bases** were covered.

411. The **sentence** was much too wordy.

412. The **liquor** store was closed.

413. The **director** hired some extras.

414. The **survey** was finally over.

415. The **contest** ended in a draw.

416. Their **doctrine** is now obsolete.

417. I will buy one **bushel** of apples.

418. We shall **overcome.**

419. The light will **fade** away.

420. The **magic** show was sold out.

421. She acted like a **princess.**

422. Her **instinct** to flee was strong.

423. That **belief** is inaccurate.

424. We must **rid** ourselves of that.

425. They would **toil** all day in the field.

426. Her **explanation** was not enough.

427. They had a **solid** defense.

428. The **joke** was on me.

429. She is a **damsel** in distress.

430. I **differ** in my opinion.

431. The **mirror** was broken.

432. Please show some **consideration.**

433. That was **characteristic** of him.

434. He **ribbed** her mercilessly.

435. She is one **bold** person.

436. This will **enable** us to go on.

437. Do not **disturb** the peace.

438. The **freight** train kept rolling.

439. His **brow** was wrinkled.

440. The had a bumper **wheat** crop.

441. The **image** lives in the mind.

442. The pants are too **tight.**

443. They provided **security** for us.

444. She is **thirteen** today.

445. The **equipment** was delivered late.

446. The **supreme** command surrendered.

447. Do not give in to **despair.**

448. **Divine** grace guides our lives.

449. The **visitor** didn't give his name.

450. I always wanted a **pony.**

451. We must **factor** in all the variables.

452. Her **occupation** is about to change.

453. We felt the **blast** this far away.

454. There is little **literature** about it.

455. He **beheld** an incredible vision.

456. The **rice** paddy is green.

457. Do not **weep** for me.

458. The **coach** blew his whistle.

459. The king sat on his **throne**.

460. I want to **join** the army.

461. He called her a **dame**.

462. My class has only one **male**.

463. Coal is a **mineral**.

464. I made a **deposit** in the bank.

465. We will **trim** the tree.

466. They will **perish** in this cold.

467. He took the **plunge** into the water.

468. She will **arise** early.

469. You seem **nervous** today.

470. We had a hard **freeze**.

471. The scientist is **brilliant**.

472. The **agency** was closed.

473. I want to **illustrate** my point.

474. The arrow is an ancient **weapon**.

475. I give it my **seal** of approval.

476. One **penny** won't buy much.

477. The great Oz has **spoken**.

478. We rolled the **barrel** over.

479. He flew off the **cliff**.

480. I heard the twig **snap**.

481. I have a **vision**.

482. I can **relate** to that statement.

483. You have an **extreme** case of the flu.

484. The **platform** was full of bags.

485. We left the **previous** day.

486. I cannot quite **grasp** the handle.

487. He finally received his **discharge**.

488. She won the blue **ribbon**.

489. I want to **acquire** some real estate.

490. The **climate** here is ideal.

491. The young man left on a **voyage**.

492. The **jewel** was not worth much.

493. The **damage** was extensive.

494. They **fled** the fire.

495. She has a **mild** disposition.

496. The handle **grip** was torn.

497. You need **treatment** for that cut.

498. His **performance** was outstanding.

499. Let's pause and **reflect** for a moment.

500. The **argument** got much louder.

Word List C

501. He kept a **pigeon** as a pet.

502. The boy turned **fourteen** today.

503. The **bride** was radiant.

504. The head master was **cruel.**

505. The **shirt** was freshly starched.

506. I have **absolute** faith in you.

507. The **screen** door was open.

508. He wore an artificial **limb.**

509. There is garbage **heap** outside.

510. We will **summon** him to appear.

511. The storm is very **fierce.**

512. She was a damsel in **distress.**

513. The **violet** looked beautiful.

514. We all are **alike** in our hearts.

515. His progress was **extraordinary.**

516. We put **rat** poison in the basement.

517. Justice will **prevail.**

518. Next year I will be in **grade** five.

519. It was the store's grand **opening.**

520. The car became **stuck** in the mud.

521. We entered through the **arch.**

522. The path was **rocky.**

523. She is **delightful** company.

524. He wore his **jeans** to the concert.

525. Her **dad** is late.

526. He blew into his **handkerchief.**

527. Who can hear in the **midst** of this?

528. They were **fed** lunch.

529. That town is a speed **trap.**

530. I go to the park and **skate.**

531. I need a **saddle** for my horse.

532. Don't **argue** with him.

533. May I **quote** you?

534. The soda **fountain** was crowded.

535. The **brick** house sold fast.

536. Put some **cash** in your pocket.

537. Your place is **ideal.**

538. I was not **aware** of that.

539. The **annual** game was canceled.

540. The water **lily** was in bloom.

541. I will **invent** a better mouse trap.

542. Do you have a **suggestion**?

543. We walked through the **grove.**

544. You will **distinguish** yourself.

545. The tomato **vine** is dying.

546. The **staff** had a meeting.

547. I want **extra** cheese.

548. The **timber** company hired me.

549. Let's **pretend** we didn't know.

550. My **gown** needs to be altered.

551. Plug in the **cord.**

552. His **rib** cage is bruised.

553. What is the seating **capacity** here?

554. You are too **clever** for your own good.

555. Her **waist** is slim.

556. I feel simply **marvelous.**

557. We **mostly** just talked.

558. The **interior** designer arrived.

559. The **messenger** delivered it.

560. We are **grateful** to you.

561. The **traffic** was intense.

562. The general ordered a **retreat.**

563. The **emotion** in the room was strong.

564. We went to a fishing **lodge.**

565. They settled their **dispute.**

566. I forgot to **remind** you.

567. The **brass** band was popular.

568. Those colors make a good **contrast.**

569. The **hut** stood abandoned.

570. The irrigation **canal** was blocked.

571. Try not to **scratch** your wound.

572. The **lightning** hit the tree.

573. Her **majesty** received the guests.

574. We will **submit** to a court of law.

575. That is a very **rare** coin.

576. He has a **distinct** accent.

577. The **victim** sued the company.

578. The **torn** pillow was thrown out.

579. To what **extent** will you commit?

580. Let's visit **sometime** this year.

581. The tire's **pressure** was low.

582. They never solved that **mystery.**

583. The light soon grew **dim.**

584. No **reward** was offered.

585. I will **construct** a house for you.

586. The **clay** soil was not good for plants.

587. The **slope** was used for sledding.

588. He put an **ornament** on his dash.

589. That is one dangerous **curve.**

590. The **luxury** ship was full.

591. You have a lot of **responsibility.**

592. We heard an **echo.**

593. He had a **relative** visit him.

594. I will sharpen my **pencil.**

595. **Tobacco** is not good for you.

596. I do not **approve** of this behavior

597. I lather myself with **soap.**

598. **Formerly** she was a student.

599. Don't **bother** with the details.

600. The **flock** flew away.

601.	His **hunger** was obvious.	626.	**Peer** pressure is strong.
602.	The patient was not **conscious.**	627.	This runs **contrary** to the law.
603.	That boy **scout** is very polite.	628.	He filled out an **application** form.
604.	Go **lightly** on the butter.	629.	We will **pursue** him.
605.	This coat was a real **bargain.**	630.	Hold the **fork** properly.
606.	I will go **anywhere** for a job.	631.	I would like to **borrow** some money.
607.	The **chimney** was built of stone.	632.	We will **endeavor** to do our best.
608.	I want a **slice** of pizza.	633.	His **humor** was very sarcastic.
609.	**Fasten** your seat belt.	634.	The **delicate** butterfly flew away.
610.	The **western** province was lost.	635.	He had **scorn** in his voice.
611.	Don't **expose** us to your cold.	636.	The **lieutenant** saluted the captain.
612.	The **tide** swept in to the shore.	637.	This story's **plot** is confusing.
613.	We will make **preparation** for her.	638.	The **structure** is still solid.
614.	Your **goodness** is refreshing.	639.	Our **neighborhood** threw a party.
615.	Let me **entertain** you.	640.	You must **dispose** of your trash.
616.	The law **review** was published.	641.	She memorized the **verse.**
617.	His **description** was accurate.	642.	He had great **affection** for his dog.
618.	She showed him great **kindness.**	643.	Would you like to sit in my **lap**?
619.	The water **slide** was fun.	644.	Her arm was **weak** from disuse.
620.	I want to enter **politics.**	645.	Bad news will **precede** you.
621.	It is not polite to **curse.**	646.	I lost my **glove.**
622.	I don't want to **oblige** myself.	647.	Be a leader not a **follower.**
623.	The judge showed **mercy.**	648.	The **stove** was red hot.
624.	They had a brief **encounter.**	649.	I want to join the **navy.**
625.	I am, **alas,** unable to help you.	650.	**Purple** is not my favorite color.

651.	I don't want to **involve** you in this.	676.	Her **absence** was sorely missed.
652.	I'll **starve** before I eat that.	677.	Don't **preach** what you don't do.
653.	I like the girl with the **curl.**	678.	The **glorious** sunshine appeared.
654.	**Pitch** me the ball.	679.	I hate **poison** ivy.
655.	He belongs in the **mental** ward.	680.	Someday I will **retire.**
656.	The **eagle** is a predator.	681.	My dog will **fetch** my paper.
657.	Your **beard** needs trimming.	682.	There is a **chill** in the air.
658.	He has a **peculiar** attitude.	683.	The **slender** woman jogged daily.
659.	**Acid** rain destroys vegetation.	684.	The ship **sank** in minutes.
660.	The **apartment** was tiny.	685.	**Curiosity** killed the cat.
661.	That food will **attract** bugs.	686.	The **rapid** advance surprised us all.
662.	**Hell** is a hot place.	687.	You must take your **medicine.**
663.	This **boot** is tight.	688.	She is too **eager** for her own good.
664.	How can I **finance** this purchase?	689.	I keep a lot of junk in the **cellar.**
665.	The wolf would **howl** at night.	690.	The **peasant** worked constantly.
666.	**Eighteen** is a great age.	691.	Everyone look **lively.**
667.	The **scientific** journal was dull.	692.	Put some **cheese** on the sandwich.
668.	We do this **lest** we forget.	693.	My clothes are **dirty.**
669.	He was **reckless** in his ways.	694.	He put a needle in his **vein.**
670.	They did not pick me in the **draft.**	695.	Be careful not to **drown** in the surf.
671.	The **physician** ordered more tests.	696.	**Hail** to the chief.
672.	Let's sit down and **discuss** this.	697.	The **host** was warm to all present.
673.	The **venture** turned into a disaster.	698.	He failed to make his **connection.**
674.	I love to take a hot **bath.**	699.	The trail was **steep** in places.
675.	The **expert** testified in court.	700.	Would you be able to **lend** us aid?

701. Place the groceries in the **sack.**

702. He put **straw** on the floor.

703. I like to work a **puzzle** occasionally.

704. Please don't **hesitate** to ask for help.

705. The jacket was made of **velvet.**

706. My **career** is in transition.

707. The mountain **expedition** failed.

708. **Autumn** is my favorite season.

709. Put the **pot** on the stove to boil.

710. The **globe** is a round sphere.

711. We had an **interval** between class.

712. I want to **retain** my credit.

713. She is **lonely** and depressed.

714. The **chest** wound was fatal.

715. His **skill** was truly remarkable.

716. The **spy** was shot.

717. She has found a **cure.**

718. The **rubber** plantation was large.

719. They need **medical** help.

720. People are **dying** from starvation.

721. I hope I can **convince** you.

722. Their **arrival** was a total surprise.

723. He put the **canoe** into the water.

724. The **ant** carried a piece of food.

725. He acted **purely** from greed.

726. All **mankind** is linked together.

727. The woman began to **boast.**

728. Her great **intelligence** was obvious.

729. The man told his story of **horror.**

730. I have great **confusion** about it.

731. The **cottage** was solid and secure.

732. Each **layer** adds more warmth.

733. Throw the **spear** with caution.

734. An **angel** appeared on high.

735. We made no **provision** for them.

736. **Sixty** people attended the festival.

737. How much do you **weigh?**

738. The **continent** is vast.

739. His **existence** was never proven.

740. One **female** cried out for help.

741. There is a slight **possibility** of rain.

742. All that **glitters** is not gold.

743. The painting is **magnificent.**

744. I hope to **restore** my good name.

745. The **institution** was insolvent.

746. The **cherry** tree was cut down.

747. Sometimes you must **assert** yourself.

748. A **ton** equals 2,000 pounds.

749. I will **cultivate** roses.

750. I have a **solution** for the problem.

751. **Meanwhile** we must wait.

752. We **dwell** in a quiet neighborhood.

753. Take a shovel and help **dig.**

754. He ordered split **pea** soup.

755. You must make **constant** effort.

756. I will **creep** up on them.

757. You must accept your **punishment.**

758. The **organ** is related to the piano.

759. The **blossom** of the flower fell.

760. Put the **lumber** in a neat pile.

761. Who can do the kangaroo **hop**?

762. We will solve the **conflict.**

763. He turned the **wheel** slowly.

764. The **lawyer** was very slick.

765. May I **acquaint** you with the facts.

766. The woman was **stout.**

767. The **naked** baby started to cry.

768. He put the **needle** in his arm.

769. The woman wore a **veil.**

770. He is **desperate** to succeed.

771. The **executive** was promoted.

772. We will divide and **conquer.**

773. The **pool** looks inviting.

774. We walked the **ridge** for hours.

775. I find his answer **odd.**

776. You are **responsible** for your actions.

777. The **museum** is open every day.

778. His **invention** changed the world.

779. The **reform** school was harsh.

780. The whistle **blew** occasionally.

781. The machine will **crush** the can.

782. What is the **thrust** of the argument?

783. I **truly** want to participate.

784. He made a **dumb** remark.

785. The **engineer** studied the problem.

786. My **payment** was made on time.

787. He tried to measure the **depth.**

788. He always had an **angle** to work.

789. We don't want to **punish** anyone.

790. He **pointed** his finger at me.

791. The **bloom** of that cactus is red.

792. I like tomato **soup.**

793. He caught the fish with a **hook.**

794. I **confess** that I am guilty.

795. They made an **agreement.**

796. He likes to work on his **lawn.**

797. We all sometimes are **weary.**

798. You walk with a **stoop.**

799. The man tried to **rob** us.

800. She scratched her **forehead.**

Word List A Answer Key

1. a
   2

2. vi-1-s̲it
   2̲ 1

3. p̲e̲a̲ce
   4

4. l̲o̲w̲
   4

5. end
   1

6. la-1-dy̲
   2 2

7. sil-2-v̲e̲r
   1   5

8. from
   1

9. ex-1̲-am-2-pl̲e̲
   1   1   7

10. bed
    1

11. hill
    1

12. in
    1

13. a̲r̲t
    5

14. I
    2

15. sat
    1

16. prin̲c̲e̲
    1

17. m̲o̲u̲th
    6

18. prac-2-ti̲c̲e̲
    1   1

19. him
    1

20. fir̲s̲t
    5

21. s̲h̲ip
    1

22. was̲
    8

23. add
    1

24. h̲o̲r̲se
    5

25. a̲r̲-1-ti-1-cl̲e̲
    5   2   7

26. en-2-t̲e̲r
    1   5

27. hi̲s̲
    1

28. c̲h̲air
    4

29. b̲o̲a̲t
    4

30. spik̲e̲
    3

31. sto̲c̲k̲
    1

32. put
    8

33. dar̲e̲
    3

34. se-1-v̲e̲r-3-al
    2̲   5   8

35. his-2-t̲o̲r̲-3-y̲
    1   5   2

36. but-2-t̲e̲r
    1   5

37. siz̲e̲
    3

38. t̲h̲o̲u̲-1-s̲and
    6   1

39. al-2-so
    8   2

40. mor̲e̲
    3

41. dif-2-f̲e̲r-3-en̲c̲e̲
    1   5   1

42. pe-1-ri-3-od
    2   2̲   1

43. r̲o̲o̲f
    6

44. c̲a̲r̲
    5

45. did
    1

46. felt
    1

47. com-2-pa-1-ny̲
    1   2   2

48. de-1-p̲a̲r̲t-2-ment
    2   5   1

49. ac-2-c̲ept
    1   1

50. mo-1-ne̲y̲
    2̲   4

51. c̲o̲u̲nt
    6

52. liv̲e̲
    3

53. stra̲i̲g̲ht
    4

54. ca̲t̲c̲h
    1

55. job
    1

56. kept
    1

57. t̲h̲is
    1

58. co-1-l̲o̲r̲
    2̲   5

59. ba-1-by̲
    2   2

60. and
    1

61. ac-2-c̲o̲r̲-1-din̲g̲
    1   5   1

62. a-1-lon̲g̲
    2   1

63. ve-1-ry̲
    2̲   2

64. f̲e̲a̲r
    4

65. w̲h̲o
    8

66. tr̲i̲e̲d̲
    4

67. n̲e̲w̲s̲
    6

68. left
    1

69. com̲e̲
    3̲

240

70. line
    3

71. kill
    1

72. three
    4

73. com-2-mon
    1   1

74. ad-2-vance
    1   1

75. ten
    1

76. ei-1-ther
    4   5

77. de-1-stroy
    2 ⌣ 6

78. sta-1-tion
    2   1

79. ci-1-ty
    2   2

80. pro-1-du-1-cer
    2   2   5

81. be-1-tween
    2 ⌣ 4

82. per-1-son
    5   1

83. share
    3

84. sort
    5

85. rule
    3

86. lie
    4

87. pret-2-ty
    x   2

88. bat-2-tle
    1   7

89. lift
    1

90. food
    6

91. came
    3

92. hole
    3

93. grew
    6

94. ho-1-nor
    2   5

95. gen-2-tle-1-man
    1   7   1

96. we
    2

97. sweet
    4

98. fact
    1

99. ex-2-cept
    1   1

100. con-2-ti-1-nue
     1   2   4

101. her-1-self
     5   1

102. leave
     4

103. if
     1

104. side
     3

105. starred
     5

106. at-2-ten-2-tion
     1   1   1

107. mile
     3

108. her
     5

109. ra-1-ther
     2   5

110. found
     6

111. cot-2-ton
     1   1

112. check
     1

113. knew
     6

114. cloud
     6

115. late
     3

116. take
     3

117. cast
     1

118. free
     4

119. ge-1-ner-3-al
     2   5   8

120. sup-2-ply
     1   2

121. lis-2-ten
     1   ~1

122. un-2-der-1-stand
     1   5   ⌣1

123. best
     1

124. hu-1-man
     2   1

125. let
     1

126. gone
     3

127. hun-2-dred
     1   1

128. rest
     1

129. tree
     4

130. mor-1-ning
     5   1

131. ex-2-press
     1   1

132. whom
     x 8

133. so-1-ci-3-e-1-ty
     2   2   2   2

134. stor-3-y
     5   2

135. warm
     5

136. sub-2-ject
     1   1

137. hard
     5

138. men
     1

139. class
     1

140. find
     <u>1</u>

141. be-1-hind
     2   <u>1</u>

142. <u>cir</u>-1-c<u>le</u>
     5   7

143. s<u>lee</u>p
     4

144. hot
     1

145. pass
     1

146. want
     8

147. stran<u>ge</u>
     3

148. be-3-<u>ing</u>
     2   1

149. su<u>g</u>-2-gest
     1   1

150. d<u>ai</u>-1-l<u>y</u>
     4   2

151. pl<u>ea</u>-1-<u>s</u>ant
     6   1

152. f<u>or</u>-1-w<u>ar</u>d
     5   5

153. in-2-t<u>er</u>-3-est
     1   5   1

154. run
     1

155. f<u>orce</u>
     5

156. sys-2-tem
     1   1

157. r<u>ea</u>d
     4

158. w<u>ea</u>r
     6

159. in-2-clu<u>de</u>
     1   3

160. no-1-ti<u>ce</u>
     2   1

161. can-2-not
     1   1

162. gi<u>v e</u>
     1

163. pic-2-tur<u>e</u>
     1   3

164. lo<u>ng</u>
     1

165. <u>k</u>n<u>igh</u>t
     4

166. o-1-<u>ther</u>
     <u>2</u>   5

167. i-1-de-3-a
     2   2   8

168. to-1-ge-1-<u>ther</u>
     8   <u>2</u>   5

169. co-1-l<u>or</u>-3-<u>ing</u>
     2   5   1

170. tall
     8

171. s<u>qua</u>re
     3

172. m u<u>ch</u>
     1

173. <u>sh</u>op
     1

174. smil<u>e</u>
     3

175. men-2-<u>tio</u>n
     1   1

176. un-2-d<u>er</u>
     1   5

177. <u>oi</u>l
     6

178. be-1-gan
     2   1

179. it
     1

180. wa<u>v e</u>
     3

181. de-1-<u>c</u>id<u>e</u>
     2   3

182. e-1-ne-1-m<u>y</u>
     <u>2</u>   2   <u>2</u>

183. lak<u>e</u>
     3

184. held
     1

185. t<u>ear</u>
     6

186. dis-2-tan<u>ce</u>
     1   1

187. six
     1

188. tell
     1

189. fa<u>ce</u>
     3

190. ta-1-ken
     2   1

191. trip
     1

192. r<u>ai</u>l-2-r<u>oa</u>d
     4   4

193. set
     1

194. to-1-w<u>ar</u>d
     8   5

195. n<u>ow</u>
     6

196. h<u>ur</u>t
     5

197. w<u>ay</u>
     4

198. <u>ar</u>-1-m<u>y</u>
     5   2

199. a-1-lon<u>e</u>
     2   3

200. pos-2-si-1-b<u>le</u>
     1   <u>2</u>   7

201. clo<u>s e</u>
     3

202. t<u>ea</u>-1-<u>cher</u>
     4   5

203. ne-1-<u>c</u>es-2-sa-1-r<u>y</u>
     <u>2</u>   1   2   2

204. ri<u>ng</u>
     1

205. ha<u>ng</u>
     1

206. re-1-c<u>or</u>d
     <u>2</u>   5

207. bl<u>ue</u>
     4

208. ea̲ch
     4

209. e-1-ve̲r-3-y̲
     2̲   5   2

210. ho̲w
     6

211. ea̲r-1-ly̲
     5   2

212. pla̲y
     4

213. be
     2

214. co-1-mi̲ng
     2̲ 1

215. fi-1-s̲h̲ing
     2̲ 1

216. dre̲am
     4

217. of-2-ten
     1 1

218. la̲y
     4

219. e-1-ven
     2 1

220. rid̲e
     3

221. num-2-be̲r
     1 5

222. w̲h̲at-1-e-1-ve̲r
     8   2̲   5

223. lo̲rd
     5

224. mad̲e
     3

225. clot̲h̲es̲
     3

226. be-1-cam̲e
     2 3

227. im-2-po̲r-1-tant
     1   5   1

228. cas̲e
     3

229. let-2-te̲r
     1 5

230. m o̲v̲e
     8

231. da̲y̲
     4

232. ho̲use
     6

233. fell
     1

234. be-1-cau̲s̲e
     2   6

235. mo-1-t̲h̲er
     2̲   5

236. club
     1

237. a-1-ro̲und
     2   6

238. grass
     1

239. twen-2-ty̲
     1   2

240. af-2-te̲r
     1   5

241. hea̲r
     4

242. no̲r
     5

243. t̲h̲ou̲gh
     4

244. ac-2-cou̲n̲t
     1   6

245. voi̲ce
     6

246. goo̲d
     6

247. si̲r
     5

248. clai̲m
     4

249. bro̲wn
     6

250. sell
     1

251. a-1-mo̲unt
     2   6

252. ho̲ur
     ~ 6

253. rol-2-li̲ng
     1̲ 1

254. dea̲r
     4

255. ai̲r
     4

256. coo̲l
     6

257. nei̲gh-1-bo̲r
     6   5

258. t̲h̲em-2-selve̲s̲
     1   3̲

259. tro̲u-1-bl̲e
     6   7

260. du̲e̲
     4

261. nar-2-ro̲w
     1   4

262. ri̲ght
     4

263. bad
     1

264. pa-1-pe̲r
     2   5

265. c̲h̲ief̲
     6

266. com-2-mand
     1   1

267. miss
     1

268. see̲m
     4

269. wind
     1

270. t̲h̲ere
     3̲

271. pi̲c̲k
     1

272. to̲o
     6

273. dat̲e
     3

274. t̲h̲an̲k
     1

275. m o̲y̲
     4

276. fo̲r-3-est
     5   1

277. n o
2
278. gr<u>ay</u>
4
279. no-1-<u>thing</u>
2   1
280. dr<u>aw</u>
6
281. m<u>ar</u>ch
5
282. cros-2-sing
1   1
283. r<u>ea</u>-1-<u>so</u>n
4   1
284. her<u>e</u>
3
285. <u>sh</u>ort
5
286. t<u>hirs</u>-2-t<u>y</u>
5   2
287. sub-2-ject
1   1
288. to-1-mor-2-r<u>ow</u>
8   1   4
289. dog
1
290. si<u>ck</u>
1
291. n<u>ew</u>
6
292. bo-1-d<u>y</u>
2   2
293. is-2-land
<u>1</u>~ 1
294. old
<u>1</u>
295. els<u>e</u>
<u>3</u>
296. stro<u>ng</u>
1
297. de-1-clar<u>e</u>
2 ~3
298. on
1
299. fa-1-v<u>or</u>
2   5

300. st<u>ar</u>
5
301. go-3-ing
2   1
302. re-1-ply
2 ˘2
303. us<u>e</u>
3
304. f<u>air</u>
4
305. <u>c</u>or-1-n<u>er</u>
5   5
306. by
2
307. <u>thr</u>ew
6
308. sim-2-p<u>le</u>
1   7
309. ha<u>ve</u>
1
310. gam<u>e</u>
3
311. sent
1
312. went
1
313. m<u>ar</u>k
5
314. still
1
315. trust
1
316. in-2-dus-2-try
1   1   2
317. re-1-<u>ceive</u>
2   4
318. r<u>ou</u>nd
6
319. les-2-son
1   1
320. pro-1-p<u>er</u>
<u>2</u>   5
321. a-1-ni-1-mal
<u>2</u>   <u>2</u>   8
322. f<u>igh</u>t
4

323. wild
<u>1</u>
324. b<u>oa</u>rd
4
325. di-1-rect
2   1
326. <u>ow</u>n
4
327. gr<u>ea</u>t
x
328. red
1
329. r<u>ea</u>d
6
330. dis-2-cuss
1   1
331. tr<u>ai</u>n
4
332. <u>c</u>en-2-t<u>er</u>
1   5
333. d<u>ee</u>p
4
334. pre-1-<u>si</u>-1-dent
<u>2</u>   <u>2</u>   1
335. na-1-<u>tio</u>n
2   1
336. hap-2-pen
1   1
337. next
1
338. le<u>ngth</u>
1
339. <u>sh</u>or<u>e</u>
3
340. di-1-vid<u>e</u>
<u>2</u>   3
341. re-1-m<u>ai</u>n
2   4
342. up
1
343. mo-1-ment
2   1
344. s<u>ui</u>t
4
345. fre<u>sh</u>
1

346. be-1-<u>low</u>
    2   4
	369. wa<u>tch</u>
	    8
		392. dry
		    2

347. o-1-pen
    2 1
	370. <u>s</u><u>oi</u>l
	    6
		393. nam<u>e</u>
		    3

348. <u>third</u>
    5
	371. <u>p</u>a<u>th</u>
	    1
		394. go-1-v<u>e</u>rn-2-ment
		    <u>2</u> 5 1

349. co-1-l<u>ored</u>
    <u>2</u> 5
	372. <u>th</u>em
	    1
		395. man
		    1

350. fa-1-m<u>ou</u>s
    2   6
	373. fu-1-tur<u>e</u>
	    2 3
		396. f<u>ee</u>l
		    4

351. wast<u>e</u>
    3
	374. but
	    1
		397. n<u>ee</u>d
		    4

352. car<u>e</u>
    3
	375. p<u>ai</u>nt
	    4
		398. <u>ou</u>t-2-side
		    6 3

353. con-2-duct
    1   1
	376. <u>wh</u>en
	    1
		399. st<u>oo</u>d
		    6

354. str<u>ee</u>t
    4
	377. n<u>or</u>-1-mal
	    5 8
		400. spr<u>ea</u>d
		    6

355. f<u>ur</u>-1-<u>th</u>er
    5   5
	378. fen<u>ce</u>
	    1
		401. a-1-fr<u>ai</u>d
		    2 ˘4

356. ra<u>c</u><u>e</u>
    3
	379. w<u>e</u>r<u>e</u>
	    5
		402. <u>ch</u>ild
		    <u>1</u>

357. j<u>oy</u>
    6
	380. hold
	    <u>1</u>
		403. <u>qu</u><u>ee</u>n
		    4

358. front
    1
	381. bro-1-<u>th</u>er
	    <u>2</u> 5
		404. si-1-len<u>ce</u>
		    2 1

359. of-2-f<u>er</u> 1 5	382. ga-1-<u>th</u>er <u>2</u> 5	405. ne-1-v<u>er</u> <u>2</u> 5

360. <u>ch</u>il-2-dren
    1   1
	383. un-2-less
	    1 1
		406. not
		    1

361. l<u>ea</u>d
    4
	384. al-2-<u>low</u>
	    1 6
		407. n<u>os</u><u>e</u>
		    3

362. ex-2-pl<u>ai</u>n
    1   4
	385. fol-2-<u>low</u>
	    1 4
		408. mas-2-t<u>er</u>
		    1 5

363. till
    1
	386. sign
	    <u>1</u>
		409. l<u>ea</u>st
		    4

364. <u>sh</u><u>ou</u>t
    6
	387. h<u>ai</u>r
	    4
		410. <u>kn</u>o<u>ck</u>
		    1

365. stu-1-d<u>y</u>
    <u>2</u>   2
	388. b<u>or</u>n
	    5
		411. of-2-fi<u>ce</u>
		    1 1

366. pro-1-vid<u>e</u>
    2   3
	389. in-2-struct
	    1 1
		412. all
		    8

367. cap-2-t<u>ai</u>n
    1   4
	390. f<u>ew</u>
	    6
		413. step
		    1

368. f<u>ai</u>l
    4
	391. e-1-v<u>er</u>-3-<u>y</u>-1-<u>thing</u>
	    <u>2</u> 5 <u>2</u> 1
		414. do
		    8

415. f__o__rm
    5

416. sti__ck__
    1

417. con-2-di-1-__tio__n
    1   2   1

418. spi-1-rit
    2   1

419. driv__e__
    3

420. dan__ce__
    1

421. __sh__ap__e__
    3

422. sens__e__
    __3__

423. p__ay__
    4

424. u__n__-2-c__le__
    1   7

425. ro__ck__
    1

426. us
    1

427. lif__e__
    3

428. m e
    2

429. fil-2-lin__g__
    1   1

430. spra__ng__
    1

431. af-2-t__er__-1-n__oo__n
    1   5   6

432. bl__ow__
    4

433. ma-1-n__y__
    2   2

434. plan
    1

435. a-1-cross
    2 ~ 1

436. b__ir__d
    5

437. roll
    __1__

438. __b__eat
    4

439. cut
    1

440. not__e__
    3

441. __th__ink
    1

442. n__ear__
    4

443. gr__ou__nd
    6

444. sold
    __1__

445. pl__ai__n
    4

446. west
    1

447. tir__e__d
    3

448. ri-1-din__g__
    2   1

449. an
    1

450. cross
    1

451. su__ch__
    1

452. ta-1-b__le__
    2   7

453. col-2-leg__e__
    1   1

454. t__ea__ch
    4

455. wid__e__
    3

456. walk
    8~

457. k__ee__p
    4

458. gr__ow__l
    6

459. cost
    1

460. dol-2-l__ar__
    1   5

461. told
    __1__

462. t__ie__
    4

463. met
    1

464. __th__en
    1

465. s__ee__
    4

466. fi-1-ni__sh__ed
    2   1

467. re-1-__qu__ire
    2   3

468. sum-2-m__er__
    1   5

469. full
    8

470. be-1-com__e__
    2   __3__

471. st__or__m
    5

472. __or__
    5

473. ex-1-__er__-1-c__i__s__e__
    1   5   3

474. sp__ea__k
    4

475. h__ur__-1-r__y__
    5   2

476. f__or__-1-m__er__
    5   5

477. pip__e__
    3

478. br__ea__k
    x

479. p__oi__nt
    6

480. son
    1

481. press
    1

482. __ea__t
    4

483. ty-3-in__g__
    2   1

484. sh<u>ow</u>
       4

485. pre-1-s<u>e</u>nt
       <u>2</u> 1

486. dr<u>u</u>g
       1

487. r<u>ea</u>ch
       4

488. be-1-sid<u>e</u>
       2 3

489. p<u>oo</u>r
       6

490. fa-1-<u>the</u>r
       8   5

491. t<u>o</u>
       8

492. b<u>oy</u>
       6

493. win
       1

494. fa-1-v<u>ored</u>
       2 5

495. a-1-no-1-<u>the</u>r
       2 <u>2</u> 5

496. dis-2-co-1-v<u>er</u>
       1 <u>2</u> 5

497. r<u>oa</u>d
       4

498. fa-1-mi-1-l<u>y</u>
       <u>2</u> <u>2</u> <u>2</u>

499. mi<u>gh</u>t
       4

500. l<u>ea</u>-1-d<u>er</u>
       4   5

501. m<u>o</u><u>th</u>
       1

502. l<u>ea</u>d
       6

503. car-2-r<u>y</u>
       1   2

504. fi-1-ni<u>sh</u>
       <u>2</u> 1

505. de-1-s<u>ire</u>
       2   3

506. t<u>oo</u>k
       6

507. l<u>a</u>nd
       1

508. cr<u>ay</u>-3-on
       4   1

509. b<u>ea</u>r
       6

510. sn<u>ow</u>
       4

511. <u>wh</u>ole
       3

512. h<u>e</u>
       2

513. r<u>ai</u>s<u>e</u>
       4

514. <u>c</u>er-1-t<u>ai</u>n
       5   4

515. a-1-b<u>o</u>v<u>e</u>
       2 1

516. fif-2-t<u>y</u>
       1   2

517. br<u>igh</u>t
       4

518. sud-2-den
       1   1

519. m<u>oo</u>n
       6

520. fi<u>sh</u>
       1

521. cl<u>ea</u>r
       4

522. lik<u>e</u>
       3

523. a-1-mon<u>g</u>
       2   1

524. suf-2-f<u>er</u>
       1   5

525. pre-1-s<u>e</u>nt
       2   1

526. wa-1-t<u>er</u>
       8   5

527. some-1-tim<u>es</u>
       <u>3</u>   3

528. <u>wh</u>ere
       <u>3</u>

529. sup-2-po<u>se</u>
       1   3

530. con-2-trol
       1   <u>1</u>

531. <u>church</u>
       5

532. spend
       1

533. s<u>ee</u>k
       4

534. e<u>dg</u>e
       1

535. ru<u>sh</u>
       1

536. b<u>ea</u>-3-u-1-t<u>y</u>
       4 2 2

537. well
       1

538. gav<u>e</u>
       3

539. r<u>ea</u>l-2-l<u>y</u>
       4   2

540. led
       1

541. s<u>oo</u>n
       6

542. just
       1

543. fill
       1

544. con-2-t<u>ai</u>n
       1   4

545. but-2-ton
       1   1

546. skin
       1

547. c<u>oo</u>k
       6

548. li<u>gh</u>t
       4

549. ni<u>gh</u>t
       4

550. <u>g</u>irl
       5

551. of-2-fi-1-<u>c</u>er
       1 <u>2</u> 5

552. d<u>ea</u>d
       6

553. st**ar**t 5	576. am 1	599. fly 2
554. tast**e** 3	577. s**aw** 6	600. **ear** 4
555. ex-2-pe-1-ri-3-en**ce** 1 2 **2** 1	578. **g**uard 5	601. s**ou**th 6
556. **the** 2	579. glass 1	602. ac-2-**ti**on 1 1
557. **are** 5	580. re-1-p**or**t 2 5	603. ri**se** 3
558. be-1-li**e**v**e** 2 6	581. tru**th** 8	604. my-1-self 2 1
559. o-1-v**er** 2 5	582. **the**s**e** 3	605. doc-2-t**or** 1 5
560. **ar**m 5	583. p**ar**-1-t**y** 5 2	606. mi-1-nut**e** **2** **3**
561. pa**ge** 3	584. spa**ce** 3	607. **g**uess 1
562. l**ow**-3-**er** 4 5	585. egg 1	608. in-2-to 1 8
563. f**oo**t 6	586. mo-1-d**er**n **2** 5	609. p**ur**-1-pos**e** 5 **3**
564. ar-2-riv**e** 1 3	587. sit 1	610. drop 1
565. ill 1	588. green 4	611. m**ou**nt 6
566. **wh**ite 3	589. God 1	612. de-1-gr**ee** 2 4
567. l**ar**g**e** 5	590. camp 1	613. d**ee**r 4
568. p**ai**d 4	591. d**ar**k 5	614. m**ea**t 4
569. **the**ir 6	592. **qu**ar-1-ter 5 5	615. tra-1-vel**e**d **2** 1
570. hat 1	593. cl**ea**n 4	616. co-1-v**er** **2** 5
571. will 1	594. **qu**ite 3	617. a-1-b**ou**t 2 6
572. stri**ng** 1	595. c**au**s**e** 6	618. fel-2-l**ow** 1 4
573. d**ea**l 4	596. ha**s** 1	619. c**oa**t 4
574. strik**e** 3	597. loss 1	620. dif-2-f**er**-3-ent 1 5 1
575. **th**at 1	598. t**ur**n 5	621. sam**e** 3

622. sun 1	645. si<u>ng</u> 1	668. mid-2-d<u>le</u> 1 7
623. top 1	646. re-1-t<u>ur</u>n 2 5	669. ap-2-p<u>ear</u> 1 4
624. sav<u>e</u> 3	647. spe-1-<u>ci</u>al <u>2</u> 8	670. ball 8
625. bri<u>dge</u> 1	648. <u>th</u>an 1	671. lo<u>ve</u> 1
626. <u>thi</u>n 1	649. ni<u>ce</u> 3	672. ad-2-mit 1 1
627. pre-1-par<u>e</u> 2 3	650. be-1-n<u>ea</u><u>th</u> 2 4	673. s<u>ay</u> 4
628. ro-1-bot 2 1	651. h<u>us</u>-2-band 1 1	674. re-1-fu<u>se</u> 2 3
629. ran 1	652. <u>ou</u>n<u>ce</u> 6	675. r<u>ea</u>-1-d<u>y</u> 6 2
630. u-1-pon <u>2</u> 1	653. p<u>air</u> 4	676. most <u>1</u>
631. ask 1	654. s<u>ch</u><u>oo</u>l 6	677. leg 1
632. stat<u>e</u> 3	655. in-2-d<u>ee</u>d 1 4	678. fir<u>e</u> 3
633. lo<u>se</u> 8	656. f<u>ee</u>t 4	679. suc-2-<u>ce</u>ss 1 1
634. s<u>ur</u>-1-pri<u>se</u> 5 ˘3	657. pas-2-sage 1 3	680. <u>ce</u>nt 1
635. j<u>u</u><u>dge</u> 1	658. hall 8	681. w<u>ai</u>t 4
636. sin<u>ce</u> 1	659. <u>ou</u>t 6	682. i<u>s</u> 1
637. bri<u>ng</u> 1	660. val-2-l<u>ey</u> 1 4	683. en-2-j<u>oy</u> 1 6
638. st<u>ay</u> 4	661. s<u>ai</u>l 4	684. <u>through</u> 6
639. <u>sh</u><u>ou</u>l-2-d<u>er</u> 4 5	662. <u>sh</u>e 2	685. e-1-le-1-<u>ph</u>ant <u>2</u> <u>2</u> 1
640. to-1-d<u>ay</u> 8 4	663. <u>wh</u>at 8	686. mem-2-b<u>er</u> 1 5
641. al-2-r<u>ea</u>-1-d<u>y</u> 8 6 2	664. din-2-n<u>er</u> 1 5	687. du-1-ri<u>ng</u> 2 1
642. help 1	665. dan-2-g<u>er</u> <u>1</u> 5	688. ef-1-f<u>or</u>t 1 5
643. stop 1	666. h<u>ea</u>d 6	689. spot 1
644. hap-2-p<u>y</u> 1 2	667. n<u>ei</u>-1-<u>th</u>er 4 5	690. sup-2-p<u>or</u>t 1 5

691. af-2-fair
     1   4
692. a-1-gree
     2 ⌣ 4
693. down
     6
694. ice
     3
695. true
     4
696. milk
     1
697. be-1-fore
     2   3
698. meet
     4
699. try
     2
700. re-3-a-3-lize
     2   2   3
701. lost
     1
702. guide
     3
703. pro-1-duce
     2   3
704. sky
     2
705. store
     3
706. heat
     4
707. price
     3
708. re-1-gard
     2   5
709. those
     3
710. field
     6
711. tire
     3
712. whose
     8
713. burn
     5

714. plant
     1
715. group
     6
716. eight
     6
717. ob-2-ject
     1   1
718. for
     5
719. a-1-way
     2   4
720. be-1-gin
     2   1
721. e-1-ver
     2   5
722. last
     1
723. pain
     4
724. coun-2-try
     6   2
725. ob-2-ject
     1   1
726. gulf
     1
727. gate
     3
728. learn
     5
729. cold
     1
730. un-2-til
     1   1
731. bank
     1
732. at-2-tempt
     1   1
733. ob-2-tain
     1   4
734. nine
     3
735. spring
     1
736. fit
     1

737. thing
     1
738. re-1-sult
     2   1
739. as
     1
740. kind
     1
741. off
     1
742. while
     3
743. bro-1-ken
     2   1
744. branch
     1
745. can
     1
746. which
     1
747. vil-2-lage
     1   3
748. hope
     3
749. dress
     1
750. act
     1
751. re-1-move
     2   8
752. se-1-ven
     2   1
753. gain
     4
754. wall
     8
755. seen
     4
756. com-2-plete
     1   3
757. moun-2-tain
     6   4
758. soft
     1
759. bet-2-ter
     1   5

760. shall
1

761. real
4

762. va-1-ri-3-ous
2 2 6

763. neck
1

764. prob-2-lem
1 1

765. huge
3

766. inch
1

767. drink
1

768. health
6

769. in-2-crease
1 4

770. tear
4

771. al-2-ways
8 4

772. gi-1-ven
2 1

773. north
5

774. trade
3

775. win-2-dow
1 4

776. must
1

777. val-1-ue
1 4

778. close
3

779. flow-3-er
6 5

780. be-1-long
2 1

781. crowd
6

782. lot
1

783. ser-1-vice
5 1

784. go
2

785. a-1-ble
2 7

786. whe-1-ther
2 5

787. rate
3

788. time
3

789. look
6

790. mat-2-ter
1 5

791. sis-2-ter
1 5

792. join
6

793. fool
6

794. king
1

795. chance
1

796. la-1-bor
2 5

797. rich
1

798. less
1

799. fine
3

800. at
1

1. ac-2-c̲i̲-1-dent
     1 **2** 1

2. di-1-rect-2-ly
     2 1˘ 2

3. vic-2-t̲o̲r-3-y
     1 5 2

4. ho-1-nest
    ~**2** 1

5. pro-1-fes-2-s̲o̲r
     2 1 5

6. in-2-fl̲u̲-3-en̲c̲e
     1 **2** 1

7. m̲i̲g̲h̲-1-ty
     4 2

8. be-1-gun
    2 1

9. m̲e̲a̲l
     4

10. ac-2-tu-3-al
      1 2 8

11. tax
     1

12. p̲a̲r-1-ti-1-cu-1-l̲a̲r
      5 **2** 2 5

13. i-1-ma-1-g̲i̲n̲e̲
     2 **2** **3**

14. v̲i̲r-1-t̲u̲e̲
      5 4

15. f̲o̲u̲n-2-da-1-t̲i̲on
      6 2 1

16. re-1-call
      2 8

17. a̲u̲-1-t̲h̲o̲r-3-i-1-ty̲
      6 5 **2** 2

18. sm̲a̲r̲t
      5

19. gun
     1

20. sa-1-cri-1-fi̲c̲e̲
      2 ~**2** 3

21. s̲e̲e̲d
      4

22. l̲e̲a̲g̲u̲e̲
      4

23. c̲e̲a̲s̲e̲
      4

24. stamp
      1

25. ex-2-pen̲s̲e̲
      1 **3**

26. crop
      1

27. ac-2-com-2-pa-1-ny
      1 1 **2** 2

28. n̲u̲rs̲e̲
      5

29. e-1-lec-2-tric
      2 1 1

30. h̲o̲u̲s̲e̲-1-hold
      6   **1**

31. pos-2-s̲e̲s-2-s̲i̲o̲n
      1~ 1 1

32. f̲o̲r-1-got
      5 1

33. a̲n̲-2-g̲e̲r
      1 5

34. re-1-pre-1-s̲e̲nt
     2 ˘2 1

35. slav̲e̲
      3

36. b̲o̲r-1-d̲e̲r
      5 5

37. r̲o̲u̲te
      6

38. in-2-di-1-vi-1-du-3-a̲l̲
     1 **2** **2** 2

39. co-1-lo-1-ny
      2 **2** **2**

40. car̲e̲-1-ful
      3 8

41. re-1-gu-1-l̲a̲r
      2 2 5

42. bak̲e̲
      3

43. t̲a̲u̲g̲h̲t
      6

44. pos-2-sib-2-ly
      1 1 **2**

45. re-1-li-1-g̲i̲o̲u̲s
      2 **2** 6

46. w̲o̲u̲nd
      6

47. con-2-fi-1-den̲c̲e̲
      1 **2** 1

48. cri̲e̲d
      4

49. f̲a̲r-1-t̲h̲er
      5 5

50. a̲u̲-1-t̲h̲or
      6 5

51. y̲e̲a̲r
      4

52. g̲uest
      1

53. sim-2-pl̲y̲
      1 **2**

54. se-1-cur̲e̲
      2 3

55. l̲e̲a̲-1-d̲i̲n̲g̲
      4 1

56. c̲o̲r-1-rect
      5 1

57. st̲a̲i̲r̲s̲
      4

58. calm
      8

59. crim̲e̲
      3

60. com-2-mu-1-ni-1-ty̲
      1 2 **2** 2

61. n̲u̲-1-m̲e̲r-3-o̲u̲s
      2 5 6

62. e-1-lect
      2 1

63. l̲o̲a̲d
      4

64. pos-2-sess
      1~ 1

65. hir̲e̲
      3

66. an-2-c̲ient
      1 1

67. re-1-p̲e̲a̲t
      2 4

68. suf-2-fi-1-c̲ient
      1 **2** 1

69. j̲o̲u̲r-1-n̲e̲y̲
      5 4

70. shut
1

71. in-2-di-1-cate
1   2   3

72. ca-1-len-2-dar
2   1   5

73. con-2-tract
1   1

74. match
1

75. burst
5

76. task
1

77. pan
1

78. slow
4

79. ves-2-sel
1   1

80. li-1-ber-1-ty
2   5   2

81. fare
3

82. aunt/aunt
6   x

83. trick
1

84. growth
4

85. stuff
1

86. sec-2-tion
1   1

87. lat-2-ter
1   5

88. won-2-der
1   5

89. sai-1-lor
4   5

90. va-1-ry
2   2

91. boil
6

92. ti-1-tle
2   7

93. tick-1-et
1   1

94. pock-1-et
1   1

95. kid
1

96. nail
4

97. po-1-si-1-tion
2   2   1

98. lean
4

99. a-1-live
2   3

100. e-1-le-1-ment
2   2   1

101. treat
4

102. bond
1

103. strip
1

104. po-1-lice
2   x

105. col-2-lect
1   1

106. de-1-vil
2   1

107. mass
1

108. com-2-pare
1   3

109. tale
3

110. pale
3

111. pipe
3

112. ve-1-ge-1-ta-1-ble
2   2   2   7

113. pro-1-fit
2   1

114. fan-2-cy
1   2

115. at-2-ti-1-tude
1   2   3

116. wrong
1

117. grown
4

118. trace
3

119. se-1-cret
2   ~1

120. lan-2-guage
1   x 3

121. fac-2-tor-3-y
1   5   2

122. dawn
6

123. desk
1

124. cre-1-dit
2   1

125. thy
2

126. qua-1-li-1-ty
8   2   2

127. e-1-du-1-ca-1-tion
2   2   2   1

128. per-1-so-1-nal
5   2   8

129. por-1-tion
5   1

130. fold
1

131. pi-1-ty
2   2

132. splen-2-did
1   1

133. hol-2-low
1   4

134. pro-1-duct
2   1

135. famed
3

136. im-2-prove
1   8

137. coin
6

138. ex-1-ist
1   1

139. mar-1-ried
     1   6

140. le-1-vel
     2   1

141. tail
     4

142. pa-1-lace
     2   1

143. proud
     6

144. vast
     1

145. ad-2-ven-2-ture
     1   1   3

146. fan-2-cied
     1   6

147. de-1-fend
     2   1

148. af-2-ford
     1   5

149. greet
     4

150. worse
     5

151. search
     5

152. lamp
     1

153. fun-2-ny
     1   2

154. sport
     5

155. ex-1-a-1-mine
     1   2   3

156. glow
     4

157. throw
     4

158. sand
     1

159. e-1-di-1-tor
     2   2   5

160. pro-1-per-1-ty
     2   5   2

161. port
     5

162. flour
     6

163. be-1-neath
     2   4

164. re-1-li-1-gion
     2   2   1

165. cam-2-paign
     1   4

166. bob
     1

167. shook
     6

168. im-2-pos-2-si-1-ble
     1   1   2   7

169. cof-2-fee
     1   4

170. free-1-dom
     4   1

171. mar-2-riage
     1   1~

172. e-1-vent
     2   1

173. sword
     ~ 5

174. ter-2-ri-1-ble
     1   2   7

175. con-2-clude
     1   3

176. bless
     1

177. cream
     4

178. throat
     4

179. at-2-tack
     1   1

180. bee
     4

181. grave
     3

182. ac-2-tive
     1   1

183. cheek
     4

184. lack
     1

185. h un-2-gry
     1   2

186. spoil
     6

187. for-1-ty
     5   2

188. cre-3-ate
     2   3

189. through-3-out
     6   6

190. slip
     1

191. e-1-co-1-no-1-mic
     2   2   2   1

192. wor-1-thy
     5   2

193. porch
     5

194. flood
     x

195. cat
     1

196. re-1-lief
     2   6

197. bare
     3

198. block
     1

199. work
     5

200. love-1-ly
     1   2

201. coast
     4

202. hos-2-pi-1-tal
     1   2   8

203. map
     1

204. folk
     1~

205. swing
     1

206. pace
     3

207. si-1-tu-3-a-1-tion
     2   2   2   1

208. ci̱-1-ti-1-zen
   1 2 1

209. rope̲
   3

210. fame̲
   3

211. ate̲
   3

212. ca-1-pi-1-tal
   2 2 8

213. grand
   1

214. a-1-wake̲
   2   3

215. sci-3-ence̲
   2 1

216. knock
   1

217. wor̲th
   5

218. ut-2-ter̲
   1   5

219. pri-1-so̲n
   2 1

220. shel-2-ter̲
   1   5

221. plate̲
   3

222. sup-2-per̲
   1   5

223. ea̲-1-stern̲
   4 ⌣5

224. silk
   1

225. po-1-pu-1-la-1-tio̲n
   2 2 2 1

226. re-1-vo-1-lu̲-1-tio̲n
   2 2 2 1

227. co-1-py̲
   2 2

228. re-1-la-1-tio̲n
   2 2 1

229. bin
   1

230. blind
   1

231. shi̲ne
   3

232. noi̲se̲
   6

233. clo̲th
   1

234. li-3-on
   2 1

235. tem-2-per̲-3-a-1-ture̲
   1   5 2 3

236. de-1-li-1-ver̲
   2 2 5

237. un-2-der̲-1-stoo̲d
   1   5 ⌣6

238. ow̲-1-ner̲
   4   5

239. suc-2-ceed̲
   1   4

240. val-1̲-u-3-a-1-ble̲
   1 2 2 7

241. shoot̲
   6

242. false̲
   8

243. as-2-sure̲
   1 x 3

244. h ung
   1

245. grace̲
   3

246. bru̲sh
   1

247. scat-2-ter̲
   1   5

248. king-2-dom
   1   1

249. net
   1

250. spite̲
   3

251. les-2-son
   1   1

252. co̲w̲
   6

253. thr̲ea̲-1-ten
   6   1

254. tri-3-al
   2 8

255. ea̲-1-si̲-1-ly̲
   4 2 2

256. strug-2-gle̲
   1   7

257. po-1-pu-1-lar̲
   2 2 5

258. fli̲ght
   4

259. dif-2-fi-1-cult
   1 2 1

260. spare̲
   3

261. prize̲
   3

262. broo̲k
   6

263. fur̲-1-ni-1-ture̲
   5 2 3

264. as-2-so-1-ci-3-a-1-tio̲n
   1 2 2 2 1

265. close̲-1-ly̲
   3   2

266. m ur̲-1-der̲
   5   5

267. ma-1-nage̲
   2 3

268. de-1-li̲ght
   2 4

269. be-1-ne-1-fit
   2 2 1

270. owe̲
   4

271. tra-1-ve-1-ler̲
   2 2 5

272. vai̲n
   4

273. pri-1-vate̲
   2 3

274. fal-2-len
   8   1

275. as-2-su̲me̲
   1   3

276. de-1-ve-1-lop
   2 2 1

277. go-1-v<u>er</u>-1-n<u>or</u>
    <u>2</u>   5   5

278. e-1-v<u>er</u>-3-y-1-bo-1-dy
    <u>2</u>   5   <u>2</u>   <u>2</u>   2

279. scar<u>ce</u>-1-l<u>y</u>
     3   2

280. kind-2-l<u>y</u>
    <u>1</u>~   2

281. pin<u>e</u>
   3

282. spent
   1

283. mix
   1

284. c<u>ou</u>-1-<u>si</u>n
    6   1

285. <u>thr</u>ead
    6

286. <u>wr</u>i-1-t<u>er</u>
    2   5

287. p<u>ow</u>-1-d<u>er</u>
    6   5

288. to-1-tal
   2   8

289. po-1-li-1-ti-1-cal
   2 <u>2</u>   <u>2</u>   8

290. fl<u>ew</u>
   6

291. ex-2-pres-2-<u>si</u>on
   1   1   1

292. re-1-<u>gi</u>on
   2   1

293. de-1-<u>ser</u>t
   <u>2</u>   5

294. blam<u>e</u>
    3

295. <u>sh</u>ell
   1

296. twi<u>ce</u>
   3

297. clo<u>ck</u>
   1

298. p<u>er</u>-1-f<u>or</u>m
   5   5

299. ma-1-<u>jor</u>-3-i-1-ty
   <u>2</u>   5   <u>2</u>   2

300. de-1-l<u>ay</u>
   2   4

301. <u>ai</u>d
   4

302. <u>our</u>-2-selv<u>es</u>
   6   <u>3</u>

303. hit
   1

304. bid
   1

305. <u>oa</u>k
   4

306. <u>th</u>e-3-<u>or</u>-3-y
    2   5   2

307. b<u>ea</u>ch
    4

308. ex-2-cu<u>se</u>
   1   3

309. go<u>es</u>
    4

310. de-1-mo-1-cra-1-tic
   2   2   ~<u>2</u> 1

311. scal<u>e</u>
   3

312. pre-1-<u>ci</u>o<u>us</u>
    <u>2</u>   6

313. pro-1-tect
   2   1

314. sp<u>ee</u>d
    4

315. p<u>au</u><u>se</u>
    6

316. c<u>our</u>-3-a<u>ge</u>
   5   3

317. <u>th</u>i<u>ck</u>
   1

318. ad-2-vi<u>ce</u>
   1   3

319. <u>ear</u>n
   5

320. w<u>or</u>n
   5

321. som<u>e</u>-1-<u>wh</u>ere
    <u>3</u>   <u>3</u>

322. stan-2-d<u>ar</u>d
   1   5

323. ful-2-l<u>y</u>
   8   2

324. re-1-du<u>ce</u>
   2   3

325. e-1-vi-1-den<u>ce</u>
   <u>2</u>   <u>2</u>   1

326. bit-2-t<u>er</u>
   1   5

327. <u>sh</u>eet
   4

328. sa-1-la-1-r<u>y</u>
   <u>2</u>   <u>2</u>   2

329. climb
   <u>1</u> ~

330. si-1-mi-1-l<u>ar</u>
   <u>2</u>   <u>2</u>   5

331. ma-1-<u>jor</u>
   2   5

332. de-1-fen<u>se</u>
   2   <u>3</u>

333. be-1-hold
   2   <u>1</u>

334. o-1-<u>th</u>er-1-wi<u>se</u>
   <u>2</u>   5   3

335. ad-2-di-1-<u>ti</u>on
   1   <u>2</u>   1

336. u-1-<u>su</u>-3-al
   2   <u>2</u>   8

337. print
   1

338. im-2-me-1-di-3-at<u>e</u>
   1   2   <u>2</u> <u>3</u>

339. had
   1

340. f<u>our</u><u>th</u>
   4

341. <u>g</u>oat
   4

342. br<u>oa</u>d
   x

343. smell
   1

344. k<u>ey</u>
   4

345. sad
   1

346. up-2-p<u>er</u>
    1   5

347. pre-1-vent
      2   1

348. com-2-bin<u>e</u>
    1   3

349. sum
    1

350. <u>ci</u>-1-vil
    <u>2</u>   1

351. dust
    1

352. ac-2-com-2-pli<u>sh</u>
    1   1   1

353. pol<u>e</u>
    3

354. fl<u>ee</u>t
    4

355. h<u>uge</u>
    3

356. re-1-co-1-v<u>er</u>
    2   <u>2</u>   5

357. p<u>er</u>-1-fect
    5   1

358. b<u>ir</u><u>th</u>
    5

359. <u>sh</u><u>ee</u>p
    4

360. slept
    1

361. cl<u>er</u>k
    5

362. r<u>ow</u>
    4

363. m<u>ai</u>n
    4

364. h<u>ar</u>m
    5

365. cast
    1

366. <u>or</u>-3-i-1-gi-1-nal
    5   <u>2</u> <u>2</u>   8

367. ba-1-lan<u>ce</u>
    <u>2</u>   1

368. us<u>e</u>-1-ful
    3   8

369. prin-2-<u>ci</u>-1-p<u>le</u>
    1   <u>2</u>   7

370. l<u>oo</u>se
    6

371. pat-2-t<u>er</u>n
    1   5

372. ho-1-n<u>ey</u>
      <u>2</u>   4

373. of-2-fi-1-<u>ci</u>al
    1   <u>2</u> 8

374. br<u>ief</u>
    6

375. swell
    1

376. jus-2-ti-1-fy
    1 <u>2</u> 2

377. sin
    1

378. s<u>ou</u>-1-<u>th</u><u>er</u>n
    6   5

379. mill
    1

380. c<u>ou</u>n-2-<u>ci</u>l
    6   1

381. <u>the</u>-3-a-1-t<u>er</u>
    2 2   5

382. de-1-ve-1-lop-2-ment
    2 <u>2</u> 1   1

383. d<u>uke</u>
    <u>3</u>

384. a-1-v<u>er</u>-3-ag<u>e</u>
    <u>2</u> 5   3

385. po-3-et
    2 1

386. flat
    1

387. lo-1-cal
    2   8

388. re-1-cog-2-niz<u>e</u>
    <u>2</u> 1   3

389. mid-2-n<u>igh</u>t
    1   4

390. f<u>ur</u>
    5

391. sal<u>e</u>
    3

392. ar-2-ran<u>g</u>e
    1   3

393. mo-1-<u>tio</u>n
    2   1

394. s<u>igh</u>
    4

395. ma-1-ga-1-zin<u>e</u>
     <u>2</u> <u>2</u>   x

396. de-1-f<u>ea</u>t
    2   4

397. con-2-ven-2-<u>tio</u>n
    1   1   1

398. <u>or</u>-1-ga-1-ni-1-za-1-<u>tio</u>n
    <u>5</u> <u>2</u> <u>2</u> 2   1

399. bu-1-r<u>y</u>
    x   <u>2</u>

400. fa-1-<u>sh</u>i<u>o</u>n
    <u>2</u>   ~1

401. prid<u>e</u>
    3

402. no-1-bo-1-d<u>y</u>
    2 <u>2</u> <u>2</u>

403. <u>ar</u>-1-tist
    5   1

404. lik<u>e</u>-1-l<u>y</u>
    3   <u>2</u>

405. gl<u>or</u>-3-<u>y</u>
    5   <u>2</u>

406. br<u>ea</u><u>the</u>
    4

407. tr<u>oo</u>p
    6

408. jus-2-ti<u>ce</u>
    1   1

409. bas-2-ket
    1   1

410. s<u>our</u><u>ce</u>
    4

411. mi-1-li-1-ta-1-r<u>y</u>
     <u>2</u> <u>2</u> <u>2</u> <u>2</u>

412. di-1-sap-2-p<u>ear</u>
    <u>2</u> 1   4

413. test
    1

414. con-2-nect
    1   1

415. dro<u>ve</u>
3

416. brok<u>e</u>
3

417. po-3-em
2 1

418. fla<u>sh</u>
1

419. ne-1-<u>c</u>es-2-si-1-t<u>y</u>
<u>2</u> 1 <u>2</u> 2

420. re-1-<u>c</u>ent
2 1

421. <u>l</u>eap
4

422. be-1-sid<u>es</u>
2 3

423. <u>sh</u>a<u>me</u>
3

424. tr<u>ea</u>-1-t<u>y</u>
4 2

425. fen-2-<u>c</u>ing
1 1

426. strok<u>e</u>
3

427. mad
1

428. d<u>ee</u>d
4

429. de-1-vot<u>e</u>
2 3

430. <u>or</u>-3-ange
5 1

431. com-2-pel
1 1

432. cat-2-t<u>le</u>
1 7

433. set-2-t<u>le</u>-1-ment
1 7 1

434. b<u>ou</u>nd
6

435. ex-2-<u>ch</u>ange
1 3

436. drag
1

437. glan<u>ce</u>
1

438. br<u>ea</u><u>th</u>
6

439. <u>wr</u>ot<u>e</u>
3

440. jump
1

441. tra<u>ck</u>
1

442. s<u>ou</u><u>gh</u>t
6

443. ti-1-n<u>y</u>
2 2

444. f<u>ai</u>nt
4

445. ter-2-ri-1-t<u>or</u>-3-y
1 <u>2</u> 5 2

446. de-1-t<u>ai</u>l
2 4

447. dr<u>ew</u>
6

448. wor<u>e</u>
3

449. <u>qu</u>an-2-ti-1-t<u>y</u>
8 <u>2</u> 2

450. flam<u>e</u>
3

451. p<u>ie</u>
4

452. bon<u>e</u>
3

453. mi-1-nis-2-t<u>er</u>
<u>2</u> 1 5

454. bent
1

455. <u>sh</u>ak<u>e</u>
3

456. w<u>ou</u>nd
6

457. c<u>i</u>r-1-cum-2-stan<u>ce</u>
5 1 1

458. ton<u>e</u>
3

459. ma-1-<u>chi</u>-1-n<u>er</u>-3-y
<u>2</u> x 5 2

460. de-1-clin<u>e</u>
2 3

461. no-1-b<u>le</u>
2 7

462. op-2-po-1-site
1 2 <u>3</u>

463. de-1-pend
2 1

464. pro-1-po<u>se</u>
2 3

465. pre-1-s<u>erv</u>e
2 5

466. pub-2-li<u>sh</u>
1 1

467. a-1-ro<u>se</u>
2 3

468. p<u>er</u>-1-fect
5 1

469. gift
1

470. br<u>ea</u>st
6

471. cr<u>ow</u>n
6

472. ju<u>dg</u>-2-ment
1 1

473. w<u>or</u>-1-<u>sh</u>ip
5 1

474. s<u>or</u>-1-r<u>y</u>
x 2

475. pr<u>ay</u>-3-<u>er</u>
4 5

476. suc-2-<u>c</u>ess-2-ful
1 1 8

477. b<u>ar</u>k
5

478. <u>ch</u>o<u>ice</u>
6

479. stre<u>tch</u>
1

480. w<u>or</u>d
5

481. sa-1-tis-2-fy
<u>2</u> 1 2

482. flag
1

483. pro-1-p<u>or</u>-1-<u>ti</u>on
2 5 1

484. rear 4	507. me-1-tal 2 8	530. skirt 5
485. cell 1	508. hunt 1	531. ap-2-proach 1 4
486. di-1-sease 2 4	509. term 5	532. rough 6
487. sha-1-dow 2 4	510. fought 6	533. ge-1-ner-3-al-2-ly 2 5 8 2
488. a-1-dopt 2 1	511. do-1-zen 2 1	534. bread 6
489. chose 3	512. wool 6	535. card 5
490. wor-1-ker 5 5	513. a-1-larm 2 5	536. in-2-vite 1 3
491. ly-3-ing 2 1	514. fix 1	537. aw-1-ful 6 8
492. deck 1	515. ru-3-in 2 1	538. a-1-ny-1-way 2 2 4
493. friend-2-ly x ˘ 2	516. rea-1-der 4 5	539. mes-2-sage 1 3
494. op-2-pose 1 3	517. heel 4	540. log 1
495. ho-1-li-1-day 2 2 4	518. pink 1	541. tent 1
496. un-2-known 1 4	519. tend 1	542. ho-1-ly 2 2
497. pre-1-fer 2 5	520. ap-2-point 1 6	543. di-1-vi-1-sion 2 2 1
498. saint 4	521. shown 4	544. wood 6
499. a-1-re-3-a 2 2 8	522. de-1-part 2 5	545. sur-1-face 5 1
500. pro-1-duc-2-tion 2 1 1	523. lo-1-ver 2 5	546. firm 5
501. gi-3-ant 2 1	524. debt 1~	547. trail 4
502. break-2-fast 6 1	525. ho-1-tel 2 1	548. ray 4
503. beg 1	526. op-2-por-1-tu-1-ni-1-ty 1 5 2 2 2	549. hate 3
504. stage 3	527. for-3-e-1-ver 5 2 5	550. corn 5
505. ac-2-ti-1-vi-1-ty 1 2 2 2	528. u-1-ni-1-ver-1-si-1-ty 2 2 5 2 2	551. ser-1-vant 5 1
506. sor-1-row x 4	529. state-1-ment 3 1	552. cake 3

553. <u>chi</u>c<u>k</u>-1-en
    1   1

554. stran-2-g<u>er</u>
    <u>1</u>   5

555. n<u>or</u>-1-<u>th</u>ern
    5   5

556. pa<u>ck</u>
    1

557. list
    1

558. o-1-p<u>er</u>-3-a-1-<u>tio</u>n
    <u>2</u>   5   2   1

559. hid<u>e</u>
    3

560. u-1-nit<u>e</u>
    2   3

561. se-1-p<u>ar</u>-3-at<u>e</u>
    <u>2</u>   5   3

562. e-1-vil
    2   1

563. mo-1-del
    <u>2</u>   1

564. dis-2-tant
    1   1

565. sc<u>ore</u>
    3

566. brav<u>e</u>
    3

567. con-2-tent
    1   1

568. in-2-tro-1-du<u>ce</u>
    1   2   <u>3</u>

569. b<u>ur</u>-1-den
    5   1

570. som<u>e</u>-1-<u>wh</u>at
    <u>3</u>   8

571. mer-2-r<u>y</u>
    1   <u>2</u>

572. ne-1-v<u>er</u>-1-<u>th</u>e-1-less
    <u>2</u>   5   2   1

573. ten-2-d<u>er</u>
    1   5

574. r<u>oy</u>-3-al
    6   8

575. dis-2-trict
    1   1

576. won-2-d<u>er</u>-1-ful
    1   5   8

577. trib<u>e</u>
    3

578. fi-1-nal
    2   8

579. st<u>u</u>-1-dent
    2   1

580. ra<u>nk</u>
    1

581. pas-2-sen-2-g<u>er</u>
    1   1   5

582. dif-2-fi-1-cul-2-t<u>y</u>
    1   <u>2</u>   1   2

583. se-1-ri-3-<u>ou</u>s
    2   <u>2</u>   6

584. con-2-duct
    1   1

585. <u>ch</u>eer
    4

586. str<u>ai</u>n
    4

587. plen-2-t<u>y</u>
    1   <u>2</u>

588. da<u>sh</u>
    1

589. m<u>ur</u>-1-m<u>ur</u>
    5   5

590. s<u>eize</u>
    4

591. en-2-tran<u>ce</u>
    1   1

592. yel-2-l<u>ow</u>
    1   4

593. pr<u>ay</u>
    4

594. tr<u>ea</u>-1-<u>su</u>r<u>e</u>
    6   3

595. ap-2-pl<u>y</u>
    1   2

596. string
    1

597. gas
    1

598. br<u>ai</u>n
    4

599. fr<u>igh</u>t
    4

600. in-2-t<u>er</u>-3-es-2-tin<u>g</u>
    1   5   1   1

601. com-2-pa-1-nion
    1   <u>2</u>   x1

602. som<u>e</u>-3-one
    <u>3</u>   x3

603. mer<u>e</u>-1-l<u>y</u>
    3   2

604. band
    1

605. ap-2-p<u>eal</u>
    1   4

606. <u>ch</u>eap
    4

607. st<u>ee</u>l
    4

608. fl<u>oa</u>t
    4

609. <u>wr</u>it-2-ten
    1   1

610. fif-2-t<u>ee</u>n
    1   4

611. t<u>ow</u>-3-<u>er</u>
    6   5

612. ran<u>ge</u>
    3

613. h<u>ar</u>d-2-l<u>y</u>
    5   2

614. ex-2-tend
    1   1

615. se-1-ri<u>es</u>
    2   6

616. de-1-<u>si</u>gn
    2   <u>1</u>

617. ma-1-nu-1-fac-2-tur<u>e</u>
    <u>2</u>   2   1   3

618. st<u>ir</u>
    5

619. pu<u>sh</u>
    8

620. d<u>ar</u>k-2-ness
    5   1

621. p<u>er</u>-1-mit
    5   1

622. oc-2-cur 1 5	645. har-1-bor 5 5	668. safe-1-ty 3 2
623. en-2-tire 1 3	646. fun 1	669. ease 4
624. aim 4	647. teeth 4	670. pro-1-ceed 2 4
625. praise 4	648. pa-1-tient 2 1	671. dish 1
626. con-2-si-1-der-3-a-1-ble 1 2 5 2 7	649. re-1-veal 2 4	672. wan-2-der 8 5
627. ap-2-ple 1 7	650. loud 6	673. beast 4
628. roar 4	651. sur-1-round 5 6	674. fence 1
629. ha-1-bit 2 1	652. dan-2-ger-3-ous 1 5 6	675. a-1-cre 2
630. bow 4	653. pro-1-gress 2 ~1	676. rail 4
631. ex-2-cuse 1 3	654. oc-2-cu-1-py 1 2 2	677. hap-2-pi-1-ness 1 2 1
632. in-2-tend 1 1	655. en-2-gine 1 3	678. pur-1-chase 5 3
633. de-1-ny 2 2	656. bell 1	679. se-1-nate 2 3
634. so-1-cial 2 8	657. prac-2-ti-1-cal 1 2 8	680. for-1-tune 5 3
635. mere 3	658. ad-2-dress 1 1	681. charm 5
636. pro-1-test 2 1	659. ap-2-pea-1-rance 1 4 1	682. steam 4
637. tem-2-ple 1 7	660. a-1-ve-1-nue 2 2 4	683. slight 4
638. pen 1	661. im-2-por-1-tance 1 5 1	684. cus-2-tom 1 1
639. dis-2-play 1 4	662. bow 6	685. row 6
640. won x	663. frame 3	686. oc-2-ca-1-sion 1 2 1
641. au-1-to-1-mo-1-bile 6 2 2 3	664. in-2-stant 1 1	687. en-2-gage 1 3
642. may-1-be 4 2	665. e-1-qual 2 8	688. cas-2-tle 1 ~7
643. wor-1-ry 5 2	666. smooth 6	689. pow-3-er-1-ful 6 5 8
644. rail-2-way 4 4	667. mer-1-chant 5 1	690. mis-2-take 1 3

691. cen-2-tral
1   8

692. dis-2-co-1-ver-3-y
1   2   5   2

693. wa-1-gon
2   1

694. ef-2-fect
1   1

695. horn
5

696. in-2-sist
1   1

697. com-2-mis-2-sion
1   1   1

698. swim
1

699. me-1-mor-3-y
2   5   2

700. sink
1

701. te-1-le-1-phone
2   2   3

702. rode
3

703. in-2-de-1-pen-2-dent
1   2   1   1

704. wake
3

705. cap
1

706. feed
4

707. a-1-void
2   6

708. qui-3-et
2   1

709. hand-2-some
1   3

710. lo-1-cate
2   3

711. self
1

712. mor-3-al
5   8

713. chap-2-ter
1   5

714. stea-1-dy
6   2

715. su-1-pe-1-ri-3-or
2   2   2   5

716. cur-1-tain
5   4

717. si-1-lent
2   1

718. ob-2-serve
1   5

719. emp-2-ty
1   2

720. con-2-ver-1-sa-1-tion
1   5   2   1

721. a-1-sleep
2   4

722. bush
8

723. a-1-part
2   5

724. re-1-spect
2   1

725. nod
1

726. bought
6

727. li-1-mit
2   1

728. in-2-side
1   3

729. com-2-merce
1   5

730. coun-2-ty
6   2

731. melt
1

732. sub-2-stance
1   1

733. an-2-gry
1   2

734. re-1-pre-1-sen-2-ta-1-tive
2   2   1   2   1

735. stare
3

736. write
3

737. con-2-sent
1   1

738. fea-1-ture
4   3

739. for-1-got-2-ten
5   1   1

740. quick
1

741. han-2-dle
1   7

742. nest
1

743. se-1-lect
2   1

744. lea-1-ther
6   5

745. cham-2-ber
1   5

746. at-2-tend
1   1

747. trem-2-ble
1   7

748. cur-1-rent
5   1

749. struck
1

750. o-1-bey
2   6

751. em-2-ploy
1   6

752. di-3-a-1-mond
2   2   1

753. pour
4

754. con-2-cern
1   5

755. crea-1-ture
4   3

756. re-1-serve
2   5

757. plane
3

758. bot-2-tom
1   1

759. mo-1-tor
2   5

760. in-2-f<u>or</u>-1-ma-1-<u>tio</u>n
    1   5   2   1

761. com-2-f<u>or</u>-1-ta-1-b<u>le</u>
    1   5   2   7

762. y<u>ar</u>d
   5

763. m<u>ea</u>nt
   6

764. ad-2-mir<u>e</u>
  1   3

765. t<u>ea</u>m
  4

766. pas-2-<u>sio</u>n
   1   1

767. f<u>ai</u><u>th</u>
  4

768. wag<u>e</u>
  3

769. de-1-t<u>er</u>-1-min<u>e</u>
   2   5   <u>3</u>

770. fa-1-v<u>or</u>-3-it<u>e</u>
  2   5   <u>3</u>

771. com-2-mit-2-t<u>ee</u>
   1   1   4

772. <u>qu</u><u>ar</u>-1-rel
   5   1

773. <u>sh</u><u>ar</u>p
   5

774. pil<u>e</u>
  3

775. sel-2-dom
  1   1

776. pa-1-rent
  <u>2</u>   1

777. lo<u>n</u>-1-gi-1-tu<u>de</u>
   1   <u>2</u>   <u>3</u>

778. sak<u>e</u>
  3

779. bor<u>e</u>
  3

780. cu-1-ri-3-<u>ou</u>s
  2   <u>2</u>   6

781. to-1-n<u>igh</u>t
  8   4

782. <u>ur</u><u>ge</u>
  5

783. em-2-pir<u>e</u>
  1   3

784. ex-2-pe-1-ri-1-ment
  1   <u>2</u>   <u>2</u>   1

785. po-1-ta-1-to
   2   2   2

786. de-1-scrib<u>e</u>
   2   ~~3

787. an-2-n<u>ou</u><u>n</u><u>ce</u>
  1   6

788. re-1-<u>qu</u>est
  2   1

789. pu-1-pil
  2   1

790. bot-2-t<u>le</u>
   1   7

791. styl<u>e</u>
  3

792. in-2-f<u>or</u>m
  1   5

793. com-2-f<u>or</u>t
   1   5

794. a-1-h<u>ea</u>d
  2   6

795. m<u>ea</u>-1-ni<u>ng</u>
   4   1

796. w<u>or</u>st
   5

797. t<u>ea</u>
  4

798. <u>sh</u>o<u>ck</u>
   1

799. f<u>ur</u>-1-ni<u>sh</u>
  5   1

800. vol-<u>1</u>-um<u>e</u>
   1   3

1. a-1-ban-2-don
   2   1   1

2. dip
   1

3. show-3-er
   6   5

4. up-2-ward
   1   5

5. guil-2-ty
   1   2

6. pil-2-low
   1   4

7. ho-1-nor-3-a-1-ble
   ~2   5   2   7

8. li-1-quid
   2   1

9. beam
   4

10. laugh-1-ter
    x   5

11. ab-2-so-1-lute-1-ly
    1   2   3   2

12. sto-1-mach
    2   1

13. mu-1-si-1-cal
    2   2   8

14. hea-1-vi-1-ly
    6   2   2

15. va-1-ca-1-tion
    2   2   1

16. file
    3

17. priest
    6

18. at-2-tach
    1   1

19. scare
    3

20. ghost
    1

21. raw
    6

22. re-1-solve
    2   1

23. in-2-spire
    1   3

24. chase
    3

25. sil-2-ly
    1   2

26. e-1-ner-1-gy
    2   5   2

27. crow
    4

28. a-1-bi-1-li-1-ty
    2   2   2   2

29. may-3-or
    4   5

30. duck
    1

31. har-1-vest
    5   1

32. patch
    1

33. fe-1-der-3-al
    2   5   8

34. am-2-bi-1-tion
    1   2   1

35. pro-1-vince
    2   1

36. sad-2-ly
    1   2

37. blaze
    3

38. rab-2-bit
    1   1

39. high-1-way
    4   4

40. con-2-demn
    1   1   ~

41. ca-1-tho-1-lic
    2   2   1

42. pro-1-hi-1-bi-1-tion
    2   2   2   1

43. ax
    1

44. stole
    3

45. fort
    5

46. pro-1-per-1-ly
    2   5   2

47. week
    4

48. con-2-tact
    1   1

49. crew
    6

50. ex-2-cep-2-tion
    1   1   1

51. at-2-mo-1-sphere
    1   2   ~   3

52. wheeled
    4

53. gent-2-ly
    1~   2

54. ru-1-ler
    2   5

55. re-1-pu-1-ta-1-tion
    2   2   2   1

56. in-2-sect
    1   1

57. cor-1-por-3-a-1-tion
    5   5   2   1

58. sig-2-nal
    1   8

59. cape
    3

60. cri-1-mi-1-nal
    2   2   8

61. con-2-science
    1   ~   1

62. mate
    3

63. drum
    1

64. in-2-ter-1-na-1-tion-1-al
    1   5   2   1   8

65. pat
    1

66. grief
    6

67. al-2-to-1-ge-1-ther
    8   8   2   5

68. pro-1-tec-2-tion
    2   1   1

69. spoon
    6

70. i-1-d<u>le</u>
    2   7
71. rod
    1
72. hid-2-den
    1   1
73. con-2-clu-1-<u>sio</u>n
    1   2̲   1
74. con-2-tri-1-but<u>e</u>
    1   2̲   3
75. lan<u>e</u>
    3
76. can-2-d<u>le</u>
    1   7
77. sto<u>ck</u>-1-ing
    1   1
78. mus-2-<u>cle</u>
    1   7
79. sa-1-vag<u>e</u>
    2̲   1
80. un-1-u-1-su-3-al
    1   2   2   8
81. in-2-stru-1-ment
    1   ˜2   1
82. ex-<u>1</u>-act
    1   1
83. as-2-so-1-<u>ci</u>-3-ate
    1   2   2̲   3
84. toss
    1
85. <u>ge</u>-1-ni-3-us
    2   2̲   1
86. sur<u>e</u>
    x3
87. re-1-pub-2-lic
    2   1   1
88. in-2-no-1-<u>cent</u>
    1   2   1
89. v<u>ice</u>
    3
90. re-1-f<u>er</u>
    2   5
91. un-<u>1</u>-a-1-b<u>le</u>
    1   2   7
92. blad<u>e</u>
    3

93. <u>th</u>rill
    1
94. ter-2-r<u>or</u>
    1   5
95. <u>ours</u>
    6
96. im-2-print
    1   1
97. ma-1-dam
    2   1
98. pas-2-tur<u>e</u>
    1   3
99. in-2-stant-2-l<u>y</u>
    1   1˜   2
100. pa-1-<u>tie</u>n<u>ce</u>
    2   1
101. pros-2-pect
    1   1
102. t<u>oe</u>
    4
103. blan<u>k</u>
    1
104. sob
    1
105. ox-<u>1</u>-en
    1   1
106. con-2-<u>ce</u>al
    1   4
107. d<u>ew</u>
    6
108. lamb
    1   ~
109. con-2-se-1-<u>que</u>n<u>ce</u>
    1   2   1
110. stiff
    1
111. mud
    1
112. o-1-p<u>er</u>-3-a
    2̲   5   8
113. u-1-ni-1-v<u>er</u>-1-sal
    2   2̲   5   8
114. pin
    1
115. e-1-t<u>er</u>-1-nal
    2   5   8

116. as-2-sist
    1   1
117. wet
    1
118. <u>ge</u>-1-n<u>er</u>-3-<u>ous</u>
    2̲   5   6
119. ti-1-g<u>er</u>
    2   5
120. re-1-p<u>air</u>
    2   4
121. in-2-ha-1-bi-1-tant
    1   2   2̲   1
122. e-1-<u>qu</u>al-2-l<u>y</u>
    2   8   2̲
123. cus-2-to-1-m<u>er</u>
    1   2   5
124. de-1-<u>serv</u>e
    2   5
125. crept
    1
126. tem-2-p<u>er</u>
    1   5
127. pond
    1
128. dri-1-v<u>er</u>
    2   5
129. ob-2-s<u>er</u>-1-va-1-<u>tio</u>n
    1   5   2   1
130. p<u>art</u>-2-n<u>er</u>
    5   5
131. <u>fea</u>-1-<u>ther</u>
    6   5
132. o-1-p<u>er</u>-3-ate
    2̲   5   3
133. <u>she</u>-1-riff
    2̲   1
134. gr<u>oa</u>n
    4
135. pig
    1
136. es-2-tat<u>e</u>
    1   3
137. h<u>er</u>d
    5
138. com-2-po<u>se</u>
    1   3

139. en-2-dur_e_
     1   3

140. lac_e_
     3

141. in-2-struc-2-_tio_n
     1   1   1

142. st_er_n
     5

143. m_ou_se
     6

144. pl_ow_
     6

145. un-2-hap-2-p_y_
     1   1   2

146. n_er_ve
     5

147. es-2-ti-1-mat_e_
     1   2   3

148. d_ar_t
     5

149. af-2-t_er_-1-w_ar_d
     1   5   5

150. g_e_-1-n_er_-3-a-1-_tio_n
     2   5 2   1

151. w_ealth_
     6

152. re-1-n_ew_
     2   6

153. in-2-dus-2-tri-3-al
     1   1   2 8

154. fond
     1

155. _sh_ift
     1

156. em-2-p_er_-3-_or_
     1   5   5

157. fr_igh_-1-ten
     4   1

158. tap
     1

159. r_eig_n
     6

160. drift
     1

161. pla-1-net
     2   1

162. p_ar_-1-l_or_
     5   5

163. f_ea_st
     4

164. bed-2-r_oo_m
     1   6

165. pr_oo_f
     6

166. cap-2-tur_e_
     1   3

167. bit_e_
     3

168. rob_e_
     3

169. hen
     1

170. com-2-pl_ai_n
     1   4

171. fi-1-nan-2-_c_ial
     2 1   8

172. _k_nit
     1

173. el-2-d_er_
     1   5

174. stem
     1

175. sun-2-l_igh_t
     1   4

176. con-2-sti-1-t_u_-1-_tio_n
     1   2 2   1

177. bind
     1

178. cr_aw_l
     6

179. swift
     1

180. as-2-sem-2-bl_y_
     1   1   2

181. ba_the_
     3

182. g_ar_-1-ment
     5   1

183. ab-2-sent
     1   1

184. _c_i-1-vi-1-li-1-za-1-_tio_n
     2 2 2 2   1

185. in-2-de-1-pen-2-den_ce_
     1 2 1   1

186. h_ay_
     4

187. _sh_i_el_d
     6

188. fe-1-v_er_
     2   5

189. cra-1-z_y_
     2   2

190. sym-2-pa-1-_thy_
     1   2   2

191. sa-1-tis-2-fac-2-_tio_n
     2 1   1   1

192. dr_ea_d
     6

193. w_ee_d
     4

194. p_ar_-1-don
     5   1

195. fas-2-te-1-nin_g_
     1 ~2 1

196. _ch_am-2-pi-3-on
     1   2 1

197. pro-1-ject
     2   1

198. b_ar_n
     5

199. bi-1-_sh_op
     2   1

200. v_ow_
     6

201. j_ar_
     5

202. com-2-mit
     1   1

203. ham-2-m_er_
     1   5

204. kit-2-ten
     1   1

205. _fea_-1-_the_red
     6   5

206. st_ee_r
     4

207. m_or_-1-tal
     5   8

208. sa-1-cr<u>ed</u>
    2 ⁓1

209. col-2-l<u>ar</u>
    1 5

210. <u>qu</u>it
    1

211. es-2-sen-2-<u>ti</u>al
    1 1 8

212. as-2-sem-2-b<u>le</u>
    1 1   7

213. car-2-ri-3-<u>age</u>
    1 <u>2</u> 1

214. fu-1-n<u>er</u>-3-al
    2 5 8

215. a-1-w<u>ai</u>t
    2 4

216. re-1-me-1-d<u>y</u>
    <u>2</u> <u>2</u> 2

217. in-2-com<u>e</u>
    1 <u>3</u>

218. wed-2-ding
    1 1

219. tum-2-b<u>le</u>
    1   7

220. <u>ph</u>o-1-to-1-gra<u>ph</u>
    2 2 ⁓1

221. ri-1-val
    2 8

222. <u>or</u>-1-ga-1-niz<u>e</u>
    5 <u>2</u> 3

223. sta-1-b<u>le</u>
    2 7

224. dr<u>aw</u>n
    6

225. r<u>u</u>d<u>e</u>
    3

226. pa-1-pa
    8 8

227. p<u>ur</u>se
    5

228. cop-2-p<u>er</u>
    1 5

229. pro-1-ject
    <u>2</u> 1

230. ca-1-pa-1-b<u>le</u>
    2 2 7

231. b<u>ir</u><u>th</u>-2-d<u>ay</u>
    5   4

232. r<u>oa</u>st
    4

233. m<u>ar</u>-1-b<u>le</u>
    5   7

234. com-2-m<u>er</u>-1-<u>ci</u>al
    1   5   8

235. in-2-ten-2-<u>tio</u>n
    1 1 1

236. stri-1-king
    2 1

237. d<u>ee</u>r
    4

238. tra-1-di-1-<u>tio</u>n
    <u>2</u> <u>2</u> 1

239. mor<u>e</u>-3-o-1-v<u>er</u>
    3 2 5

240. spell
    1

241. twist
    1

242. ro-1-bin
    <u>2</u> 1

243. er-2-r<u>or</u>
    1 5

244. a-1-<u>sha</u>m<u>ed</u>
    2   3

245. has-2-ten
    <u>1</u> ⁓1

246. fund
    1

247. cag<u>e</u>
    3

248. re-1-m<u>ar</u>-1-ka-1-b<u>le</u>
    2 5 2 7

249. in-2-clin<u>e</u>
    1 3

250. m<u>ai</u>-1-den
    4 1

251. <u>sh</u>ep-2-h<u>er</u>d
    1 5

252. in-2-struct
    1 1

253. cra<u>sh</u>
    1

254. swept
    1

255. t<u>oo</u>l
    6

256. dr<u>ai</u>n
    4

257. som<u>e</u>-1-h<u>ow</u>
    <u>3</u>   6

258. palm
    8

259. far<u>e</u>-1-well
    3   1

260. dig-2-ni-1-t<u>y</u>
    1 <u>2</u> 2

261. se-1-ver<u>e</u>
    <u>2</u> 3

262. <u>ph</u>y-1-<u>si</u>-1-cal
    <u>2</u> <u>2</u> 8

263. but-2-ton
    1 1

264. <u>for</u>-1-gi<u>ve</u>
    5 1

265. ar-2-r<u>ow</u>
    1 4

266. com-2-ment
    1 1

267. lun<u>ch</u>
    1

268. ki<u>ck</u>
    1

269. de-1-<u>ci</u>-1-<u>si</u>on
    2 <u>2</u> 1

270. be-1-gin-2-ning
    2 1 1

271. mo-1-nu-1-ment
    <u>2</u> 2 1

272. tin
    1

273. tun<u>e</u>
    3

274. <u>ph</u>ra<u>se</u>
    3

275. e-1-rect
    2 1

276. a<u>sh</u>
    1

277. de-1-struc-2-tion
    2   ˜1   1

278. func-2-tion
    1 ˘   1

279. e-1-le-1-ven
    2   2   1

280. re-1-lieve
    2   6

281. im-2-prove-1-ment
    1   8   1

282. o-1-live
    2   1

283. shed
    1

284. loan
    4

285. crack
    1

286. sweep
    4

287. wel-2-come
    1   3

288. pearl
    5

289. thun-2-der
    1   5

290. pack-1-age
    1   1

291. fan
    1

292. e-1-nor-1-mous
    2   5   6

293. pro-1-gram
    2 ˜1

294. de-1-scend
    2   1

295. be-1-tray
    2 ˜4

296. risk
    1

297. toy
    6

298. com-2-man-2-der
    1   1   5

299. no-1-vel
    2   1

300. keen
    4

301. de-1-ceive
    2   4

302. a-1-gri-1-cul-2-ture
    2 ˘2   1   3

303. m ock
    1

304. grieve
    6

305. belt
    1

306. m ean-2-time
    4   3

307. swal-2-low
    8   4

308. ba-1-sis
    2   1

309. en-2-cour-3-age
    1   5   1

310. fro-1-zen
    2   1

311. de-1-fi-1-nite
    2   2   3

312. re-1-lease
    2   4

313. per-1-ceive
    5   4

314. plead
    4

315. sew
    x

316. ne-1-glect
    2 ˜1

317. coun-2-sel
    6   1

318. sway
    4

319. ad-2-vise
    1   3

320. dot
    1

321. warm
    5

322. scream
    4

323. faith-2-ful
    4   8

324. flung
    1

325. pro-1-fes-2-sion-1-al
    2   1   1   8

326. em-2-brace
    1   3

327. bend
    1

328. ripe
    3

329. re-1-gi-1-ster
    2   2 ˜5

330. com-2-bi-1-na-1-tion
    1   2   2   1

331. rug
    1

332. jur-3-y
    5   2

333. de-1-coy
    2   6

334. bean
    4

335. mix-2-ture
    1   3

336. ac-2-cus-2-tom
    1   1   1

337. tube
    3

338. phi-1-lo-1-so-1-phy
    2   2   2   2

339. hedge
    1

340. glimpse
    3

341. film
    1

342. frost
    1

343. bu-1-reau
    2   6

344. sche me
    3

345. im-2-pres-2-sion
    1   1   1

346. rea-1-ding
    4   1

347. tri-3-umph
    2   1

348. per-1-ma-1-nent
    5   2   1

349. con-2-fer-3-ence
    1   5   1

350. sprang
    1

351. col-2-lec-2-tion
    1   1   1

352. do-1-mes-2-tic
    2   1   1

353. a-1-broad
    2 ˘ x

354. ox
    1

355. in-2-tro-1-duc-2-tion
    1   2   1   1

356. haste
    3

357. pro-1-claim
    2 ˘4

358. no-1-tion
    2   1

359. bench
    1

360. ri-1-fle
    2   7

361. sang
    1

362. co-1-lumn
    2   1 ~

363. rage
    3

364. ju-1-nior
    2   x5

365. go-1-vern
    2   5

366. cave
    3

367. mis-2-tress
    1   1

368. bade
    3

369. trunk
    1

370. per-1-su-3-ade
    5   2   3

371. in-2-vi-1-ta-1-tion
    1   2   2   1

372. ar-2-rest
    1   1

373. mea-1-dow
    6   4

374. me-1-rit
    2   1

375. bunch
    1

376. sta-1-tue
    2   4

377. im-2-port
    1   5

378. run-2-ning
    1   1

379. se-1-ven-1-ty
    2   1   2

380. li-1-ter-3-a-1-ry
    2   5   2   2

381. cor-1-re-1-spon-2-dent
    5   2 ˘1   1

382. sus-2-pect
    1   1

383. de-1-vice
    2   3

384. doll
    1

385. au-1-di-3-ence
    6   2   1

386. owl
    6

387. fail-1-ure
    4   3

388. in-2-ter-1-rupt
    1   5   1

389. pri-1-vi-1-lege
    2   2   1

390. li-1-nen
    2   1

391. foo-1-lish
    6   1

392. re-1-gret
    2 ˘1

393. ar-1-mor
    5   5

394. luck
    1

395. rub
    1

396. juice
    4

397. dar-1-ling
    5   1

398. con-2-ve-1-ni-3-ent
    1   2   2   1

399. mis-2-sing
    1   1

400. can-2-dy
    1   2

401. ex-2-cite
    1   3

402. per-1-so-1-na-1-li-1-ty
    5   2   2   2   2

403. ma-1-na-1-ger
    2   2   5

404. ar-2-range-1-ment
    1   3   1

405. in-2-su-1-rance
    1   x2   1

406. fre-1-quent
    2   1

407. bad
    1

408. to-1-wards
    8   5

409. i-1-ma-1-gi-1-na-1-tion
    2   2   2   2   1

410. ba-1-ses
    2   1

411. sen-2-tence
    1   1

412. li-1-quor
    2   5

413. di-1-rec-2-tor
    2   1   5

414. sur-1-vey
    5   6

415. con-2-test
    1   1

416. doc-2-trin<u>e</u>
    1   <u>3</u>

417. bu-1-<u>sh</u>el
    8   1

418. o-1-v<u>er</u>-1-com<u>e</u>
    2   5   <u>3</u>

419. fad<u>e</u>
    3

420. ma-1-gic
    <u>2</u>   1

421. prin-2-<u>c</u>ess
    1   1

422. in-2-sti<u>n</u>ct
    1   1

423. be-1-l<u>ie</u>f
    2   6

424. rid
    1

425. t<u>oi</u>l
    6

426. ex-2-pla-1-na-1-<u>ti</u>on
    1   <u>2</u>   2   1

427. so-1-lid
    <u>2</u>   1

428. jok<u>e</u>
    3

429. dam-2-<u>s</u>el
    1   1

430. dif-2-f<u>er</u>
    1   5

431. mir-2-r<u>or</u>
    1   5

432. con-2-si-1-d<u>er</u>-3-a-1-<u>ti</u>on
    1   <u>2</u>   5   2   1

433. <u>ch</u>a-1-rac-2-t<u>er</u>-3-is-2-tic
    <u>2</u>   1   5   1   1

434. rib<u>b</u>ed
    1

435. bold
    <u>1</u>

436. e-1-na-1-b<u>le</u>
    <u>2</u>   2   7

437. dis-2-t<u>u</u>rb
    1   5

438. fr<u>eigh</u>t
    6

439. br<u>ow</u>
    6

440. <u>wh</u><u>ea</u>t
    4

441. i-1-mag<u>e</u>
    <u>2</u>   1

442. t<u>igh</u>t
    4

443. se-1-cu-1-ri-1-ty
    <u>2</u>   <u>2</u>   <u>2</u>   2

444. <u>th</u>ir-1-t<u>ee</u>n
    5   4

445. e-1-<u>qu</u>ip-2-ment
    2   1   1

446. su-1-prem<u>e</u>
    <u>2</u>   ⌣3

447. de-1-sp<u>ai</u>r
    2   ⌣4

448. di-1-vin<u>e</u>
    <u>2</u>   3

449. vi-1-si-1-t<u>or</u>
    <u>2</u>   <u>2</u>   5

450. po-1-n<u>y</u>
    2   2

451. fac-2-t<u>or</u>
    1   5

452. oc-2-cu-1-pa-1-<u>ti</u>on
    1   2   2   1

453. blast
    1

454. li-1-t<u>er</u>-3-a-1-tur<u>e</u>
    <u>2</u>   5   2   3

455. be-1-held
    2   1

456. ri<u>c</u><u>e</u>
    3

457. w<u>ee</u>p
    4

458. <u>c</u><u>oa</u><u>ch</u>
    4

459. <u>thr</u>on<u>e</u>
    3

460. j<u>oi</u>n
    6

461. dam<u>e</u>
    3

462. mal<u>e</u>
    3

463. mi-1-n<u>er</u>-3-al
    <u>2</u>   5   8

464. de-1-po-1-sit
    2   <u>2</u>   1

465. trim
    1

466. pe-1-ri<u>sh</u>
    <u>2</u>   1

467. plung<u>e</u>
    1

468. a-1-ri<u>s</u><u>e</u>
    2   3

469. n<u>er</u>-1-v<u>ous</u>
    5   <u>6</u>

470. fr<u>ee</u>z<u>e</u>
    4

471. bril-2-li-3-ant
    1   <u>2</u>   1

472. a-1-gen-2-<u>c</u><u>y</u>
    2   1   <u>2</u>

473. il-2-lu-1-strat<u>e</u>
    1   <u>2</u>   ⌣⌣3

474. w<u>ea</u>-1-pon
    6   1

475. <u>s</u><u>ea</u>l
    4

476. pen-2-n<u>y</u>
    1   2

477. spo-1-ken
    2   1

478. bar-2-rel
    1   1

479. cliff
    1

480. snap
    1

481. vi-1-<u>si</u>on
    <u>2</u>   1

482. re-1-lat<u>e</u>
    2   3

483. ex-2-trem<u>e</u>
    1   3

484. plat-2-f<u>or</u>m
    1   5

485. pre-1-vi-3-<u>ou</u>s
    2   <u>2</u> $\overline{\overline{6}}$

486. grasp
    1

487. dis-2-<u>char</u>ge
    1   5

488. rib-2-bon
    1   1

489. ac-2-<u>qu</u>ire
    1   3

490. cli-1-mat<u>e</u>
    2   <u>3</u>

491. v<u>oy</u>-3-ag<u>e</u>
    6   1

492. j<u>ew</u>-3-el
    6   1

493. da-1-mag<u>e</u>
    <u>2</u>   1

494. fled
    1

495. mild
    <u>1</u>

496. grip
    1

497. tr<u>ea</u>t-2-ment
    4   1

498. p<u>er</u>-1-f<u>or</u>-1-man<u>ce</u>
    5   5   1

499. re-1-flect
    2 ~1

500. <u>ar</u>-1-gu-1-ment
    5   2   1

501. pi-1-g<u>eo</u>n
    <u>2</u>   1

502. f<u>ou</u>r-2-t<u>ee</u>n
    4   4

503. brid<u>e</u>
    3

504. cr<u>u</u>-3-el
    <u>2</u>   1

505. <u>shir</u>t
    5

506. ab-2-so-1-l<u>u</u>t<u>e</u>
    1   2 <u>3</u>

507. scr<u>ee</u>n
    4

508. limb
    1 ~

509. h<u>ea</u>p
    4

510. sum-2-mon
    1   1

511. f<u>ier</u>c<u>e</u>
    6

512. dis-2-tress
    1   1

513. vi-3-o-1-let
    2   2   1

514. a-1-lik<u>e</u>
    2   3

515. ex-2-tra-3-<u>or</u>-1-di-1-na-1-ry
    1 8 <u>5</u> <u>2</u> 2 $\overline{2}$

516. rat
    1

517. pre-1-v<u>ai</u>l
    2   4

518. grad<u>e</u>
    3

519. o-1-pe-1-ni<u>ng</u>
    2   <u>2</u>   1

520. stu<u>ck</u>
    1

521. <u>ar</u>ch
    5

522. ro<u>ck</u>-1-<u>y</u>
    1   2

523. de-1-li<u>ght</u>-2-ful
    2   4   8

524. j<u>ean</u><u>s</u>
    4

525. dad
    1

526. hand-2-k<u>er</u>-1-<u>chie</u>f
    1~~   5   6

527. midst
    1

528. fed
    1

529. trap
    1

530. skat<u>e</u>
    3

531. sad-2-d<u>le</u>
    1   7

532. <u>ar</u>-1-g<u>ue</u>
    5   4

533. <u>qu</u>ot<u>e</u>
    3

534. f<u>ou</u>n-2-t<u>ai</u>n
    6   4

535. bri<u>ck</u>
    1

536. ca<u>sh</u>
    1

537. i-1-d<u>ea</u>l
    2   4

538. a-1-war<u>e</u>
    2   3

539. an-2-nu-3-al
    1   2   8

540. li-1-l<u>y</u>
    <u>2</u>   2

541. in-2-vent
    1   1

542. sug-2-ges-2-<u>ti</u>on
    1   1   1

543. grov<u>e</u>
    3

544. dis-2-tin-2-g<u>ui</u><u>sh</u>
    1   1   x 1

545. vin<u>e</u>
    3

546. staff
    1

547. ex-2-tra
    1   8

548. tim-2-b<u>er</u>
    1   5

549. pre-1-tend
    2   1

550. g<u>ow</u>n
    6

551. c<u>or</u>d
    5

552. rib
    1

553. ca-1-pa-1-c<u>i</u>-1-ty 2 2 2 2	576. dis-2-t<u>in</u>ct 1 1	599. bo-1-<u>ther</u> 2 5
554. cle-1-v<u>er</u> 2 5	577. vic-2-tim 1 1	600. flo<u>ck</u> 1
555. w<u>ai</u>st 4	578. t<u>orn</u> 5	601. h<u>un</u>-2-g<u>er</u> 1 5
556. m<u>ar</u>-1-ve-1-l<u>ou</u>s 5 2 6	579. ex-2-tent 1 1	602. con-2-s<u>cious</u> 1 x 6
557. most-2-l<u>y</u> 1˜ 2	580. som<u>e</u>-1-tim<u>e</u> 3 3	603. sc<u>ou</u>t 6
558. in-2-te-1-ri-3-<u>or</u> 1 2 2 5	581. pres-2-sure 1 x3	604. l<u>igh</u>t-2-l<u>y</u> 4 2
559. mes-2-sen-2-g<u>er</u> 1 1 5	582. mys-2-t<u>er</u>-3-y 1 5 2	605. b<u>ar</u>-1-g<u>ai</u>n 5 4
560. grat<u>e</u>-1-ful 3 8	583. dim 1	606. a-1-n<u>y</u>-1-<u>wh</u>er<u>e</u> 2 2 3
561. traf-2-fic 1 1	584. re-1-w<u>ar</u>d 2 5	607. <u>ch</u>im-2-n<u>ey</u> 1 2
562. re-1-tr<u>eat</u> 2 ˜4	585. con-2-struct 1 1	608. sli<u>ce</u> 3
563. e-1-mo-1-<u>tio</u>n 2 2 1	586. cl<u>ay</u> 4	609. fas-2-ten 1 ~1
564. lo<u>dge</u> 1	587. slop<u>e</u> 3	610. wes-2-t<u>er</u>n 1 5
565. dis-2-put<u>e</u> 1 3	588. <u>or</u>-1-na-1-ment 5 2 1	611. ex-2-pos<u>e</u> 1 3
566. re-1-mind 2 <u>1</u>	589. cur<u>v</u> <u>e</u> 5	612. tid<u>e</u> 3
567. brass 1	590. lux-<u>1</u>-u-1-r<u>y</u> 1 2 2	613. pre-1-pa-1-ra-1-<u>tio</u>n 2 2 2 1
568. con-2-trast 1 1	591. re-1-spon-2-si-1-bi-1-li-1-ty 2 ˜1 2 2 2 2	614. g<u>oo</u>d-2-ness 6 1
569. hut 1	592. e-1-<u>cho</u> 2 2	615. en-2-t<u>er</u>-1-t<u>ai</u>n 1 5 4
570. ca-1-nal 2 1	593. re-1-la-1-ti<u>v</u> <u>e</u> 2 2 1	616. re-1-v<u>iew</u> 2 x6
571. scr<u>atch</u> 1	594. pen-2-<u>ci</u>l 1 1	617. de-1-scrip-2-<u>tio</u>n 2 ˜˜˜1 1
572. l<u>igh</u>t-2-ning 4 1	595. to-1-bac-2-co 2 1 2	618. kind-2-ness 1˜ 1
573. ma-1-jes-2-t<u>y</u> 2 1 2	596. ap-2-pro<u>v</u> <u>e</u> 1 8	619. slid<u>e</u> 3
574. sub-2-mit 1 1	597. s<u>oa</u>p 4	620. po-1-li-1-tics 2 2 1
575. rar<u>e</u> 3	598. f<u>or</u>-1-m<u>er</u>-1-l<u>y</u> 5 5 2	621. c<u>ur</u>s<u>e</u> 5

622. ob-2-lige 　1　　3	645. pre-1-cede 　2　　3	668. lest 　1
623. mer-1-cy 　5　2	646. glove 　1	669. reck-2-less 　1　　1
624. en-2-coun-2-ter 　1　6　　5	647. fol-2-low-3-er 　1　4　　5	670. draft 　1
625. a-1-las 　2　1	648. stove 　3	671. phy-1-si-1-cian 　2　2　　1
626. peer 　4	649. na-1-vy 　2　2	672. dis-2-cuss 　1　　1
627. con-2-tra-1-ry 　1　2　2	650. pur-1-ple 　5　7	673. ven-2-ture 　1　3
628. ap-2-pli-1-ca-1-tion 　1　2　2　1	651. in-2-volve 　1　1	674. bath 　1
629. pur-1-sue 　5　4	652. starve 　5	675. ex-2-pert 　1　5
630. fork 　5	653. curl 　5	676. ab-2-sence 　1　1
631. bor-1-row 　x　4	654. pitch 　1	677. preach 　4
632. en-2-dea-1-vor 　1　6　　5	655. men-2-tal 　1　8	678. glor-3-i-3-ous 　5　2　6
633. hu-1-mor 　2　5	656. ea-1-gle 　4　7	679. poi-1-son 　6　1
634. de-1-li-1-cate 　2　2　3	657. beard 　4	680. re-1-tire 　2　3
635. scorn 　5	658. pe-1-cu-1-liar 　2　2　x 5	681. fetch 　1
636. lieu-1-te-1-nant 　6　2　1	659. a-1-cid 　2　1	682. chill 　1
637. plot 　1	660. a-1-part-2-ment 　2　5　　1	683. slen-2-der 　1　5
638. struc-2-ture 　1　3	661. at-2-tract 　1　1	684. sank 　1
639. neigh-1-bor-1-hood 　6　　5　　6	662. hell 　1	685. cu-1-ri-3-o-1-si-1-ty 　2　2　2　2　2
640. dis-2-pose 　1　3	663. boot 　6	686. ra-1-pid 　2　1
641. verse 　5	664. fi-1-nance 　2　1	687. me-1-di-1-cine 　2　2　3
642. af-2-fec-2-tion 　1　1　1	665. howl 　6	688. ea-1-ger 　4　5
643. lap 　1	666. eigh-1-teen 　6　4	689. cel-2-lar 　1　5
644. weak 　4	667. sci-3-en-2-ti-1-fic 　2　1　2　1	690. pea-1-sant 　6　1

691. liv̲e-1-ly̲
     3   2

692. cheese̲
     4

693. dir̲-1-ty̲
     5   2

694. v<u>ei</u>n
     6

695. dr<u>ow</u>n
     6

696. h<u>ai</u>l
     4

697. host
     1

698. con-2-nec-2-t<u>io</u>n
     1   1   1

699. ste̲<u>e</u>p
     4

700. lend
     1

701. sa<u>ck</u>
     1

702. stra<u>w</u>
     6

703. puz-2-z<u>le</u>
     1   7

704. he-1-si̲-1-tat<u>e</u>
     2   2   3

705. vel-2-vet
     1   1

706. ca-1-r<u>ee</u>r
     2   4

707. ex-2-pe-1-di-1-t<u>io</u>n
     1   2   2   1

708. <u>au</u>-1-tumn
     6   1   ~

709. pot
     1

710. glob<u>e</u>
     3

711. in-2-ter̲-1-val
     1   5   8

712. re-1-t<u>ai</u>n
     2   4

713. lon<u>e</u>-1-ly̲
     3   2

714. <u>ch</u>est
     1

715. skill
     1

716. spy̲
     2

717. cur<u>e</u>
     3

718. rub-2-ber̲
     1   5

719. me-1-di-1-cal
     2   2   8

720. dy̲-3-<u>i</u>ng
     2   1

721. con-2-vin<u>ce</u>
     1   1

722. ar-2-ri-1-val
     1   2   8

723. ca-1-n<u>oe</u>
     2   x

724. ant
     1

725. pur<u>e</u>-1-ly̲
     3   2

726. man-2-kind
     1   1

727. b<u>oa</u>st
     4

728. in-2-tel-2-li-1-g<u>e</u>n<u>ce</u>
     1   1   2   1

729. h<u>or</u>-1-r<u>or</u>
     5   5

730. con-2-fu-1-s<u>io</u>n
     1   2   1

731. cot-2-tag<u>e</u>
     1   1

732. l<u>ay</u>-3-er̲
     4   5

733. sp<u>ea</u>r
     4

734. an-2-gel
     1   1

735. pro-1-vi-1-s<u>io</u>n
     2   2   1

736. six-2-ty̲
     1   2

737. w<u>eigh</u>
     6

738. con-2-ti-1-nent
     1   2   1

739. ex-1-is-2-ten<u>ce</u>
     1   1   1

740. fe-1-mal<u>e</u>
     2   3

741. pos-2-si-1-bi-1-li-1-ty̲
     1   2   2   2   2

742. glit-2-ter̲s
     1   5

743. mag-2-ni-1-fi-1-<u>ce</u>nt
     1   2   2   1

744. re-1-stor<u>e</u>
     2   ⁓3

745. in-2-sti-1-tu̲-1-t<u>io</u>n
     1   2   2   1

746. <u>ch</u>er-2-ry̲
     1   2

747. as-2-s<u>er</u>t
     1   5

748. ton
     1

749. cul-2-ti-1-vat<u>e</u>
     1   2   3

750. so-1-lu̲-1-t<u>io</u>n
     2   2   1

751. m<u>ea</u>n-2-<u>wh</u>il<u>e</u>
     4   3

752. dwell
     1

753. dig
     1

754. p<u>ea</u>
     4

755. con-2-stant
     1   1

756. cr<u>ee</u>p
     4

757. pu-1-ni<u>sh</u>-2-ment
     2   1   1

758. <u>or</u>-1-gan
     5   1

759. blos-2-som
     1   1

760. lum-2-b<u>er</u>
    1   5

761. hop
    1

762. con-2-flict
    1   1

763. <u>wh</u><u>ee</u>l
      4

764. l<u>aw</u>-1-y<u>er</u>
    4   5

765. ac-2-<u>qu</u><u>ai</u>nt
    1   4

766. st<u>ou</u>t
     6

767. na-1-k<u>ed</u>
    2   1

768. n<u>ee</u>-1-d<u>le</u>
    4   7

769. v<u>ei</u>l
    6

770. des-2-p<u>er</u>-3-at<u>e</u>
    1   5   3

771. ex-<u>1</u>-e-1-cu-1-ti<u>ve</u>
    1   <u>2</u>   2   1

772. con-2-<u>qu</u><u>er</u>
    1   5

773. p<u>oo</u>l
     6

774. ri<u>dge</u>
    1

775. odd
    1

776. re-1-spon-2-si-1-b<u>le</u>
    2 ~1   <u>2</u>   7

777. mu-1-<u>se</u>-3-um
    2   2   1

778. in-2-ven-2-<u>ti</u>on
    1   1   1

779. re-1-f<u>or</u>m
    2   5

780. bl<u>ew</u>
    6

781. cru<u>sh</u>
    1

782. <u>th</u>rust
    1

783. tr<u>u</u>-1-l<u>y</u>
    2   2

784. dumb
    1   ~

785. en-2-<u>gi</u>-1-n<u>ee</u>r
    1   <u>2</u>   4

786. p<u>ay</u>-1-ment
    4   1

787. dep<u>th</u>
    1

788. <u>an</u>-2-g<u>le</u>
    1   7

789. pu-1-ni<u>sh</u>
    <u>2</u>   1

790. p<u>oi</u>n-2-t<u>ed</u>
    6   1

791. bl<u>oo</u>m
     6

792. s<u>ou</u>p
    6

793. h<u>oo</u>k
    6

794. con-2-fess
    1   1

795. a-1-gr<u>ee</u>-1-ment
    2 ~4   1

796. l<u>aw</u>n
    6

797. w<u>ea</u>-1-r<u>y</u>
    4   2

798. st<u>oo</u>p
    6

799. rob
    1

800. for<u>e</u>-1-h<u>ea</u>d
    3   6

A Final Note

After the student has successfully completed reading all words from Section Four, he must then use additional practice material. Spelling requires a far greater amount of time to master than does decoding. Thus while one is finished with the decoding portion of this book, he will most likely need to continue developing spelling skills by working from the Word Lists A, B, and C.

As the student works from these word lists for purposes of developing spelling skills, it is important for him to continue to develop decoding skills as well. For oral reading practice the teacher must choose material that is written at a level which is sufficient to hold the interest of the student in addition to being written at a reading level which is appropriately suited for the skills of the reader.

If you are working with an older child or an adult, be sure and use material that is written specifically for an older audience. Never use children's books for older students. The library is an excellent source to find suitable reading material. There is presently available a great deal of material written at basic and intermediate levels designed for the older student. Ask your librarian for help in directing you towards such material.

To determine the suitability of reading material in terms of the appropriate reading level for a particular student, use a five per cent rule of thumb. A student should be able to read approximately ninety-five out of every one hundred words with relative ease in a given selection. If he has difficulty with many more words than that, use other material. On the other hand do not use material that is so easy for him to read that he seldom encounters a word he does not immediately recognize. The goal is to find material that will provide a good balance between the practice and review of already-learned principles of reading with the carefully controlled introduction of new and more challenging material.

Keep in mind that it is the continuity of steady practice over a sufficient period of time that is the key to the eventual and inevitable victory of two or more people forever changing their lives: one by learning to read and spell, the other by making that miracle possible.